# First Call For The Burley Express

*Ron Sheeley*

ISBN: 0692798242
ISBN 13: 9780692798249
Library of Congress Control Number: 2016917597
Sheeley Publishing, Bonita Springs, FL

Burley defined:

Bur. ley
/bar' – ley/

Noun:

1. The Chicago abbreviation for a variety show, typically including striptease
2. A 1953 Ford station wagon "transportation cooperative" that made express trips Friday and Saturday nights from the suburbs to downtown Chicago to the burlesque theatres on South State Street

# Prologue

*"We should be careful to get out of an experience only the wisdom
that is in it---and stop there; lest we will be like the cat that sits
down on a hot stove lid. She will never sit down on a hot stove-lid
again--- and that is well; but, also she will never sit down on a cold
one anymore"*
— *Mark Twain*

*"Come on,
baby don't you want to go,
back to that same old place,
Sweet Home Chicago"*
— *The Blues Brothers, 1980*

WHILE I RECEIVED a grade of "6" in senior English Class ("7" was failing), at Lyons Township High School (LTHS) in LaGrange, Illinois, I decided to write this book about what happened to 8-white guys from Western Springs, IL a rich western suburb of Chicago, the town west of LaGrange, from the start of high school in 1956 until June 10, 2015 when we gathered for one of the eight's funeral in beautiful downtown Skokie, Illinois. Someone had to tell these stories, but the guy who should have written the book, who told us it was a waste of time because no one would read it, and who brought us all together for perhaps the final time, Walter Jason "Jay" Crawford, died from a ruptured aorta on June 7, 2015 in a damp, old $600/month basement rental apartment on Irving Park Blvd. "He hated the apartment" his son Huey Crawford told us at Jay's funeral. Irving Park

Blvd, the main east-west street just north of Wrigley Field, was the same street notorious gangster John Dillinger made one of his many daring escapes on. Not that Dillinger has anything to do with this story. But Irving Park Blvd is in Chicago, and Chicago to all of us was, and always will be, Sweet Home Chicago. The Big Onion as Jay used to call it. And if there was ever a character that fit in Chicago, Jay was the guy.

# Chapter I

*"We learn by doing"*
*— Jonathan Winters, comedian*

THIS BOOK, AND what happened to these 8-guys, (Squatman, Dutchy, Admiral Baldy, Willie The Wop, John BS, Buck, Jay and myself) and what we learned along the way, from the *"First Call For The Burley Express"* (the burlesque strip-tease joint) on South State Street (at State Street and Congress Parkway as it was called then, now the Eisenhower Expressway in downtown Chicago) to Jay's death 59-years later, is dedicated to Jay, and is what this book is all about. Jay taught us all a lot---from everything he learned in the ghetto working for the City of Chicago Department of Family and Children's Services (DCFS) in Cabrini-Green and the Robert Taylor Homes and the Southside of Chicago, to how to handicap a horse race, to how to pick a 65 to 1 shot to win the NCAA Basketball championship in 2014 to foreign affairs to politics and to life far, far away from the wealthy suburb and friendly confines of Western Springs, IL. After all, how many guys do you know that would use a Hefty green plastic garbage bag for a suitcase when traveling out to Las Vegas for a reunion with his high school buddies? How many guys do you know that would have at least 5-years of the Daily Racing Form piled up in his office? How many guys do you know that could only get in his car through the rear door on the passenger side of his car? How many guys do you know, who couldn't swim, swim across a lake? And, exactly how many white guys do you know who would have spent a career walking even near Cabrini? Yet Jay spent 40-years going in and out of the projects. He also spent a lifetime chasing rainbows at the racetrack and still looking for the big score that would get him back to even. He was like a gold prospector looking for the one big payload. The payload was never discovered, but what he taught us will last the rest of our lifetime.

If you want to learn about what it was like growing up in Chicago in the 1950s and 1960s, what Wrigley Field was like in the early 1960s when no one attended any games, the excitement that the 1959 go-go White Sox at Comiskey Park brought us, the music we heard, what we learned hitchhiking on Route US 66, what the salesmen at Maxwell Street, the open air market on the near Southside of Chicago, taught us about selling, how to rise upward, and things to avoid doing, in corporate America, what a Marathon Oil gas station owner in Springfield, Illinois taught us, how to sneak down into the box seat section of any baseball park, how to hop a freight train, what the Follies Theatre on South State in Chicago taught us in our youth, how to play whiffle ball, how to order an Italian beef sandwich at Mr. Al's in Chicago, how to ride the Red Line El in Chicago, and, other things no one, and I mean no one, could possibly teach you, and a ton of things that you may have missed learning that we can refresh for you, then this is your book.

NOTICE
"It is considered bad manners and harmful to your taste buds to put ketchup on your hotdog within the city limits of Chicago"
— a sign posted on counter of Gold Coast Hotdogs,
Midway Airport food court, Chicago, Illinois, circa 2015

One thing we all learned and all agreed upon over the past 60-years …if you missed New Orleans before Katrina, you missed New Orleans; and, if you missed Wrigley before 1969, you missed Wrigley; if you missed watching a college basketball game in the Chicago Stadium you missed the best stadium of all, if you missed Bobby Hull coming down center ice in the Chicago Stadium, with the crowd going nuts and the roar increasing, you missed the best of hockey player to lace them up; if you missed the 1963 NCAA basketball championship game, you missed the most exciting overtime game ever played; if you missed Chicago Bear linebacker Larry Morris knocking NY Giants quarterback Y.A. Tittle, as tough a football player you will ever see, out in the 1963 NFL Championship game played in Wrigley Field, you missed one of the most bruising tackles of all time; if you missed shopping at Maxwell Street, you missed learning how the best salesmen sold merchandise. If you missed talking to the old men sitting in the grandstand enjoying their lunch before a game at Wrigley, you missed the best stories and advice you will ever hear; if you missed the Follies Burlesque Theatre on South State at Congress Parkway in Chicago you missed Scurvy Miller, the best stand-up comic entertainer of all time; if you missed the excitement of the go-go White Sox 1959 pennant run, you missed the best in history; if you missed a hotdog and fries in a brown paper shopping bag for 25-cents at Parky's on Roosevelt, you missed the best dog in Chicago (hold the ketchup) ; if you missed hitch hiking on The Big One, US 66, stretching from Chicago to Los Angeles you missed the experience of a lifetime; if you missed grinding burrs off of big, long steel I-beams on the grave yard shift at Ryerson Steel Company in Melrose Park, Illinois at 3:00am, you missed the best reason to return to college;  if you missed watching Gayle Sayers run against the San Francisco 49'ers on a wet, sloppy field back in the day when the Bear played at Wrigley, you missed poetry in motion;  if you missed the exhilaration of catching a southbound freight out of Champaign-Urbana, IL headed to The Big Easy, you just haven't lived; and,  if you missed the 1950s and 1960s growing up in Chicago, you missed the best of Chicago and our kind of town and you missed the best education you could have ever gotten.  And, if you missed watching the grace, speed and power of Roberto Clemente and Willie Mays when they played The Cubbies in Wrigley, like us, you will need to wait a long time before you will see two like them again, if we ever do.

We learned about the Cubs, life in Chicago in the 1940s and the importance of saving money for retirement from the old men sitting in the Grandstand Section at Wrigley Field. For some reason they always seem to congregate in Grandstand Sections 208 & 209 on the Cubs dugout side of the field. I think it was far enough away from most of the people attending their first game. They brought their brown bags with their lunch in them and they brought stories. We also all learned that it wasn't what you did that you will remember throughout life, but what you didn't do that you will remember. Here is what we all learned. Here are the things we did do and the things we did not do, that we should have done. We knew in April 1962 in Wrigley Field, when we were sneaking down to the box seats behind the visitor's dugout, that we would not see anything like this again because we knew that as it was happening. You can wish for it again, but the moment will not arrive. And, what we all agreed to over having a great steak at Gibson's restaurant in downtown Chicago (along with the now closed Stockyard Inn, the best steak in Chicago) the evening before Jay's funeral the next afternoon in Skokie, Illinois was that the things we did not do forever haunt us to this day. I think Jay knew that better than any of us because he talked about those "missed opportunities" a lot in his later years. One of Jay's biggest missed opportunities, and a story he told about it over and over in later years, was the $125 he did not spend on entertainment with a drop-dead gorgeous bar tender & hooker in Lyons, Illinois. Even Jay's Chicago buddy Rocky Duck thought he was crazy. The Duck didn't offer his opinion on many things. I thought it was interesting that in the end, the one opportunity that got away, that haunted him to the day he died was a beautiful, young prostitute in Lyons, Illinois. But that was Jay. We always loved the bars in Lyons on Ogden Ave. Seedy, but mysterious. The seedier the bar looked on the outside the more Jay wanted to see the bar on the inside. The more mysterious a massage parlor on Irving Park Blvd looked, the more Jay talked about it.

But, as you will see in this book, money had trouble leaving Jay's hands even if the bet at the racetrack was "rock solid" or a missed opportunity, with odds favoring him, presented itself. We all agreed ahead of time at a Sports Book in Vegas that a horse by the name of Texas Red was the "bet of the day" during the 2nd day of the 2014 Breeder's Cup. We gave our money to Jay to bet on Texas Red. So instead of putting $100 to win on Texas Red Jay decided to bet three dollars on the horse to win. Three dollars to win on Texas Red…it still haunts Buck, BS and me. The majority of the money Jay bet on the Texas Red that eventful day went into exactas, trifectas and superfectas. Instead of taking the money used to place these "exotic" bets as they were called, if we put the money on Texas Red to win, we would have had a "signer". A "signer" at the track means that if the winning ticket is $600 the horseplayer must complete IRS Form W-2G so the IRS knows you won and can tax you on your winnings. Yes, Texas Red won going away.

And while that wasn't the only time, it was the most recent time we missed an opportunity. 6-months before the Breeder's Cup bet, we decided to bet on Connecticut to win the NCAA Basketball Final Four. Connecticut won all right at 65/1 and Jay had $50 dollars placed on the bet or ~$16.50 per man. $16.50 per man we bet on the game should have been $100 per man bet to win on UConn. But, one thing everyone agreed on at Arlington, Sportsmen's and Hawthorn racetracks, or The Mudbug, the off-track horse racing betting parlor, nobody in Chicago was a better horse handicapper than Jay. He did his homework on what he always called "the shape of the race". And many people thought he was the best in the business. Tommy the Bookie knew Jay was the best, and Tommy knew horses and how to bet on horses.

"Oh, what a night
Late December, back in '63
What a very special time for me
As I remember, what a night"
— The Four Seasons, Oh What A Night", 1975

This story and these adventures started out in the wealthy Queen suburb of Western Springs, Illinois (the name plate displayed entering Western Springs read "Queen of the Western Suburbs") in the 1950s and mid 1960s, we grew up thinking that the residents of this wealthy suburb all thought alike. And, I look back now and am sure they did all think alike. Jay, however, was different and from the day I first met him shooting baskets at a neighbor's court at 47th and Woodland, on a drizzling rainy day when most people our age were inside, I immediately knew it. How many guys are shooting baskets in a drizzle and intermittent downpour?

Jay spent many, many years on the front line of child abuse-neglect prevention threading his way through rapid representation of the Dept of Family & Children's Services, the housing projects, the court system and the public.

For all practical purposes Jay was homeless when he died, and, like each adventure we had together throughout life from the two of us swimming across Lake Bloomington, Illinois, to listening to the detailed story of Jay and Squatman hopping a freight to New Orleans, to hitchhiking together on the big one, US 66, in the early 1960s, we all learned from each other's experience and the things we did together. 50-years later Jay could tell you the restaurant they stopped at before he and Squatman hitchhiked into Greenwood, Mississippi in 1965. There wasn't much he didn't remember, even down to the smallest detail. At the 50th LTHS high school reunion, Jay remembered the guy who tried to beat him up in 3rd grade. He could remember a horse 10-years back and quote you the odds on the race.

In case you are wondering, Dr Fager was the greatest horse he ever saw run. Dr Fager was recognized by experts and enlightened observers as the greatest horse ever to race in America bar none, including the vaunted Secretariat. On a hot August day in 1968 at Arlington Park, outside Chicago, Doctor set the mile record in 1:32 1/5 while carrying a staggering weight of 134-pounds. The Doctor was "a wild mustang running loose among saddle ponies". And, 50-years later he could tell you where driving Dave Downey of Illinois basketball fame was from and the last batter Chicago Cub pitcher Don Cardwell faced to complete his no-hitter in Wrigley Field in May, 1960.

Jay and I were in "home room" together in high school starting the day after Labor Day in 1956---Lyons Township High School South Campus (the original Lyons Township high school on Brainard was too small to accommodate all 4-grades of Freshmen through Seniors) where you started the school day so the teachers could take attendance to see who "skipped" class...it wasn't until 1959 that we "skipped"...but the cause was right...the Go-Go Sox of 1959 were playing hated Los Angeles in the World Series. Looking back, the Go-Go White Sox out of Comiskey Park at 35th and Shields on Chicago's Southside, along with the 1963 Chicago Bears, the 1963 Loyola, IL Ramblers in basketball and the 1985 Chicago Bears, who fielded the greatest defense ever put on a football field, were what made the Big Onion of Chicago the sports town that it was. In good years, and, bad, the Chicago Bears will always be The Monsters of the Midway, and it made no difference if you were a Sox fan or a Cub fan, when football started in Chicago, we were all Bear Fans, Even the Bears' fight song, "Bear Down Chicago Bears" to this day insights a roar from the crowd at Soldier Field and is one of the greatest football fight songs ever written. The Bears did not play in FedEx Field, MetLife Stadium, AT&T Stadium or Sports Authority Field at Mile High...the Bears played in Soldier Field, opened in 1924, a memorial to the U.S. soldiers who died in combat. This is Soldier Field...not Sports Authority at Mile High.

The Chicago Bears Fight Song, composed 1941

*Bear Down, Chicago Bears, Make every play, clear the way to victory!*
*Bear Down, Chicago Bears, Put up a fight with a might so fearlessly!*
*We'll never forget how you thrilled the nation, with your T-formation*
*Bear Down, Chicago Bears, and let the people know why you are wearing the crown*
*You're the pride and joy of Illinois, Chicago Bears, Bear down!*

## January...the month you "Pay The Piper" in Chicago

The weather in Chicago in the Fall during the start of football season was the best of the best or "postcard perfect" as we liked to say...cool, crisp sunny afternoons with low humidity and the leaves on the many oak, elm and maple trees starting to change from green to red and yellow. Heaven sent is what we said about it. You would have to look far and wide to see better fall colors than what the Midwest displays. Just west of Wentzville, Missouri traveling west on Interstate 70 toward Columbia, Missouri there is a big hill where the road descends down, runs flat for a while and then ascends upward. On a cool October morning passing over that stretch of I-70 is a photo opportunity you won't see in many places in this country. Rarely did it get over 90-degrees in Chicago even in July and August, and most homes did not have air conditioning in the late 50s. We didn't. Fall was the best season of the year in Chicago land, and I don't know many places that would compare with the fall weather in Chicago.

Only cool summer nights in God's Country (Minnesota and Wisconsin.) could beat Chicago in the fall. But, after fall in Chicago, we had to Pay The Piper, as the old men in the grandstand at Wrigley Field taught us, for winter was coming and winter in Chicago was as "rough as a cob" as Jay put it. Pay the Piper. Not only was it overcast most of the time from November to March, and when those January winds came down from the North, Chicago suffered mightily with temperatures well below zero. The coldest I've experienced was 26-below zero and that was before they accounted for the wind chill. You better have everything covered on your body venturing out in 26-below. Your nose freezes and frostbite is a major issue. I don't remember too many really sustained cold nights growing up in Chicago, but I do remember snow. We had a block-long driveway and when the snow fell you had to get on it right away because the temperature always dropped after a storm and you went from shoveling snow to picking ice. It was like going from lightning to the lightning bug. Winter usually tried to end toward mid-March and we went outside to play basketball. I can remember snow in early April, but it was rare and was of the heavy variety, the ball busting variety if you will, which melted quickly. The clothes (called "stuff" in Chicago) one had to wear to go outside in Chicago were noteworthy. Boots, gloves, scarf, jacket and stocking hat were the norm. When I was a mailman, on many occasions, I wore long underwear pants and two pairs of socks, a thermal long sleeve undershirt, a post office shirt, a sleeveless vest and my post office jacket. You just got used to lugging a big parka around just as you got used to the cold after a week or so in it. In later years, I learned the value of a good scarf for its versatility and warmth.

"Now get up on the floor, 'cause we're gonna boogie, oogie, oogie till we just can't boogie no more"
— Taste of Honey, 1978

## Back to 1956...

I really didn't know Jay then and it wasn't until the summer of 1958 that we became close friends, but I felt that he was a guy you could trust. Certainly Jay was a guy who could help you improve your vocabulary. One of the reasons we bonded was his love of sports and another was whiffle ball and a board game called Big League Manager (BLM). There was no baseball game ever invented that even came close to BLM...it was all based on math. If a hitter batted .270 in 1958, his chance of getting a hit was 27 out of 100. Pitchers were ranked by stats as to walks, pitching with no one on, pitching with men on base, etc. It was the best and we played it that summer in Jay's basement on his ping-pong table hour after hour. I think that summer each team completed playing 70-games (back then the season lasted 154-games). We completed a lot of BLM games considering we played baseball or basketball everyday it was nice outside. So Jay and I became close friends that summer and remained so until his death in June 2015.

One thing we knew for sure in the fall and winter of 1958, and 1959 and 1960, was that none of our LTHS classmates were listening to Scurvy Miller tells jokes on South State at the Follies Burlesque Theatre on Friday and Saturday night. What we didn't realize, until we left Western Springs after high school graduation, that not everyone grew up like we did in the confines of safe Western Springs. But, we knew that 99% of our high school classmates didn't think like we did. To even venture to downtown Chicago at night scared the crap out of most of our classmates, not to mention walking into a burlesque theatre with a lot of old men from who knows where. You didn't see many homeless in the 1950s in Chicago, at least homeless sleeping on the streets. To this day though, the most tragic sight in America is to see a 65-year old homeless woman on the streets. Most of the homeless had dogs that slept next to them. They took good care of their dogs. Newspaper was a good insulator and then used that as the mattress with cardboard boxes used to build their house. In the winter in the Windy City cardboard saved the day for the homeless living on the streets.

# Chapter 2

*"It ain't what you know that gets you in trouble,*
*it is what you know for sure that just ain't so"*
*— Mark Twain*

The Car Wash to BG burgers to Ryerson Steel…

"You might not ever get rich, but it is better than diggin' a ditch"
— Rose Royce, "Car Wash", 1978

RIGHT AFTER HIGH school Jay and I landed a job at the Western Springs car wash. When the car went through the wash, our job was to dry it off from top to bottom using small bath-type towels when the car exited the wash cycle. By noon on any given day, my arms were ready to fall off and your back got so stiff you could hardly stand up straight. Two hours into the job my socks were wet and so were the front of my pants. But the cars never stopped on a Saturday and there were no coffee breaks. So two weeks after starting there, we quit the car wash. I didn't think might right wrist would ever be quite the same. To this day, I always tip the car wash people because I walked 2-weeks in their shoes. A ball-busting two weeks I might add. But, to this day I think digging a ditch would have been easier work than the car wash.

BG Wimpy on LaGrange Road at Ogden Ave in LaGrange, IL was a restaurant that was way ahead of its time in 1959 when it first opened and I would compare it to Chili's restaurants today. In 1959 it put out classy burgers and other

American food in a restaurant that had more style than TOPS Big Boy did even though TOPS burgers were unsurpassed. When it opened, it was immediately a see-and-be-seen place for the college-aged crowd. Fred A Hale, the restaurant manager, hired me to work after school and on weekends and then during the summer months. His favorite trick, as we were about to officially check out for the evening was to have us "go back and knock out those pots and pans" as he liked to say. Even Muhammad Ali couldn't have knocked out the mountain of pots and pans awaiting us. It took Jay and I at least another hour to bring the mountain of pots to Muhammad. We did learn how to wash pans, however... always let the tough pans soak and get the easy ones first.

We "bussed" tables at BG Wimpy. Bussed is restaurant lingo for picking up the dishes and cleaning a table after customers finished eating and left the restaurant. Sometimes I wondered what some customer's kitchen tables looked like after cleaning the table where they sat and ate. On Saturday night the place was just packed and noisy, with a line stretching out the front door waiting to get in, we had to be nimble afoot and able to lift heavy trays of dirty dishes and haul them through two double doors before landing in the dishwashing section of the restaurant. Occasionally a tray slide and several dishes would go over, but we never hit any customers with dirty dishes. It was fun clearing a table next to a table of "businessmen" who were vying for the check. "I'll take it"; "no I'll take it"; "no, you took it last time". The match went on for a couple of more rounds before the "winner" insisted he would take the check. If you really want to take a check when out with a group "insist" that the check comes to you. On occasions when the short order cooks called in sick, we would take turns working the burger grill where all the burgers were fried. I think this was BG Wimpy's downfall because they insisted, or at least management did, on over frying the burger. People want juicy burgers as Wimpy's found out later from Wendy's. They missed the high school crowd because their burgers were more expensive than a TOPS Big Boy.

Flipping and watching 20-burgers at a time will teach you the lessons necessary to become a good short order guy but a long ways from being a chef of any kind. We weren't going to exchange recipes or how to cook things with the chefs at Gene and Georgetti's any time soon. Burger "tosser" yes we were. The only thing Fred A. Hale taught us was to keep moving as he was always watching. Keep moving and stay employed. We started carrying a busboy towel with us, it was a dirty job, and so anytime there was dead time out came the town and what ever was close to us got cleaned. See Fred, we are busy.

In the hot summer of 1963, at Joseph T Ryerson Steel Fabricating Co in Melrose Park, IL, working the graveyard shift as a summer employee, I worked the shot blaster machine with Willie, an African-American from the south side of Chicago. Not only was it a dirty and dusty job, we often had to lift heavy steel beams with no breaks and 45-min for dinner. But just breathing the shit in the air was too much. Willie and I worked very hard, and kept each other awake at 4:00 in the morning that seemed the time every morning we reached the ED-95 (used in the operating room to measure the time to repeat the dose). At that time, Jay and I knew nothing about the high rise ghetto projects being built in downtown Chicago. In 1970, when Jay started working at the Department of Children & Family Services, we learned from Jay, who visited the projects almost every day on the job, that it was a rough-tough neighborhood, and only going to get tougher.

It was 5-months after Jay's death that we realized that one of the truly great characters in Chicago history was gone. And, a year after Jay's death I received an email from Squatman telling me how much he missed him. Jay was a guy who brought us together and a guy who taught us many, many things about life along the way. A guy who, in our opinion, deserves to be remembered for what he did for the people of Chicago. And, 75-people, from all walks of life, agreed with me and showed up to pay their final respects at his funeral on a postcard Saturday afternoon in June in Skokie, IL which is connected to Chicago on the North.

*"Well the South Side of Chicago, Is the baddest part of town, and if you go down there, You better just beware of a man named Leroy Brown"*
— Jim Croce, *"Bad, Bad Leroy Brown"*

## The projects..."Rough as a cob"...

For the people reading this book who are not familiar with Cabrini-Green and the Robert Taylor Homes in Chicago, where Jay worked on and off as a Dept of Children & Family Services employee for 40-years, they are definitely worth noting. Cabrini-Green was composed of 10-sections built over a 20-year period. Cabrini-Green was bordered in the apex of Clybourn Ave and Halsted Street on the North, North Larrabee on the West and Chicago Ave on the South in Chicago. There aren't too many apartment buildings where the women had to roll their refrigerators in front of the door at night to keep guys out. There aren't too many apartment buildings that make national news like Cabrini-Green did in the mid 1990s when 9-year old "Girl X" was found in a 7th floor stairwell on North Larrabee Street after being raped, beaten, choked poisoned by having a can of insecticide sprayed down her throat. Girl X survived, but she was blinded and left with significant brain damage.

I remember Jay telling us the story of a crack cocaine Mother walking out the door of her Cabrini apartment leaving 6-babies locked in while she went out for more stuff. While the Mother was gone, because of the crying and screaming made by 6-infants, the neighbors broke down the door to find these half-naked babies crawling around on the kitchen floor. All hell broke out when it reached the local news and Jay feared for his job when it made it all the way up to national news with President Clinton making a really big deal out of it. Jay's comment on the babies who made national news was that he could take you to 10-more cases just like that because it happened almost weekly. To calm things down and show the world that Cabrini-Green apartments were safe, the Mayor of Chicago Jane Byrne, moved into Cabrini to show how safe living there really was. What the public didn't know is that the good Mayor had a select entrance and, more importantly, had exit doors welded shut to prevent their use. Jane stayed around 3-weeks, un-welded the doors, and made a hasty exit. But it wasn't long before the gang bangers went to school on Jane's welding shop and welded shut select exit doors at Cabrini, The years Jay spent going in and out of the ghetto took its toll on him. He hated working with and going in to court to testify on a case. He hated going into the Department of Children & Family Services (DCFS) office to deal with inept supervisors who all specialized in covering their collective asses. If it hadn't been for the racetrack I think he would have cracked looking at what he had to look at daily at what he often described "the shit in the ghetto". He said he could never do my job of hopping on and off airplanes every week, but the truth of the matter was I don't know of anyone who could or would want to do his job. The people (cases) he had to work with and help took a lot of patience. Just the thought of driving by Cabrini scared the shit out of most people. Just the word "Cabrini", if you lived in Chicago, scared the shit out of most people. We all begged Jay to write about the ineptitude of the DCFS, the case load, the inept judges, the decisions made by the courts to name a few. But, he never did. It was more fun to work on his horse track charts then write about a job he hated. And it was a lot easier for him to bitch about the entire situation than to sit down and write. I only wish I would have had a tape recorder with me when he told stories about what really happened in his job. But no one would have believed the stories he told, and the DCFS, the judges and the courts would have denounced him as a loose screw. One day someone will step forward and write about it all and then people will really know what Jay had to deal with for forty-plus years.

During the worst years, Cabrini-Green saw vandalism increase dramatically. Jay sported a scar on his forehead running from the top of his head to just above his eye on the left side of his face from a beer bottle thrown at him in Cabrini. Rats and cockroaches were everywhere because rotting garbage piled up in the trash chutes. There were plenty of boarded up windows. Jay said Cabrini looked like a hellhole. I think it was 2011 when the last Cabrini building was torn down and developers started popping up as Cabrini was close to The Super Bowl of Shopping Michigan Avenue...the Miracle Mile. Chicago was all about making money and here was a chance to take some prime real estate and build million dollar condos. Just ask the Mayor.

And, with the closing of Cabrini was the closing of Farmer Brown's Chicken restaurant, located across the street from Cabrini, which in my opinion, while only getting "take-out" twice with Jay, was the best of the best. The Colonel did not have a chance next to Farmer Brown's chicken. Jay really missed Farmer Brown's after it closed and who would blame him. The woman who owned the place for years, according to Jay, one day decided to quit. Jay once told me that the great singer Curtis Mayfield of the Impressions and the song "Gypsy Woman" fame came from Cabrini. If you haven't listened to "Gypsy Woman" do yourself a favor, Google it up, and listen to a classic.

*"I hate to see the lady go, knowing she will never know, that I love her, I love her, The Gypsy Woman"*
— The Impressions, "Gypsy Woman", 1961

The Robert Taylor Homes, a public housing project on Chicago's South side on State Street between 39th and 54th South along side the Dan ("damn") Ryan was completed in 1962 and at its peak housed 27,000 residents. Bigger than Cabrini, Jay said he once had to run for his life at the Taylor Homes and it was a very, very tough neighborhood especially in the mid 1970's. Bad, bad Leroy Brown. Rough as a cob.

# Chapter 3

*"We move forward; we don't dig in"*
*— General George Patton*

Jay's funeral...

"If you don't know me by now, you will never never never know me"
— Harold Melvin and the Blue Notes, 1972

I INVITED THE Mayor of Chicago, Rahm Emanuel to the funeral, who had time to glad hand me at the Fullerton Red Line El Station when he was running for election for the Mayor's office, to attend Jay's funeral but he was way too busy to attend. Unless you bring money, the Mayor can find other things to do. Oh yes, the Mayor's office also asked me how many people would be attending the funeral. We all thought it was nice of the good Mayor to be so concerned about a guy who did so much for the underprivileged in the Big Onion. For 40-years Jay went in and out of some of the toughest areas in Chicago saving children, and the Mayor couldn't even send a card. But I bet the Mayor sent a lot of cards to his construction friends. The "M" in mayor stood for Money in Chicago, and when questioned about possible past sins, the "M" in mayor stood for Memory as in "I don't remember". The last of the Daley mayors wanted to sell Midway like he did the parking meters in Chicago to Morgan Stanley. Yes, at one time a Wall Street bank owned the parking meters in Chicago. I wonder if they still do. The city that rubbed shoulders with Big Al Capone, Big Mike Ditka, Big Dick Butkus and John Dillinger will only bend so much dear Morgan & Stanley. Hey Western Union man.

I also invited the top guy at the Department of Children and Family Services and despite the fact that Jay was the very first worker to accept assignment as a sex abuse investigator in the State of Illinois; he too, had much too much paperwork to do on a Saturday. When you are busy, well you are busy. When you don't look good, you just don't look good. But the guys who answered the funeral call for Jay, The First Call For The Burley Express, Lyons Township High School, LaGrange, Illinois guys, later to be known as The Braidwood Bunch, ---Squatman, Buck, Willie The Wop, "John BS", Dutchy, "Baldy and me-- were there. Long time friend of Jay's, Mahoney was there. He confessed after the ceremony that, like the rest of us, he would sorely miss Jay. Jay's good friend and fellow horse handicapper, Tommy attended. . A class guy, Tommy, he told us that Jay was one of the best horse handicapper in Chicago. The Sheriff, as Jay called her, was there. She was the 7-UP Company's poster child in the 1960's and came as close to anyone to really understanding Jay. Rich Means attended. AP was there…she was a fan of Jay's for a long time. And former co-workers at the Dept of Children & Family Services, who knew Jay for many years, were there. And, a love Jay lost, Ms M was there. The people who mattered to us were there, and that is all that mattered to us. It was a nice quiet funeral attended by people who wanted to pay their last respect to Jay, and, many did not. Jay often admitted later in life that people, on first sight, either loved him or hated him…there was no middle ground. I really think he liked it that way. There were a lot of tears, but more "why" questions than anything. Squatty, who perhaps knew Jay the longest, delivered an eloquent talk about their hitch hiking through Mississippi in 1965, which he said marked the true measure of his friend Jay because of all the possible serious trouble they could have been in. If you were a white guy from the North in 1965, Greenwood, Mississippi was not your kind of town. Squatty, as I write this, still can't get over the fact that Jay is gone. I know Mahoney and Tommy feel the same. The one thing about Jay is if he counted you as a friend, you had a friend for life. He was first and foremost a true character the likes of which, and everyone who met him agreed, you only meet one time in a lifetime. The Big Onion had character, and Jay was its favorite son.

Everyone who wanted to say something about Jay got up and spoke. One of Jay's girl friends got up in front of the gathering and talked about the road trip they took together over to Dubuque, Iowa for a weekend of fun a few months before Jay died. Jay's wife, "the Missus." as he called her, sat in the first row and took it all in. It was too late for her to fight with him about that escapade. But she didn't miss many fights and we all wondered why he didn't divorce her as she offered little to his peace of mind. Buying stuff they didn't need and charging it on her credit card and not paying the bill. They lived in a 2-bedroom house, the lower level they rented out, on North Mozart in Chicago, one block west of the famous California Ave as it intersected with Irving Park Blvd. and 1 ½-blocks north of Packy Gas as Jay called the gas station at Mozart and Irving Park Blvd because the owners were from Pakistan. Jay sold the Mozart house prior to his death. A developer immediately leveled the house and planned to build a 3-condo unit of the property. Jay's "partner" pocketed the commission from the sale of the house. I won't waste your time discussing the "partner". He was anything but a partner. Not before selling it, however, Jay spent $900 on two trusty plumbers, both recommended highly by Jay's fantasy-baseball league partner, who were going to fix his pipes running out to the street. I called the plumbers Trusty I and Trusty II. Each received a check from Jay for $450 and did nothing. The 3rd plumber called by Jay to fix the problem was called "Un-Trusty" by Buck. "Un-Trusty" was never used. After "Un-Trusty" was de-selected, Buck was surprised that there were not more plumbers at Jay's front door waiting to collect $450. In the Big Onion, you paid your money and you took your chances, and you don't trust your Trusties. Buck and I, to this day, still laugh about the Trusty and Un-Trusty plumbers.

As I sat there at Jay's funeral my mind wandered back to all the adventures we had together and what made him a one-of-a-kind. And, looking at his urn at the ceremony I kept thinking about what Jay said they always said in the ghetto…"on the strength". Jay's son took the podium to begin the ceremonies and started the proceedings with Jay's favorite quote (and he had many quotes) from the movie The Cincinnati Kid, where in the final poker game, Yancey (played by Edward G. Robinson, a great actor) beat the Kid, played by Steve McQueen, with a royal flush, and said *It gets down to what it is all about, doesn't it, Kid. Making the right move at the wrong time*. Words to live by. And, speaking of Cincinnati, when you get there the very first thing you want to do is go to a Skyline Chili Parlor and order Skyline 3-Way. Or go to WalMart and buy a can of Skyline chili, some spaghetti, Kraft grated mild cheddar cheese and 1-onion and make 3-Way at home. You will thank me for it.

A lot of people who spoke about Jay at his funeral talked about what a great horse handicapper he was and what a terrible (and I do mean terrible) better he was. No one, however, knew how Jay got hooked on betting the horses, but sitting there in the audience I thought back to the night it all happened...and where.

"Just be thankful for what you've got, though you may not drive a great big Cadillac, Diamond in the back, sunroof top, Diggin' the scene, With a gansta lean, Gansta whitewalls, TV antennas in the back"
— William DeVaughn "Be Thankful For What You Got"

The year was 1964 and, with dates in tow, Jay and I decided to take them to Sportsmen's Park to watch the trotters. Sportsmen's Park had a culture all of its own, and, while Jay never went back to bet the trotters again, that night got him more than on his way to betting. As Paul Newman said in the hit movie *"The Color Of Money"*, *"money won is twice as sweet as money earned"*. We stayed longer than we thought that night at Sportsmen's Park, and, as I recall, it was the 2nd or 3rd to last race that we spotted in the program a 5-1 or 6-1 semi long shot by the name of Diploma Time out of DeKalb, Illinois. Knowing I wasn't going to graduate from Northern Illinois Univ in DeKalb, IL what a better way to remember old times but to put a couple of bucks down on Diploma Time to win. Had Jay worried more about getting a win (and place) bet down on the thousands of horses he bet on from 1964 to 2015, he would be a millionaire. But the lure of those trifectas (you must select the 1,2, 3rd horse in the exact order of finish)) and superfectas (you must select the1, 2,3,4th horse in the exacta order of finish) was just too strong to resist, and our boy, knowing that any horse in the race could finish 3rd and 4th in any given race, continued to bet "tri's" and "super's". But he could pick horses like no one else...he just couldn't pick 3rd or 4th without spending extra money on top to do so...that was his downfall. His Waterloo if you will. Over

51-years of betting horses, had he just spent money to throw two more horses in the tri and 2-more horses in the "super", there is no question in my mind that he would be up $5-million. Always trying to save money, but always trying to play the "tri's" and "super's" and throwing in as few as possible horses to finish 3$^{rd}$ or 3$^{rd}$ and 4$^{th}$ on a superfecta, always seemed to cost him dearly. He once lost at the Arlington, Illinois race track in a race called "The Million" when the horse "Storming Home" suddenly unseated the jockey just as the horse passed under the finish wire. He had plenty of other crazy losers---mispunching a Pick 4 winner, losing a winning Pick 3 bet because the horse ran off the track at the top of the stretch. As Jay would be the first to address, there are many, many ways to lose at the track, but once you get the "bug" there is no turning back.

How Jay picked the horses should have been "The Little Book On Handicapping The Horses" and its sequel "The Little Book On Betting The Horses", but neither was written. Until now. This book provides you with what I learned from Jay at Arlington Park (Chicago, IL), Churchill Downs (Louisville, K), the Naples-Ft Myers (FL) dog track, Gulfstream (Hallendale, FL), the famous off-track betting parlor, The Mudbug (Chicago, IL) with Jay's good friends Freddie and Barry, the SunCoast Sports Book (Las Vegas, NV), Sportsmen Park (Chicago, IL), the off track parlor in Gary, Indiana where we watched the great horse Cigar get beat. You get the idea, I listened; Jay taught. He would review every race on the card and explain in great detail which horse would take the lead, how many horses would take the lead (how much speed in the race?), was it "cheap" speed, who was the top closer? The best bet was a horse that would take the lead and hold it.

# Chapter 4

*"We'll make them turn their heads everywhere we go"*
*— The Ronettes, July 1963, "Be My Baby"*

"Western Springs will be next" — Conductor on the Burlington railroad

I MOVED TO The Queen Of The Western Suburbs"---Western Springs, IL---on June 15, 1956 and first met Jay the very day I moved in. It rained that day. He was shooting baskets by himself at a friends house on Woodland Ave in the 4600 block as I pulled up on my bike (the bike was named Brown Betty) and on every shot he yelled out a Purdue players name and where he was shooting from… "Willie so and so from the corner", Jake on a lay up". I knew he was different the first time I met him, and was I ever right. Few people knew the starting guard and center for the Boilermakers of Purdue in 1956 and Willie Meriweather and Jake "The Snake" Eisen will always go down as two of our favorite Big 10 players.

Western Springs, IL in 1956 was the perfect town if you were white, had a job in downtown Chicago or the suburbs, didn't want bars on your windows, and wanted a nice manicured yard, plenty of oak trees (and plenty of leaves to rake) and wanted your children to get a good preparatory college education at Lyons Township High School (LTHS), located at Cossitt and Brainerd in the next town east of Western Springs, LaGrange, IL. The town to the immediate other side of Western Springs, on the west side, was the snobby little town of Hinsdale, IL.

While Jay and I thought the high school was way, way overrated for its academic excellence, top 50 in the USA, a lot of people moved to Western Springs because of the school system and low crime rate. I can only remember one class at LTHS that I benefitted from, and it was by my good fortune that I elected to take the class as one of my electives in my senior year. It was a class on how to invest in the stock market. The 2nd choice I had for an elective course was an electricity class that taught the pupil how to screw in a light bulb and read ohms or watts or something like that. For me, with money in the Western Springs Bank that I earned on my paper route delivering Suburban Shopper newspaper, the choice of what class to take was a no brainer. From what I learned in that class I bought my first mutual fund in 1968.

The "Queen" was best remembered by passengers on the Burlington railroad (the same railroad Warren Buffett bought years later and then called The Burlington Northern Santa Fe)), which ran through the center of town separating the north from the south. On the north side of the tracks in down town Western Springs was a 4-story water tower that housed my stepmother's friend, The Chief, along with Western Springs finest police officers. If you knew the Chief of Police, you didn't pay any speeding tickets. Most of the residents in the town worked in downtown Chicago and routinely caught the 7:00am train to Union Station on Canal Street which meant getting up at 5:00am to get ready for work if you were going to have a little bite of breakfast before departing. 5:00am wake up calls weren't a blessing for anyone's sex life especially when you had a train schedule to meet and didn't return home from work until 6:00 or 6:30. Time for dinner and a little paperwork and off to bed. In those days there were no cell phones or computers or emails…everything was on paper. I do think one had more time to think in those days because the information flow was a lot slower. Just because the information flow was a lot slower back in the day did not mean that upper management in corporate America did not make big errors in deciding what to do.

Western Springs was the type of town where you quickly learned to stand up when a woman entered the room and when you walked with a woman on the sidewalk you always walked on the street side, just in case in bad weather a car splashed water on the sidewalk you were going to get wet, not the woman. And, most importantly, your spoon went out away from you when you were eating soup. Don't forget to sit up straight while you were slowly moving your soup spoon up and away from you. It was also important to be on time for the 3-block walk to church every Sunday no matter what the weather or how tight your white shirt collar was. Probably it was most important to be home in time for dinner promptly at 6:00pm. These were Lester The Pester's (my father's) rules. Manners were everything in Western Springs where it took a 9-iron from the street to reach most of the front doors. We lived in a Frank Lloyd Wright designed home which faced sideway to the Central Ave with the front door facing north toward Ogden Ave (US 34) two blocks away. US 34 was famous for the cattle trucks that rolled through in the 1950s and 1960s on the way toward the famous Chicago Stockyards. The same Stockyards Frank Sinatra sang about in "My Kind Of Town". I used to feel so sorry looking at those animals packed into those cattle trucks and so did a lot of people. They were like sardines stuffed into a can. No food or water for many miles on US 34 coming from Iowa and Nebraska. They had such sad looking eyes. I remember those sad eyes like it was yesterday. But America liked their beef in those days ("where's the beef" as the old lady from Normal, IL said in a Wendy's commercial) so the trucks rolled down US 34/ Ogden Ave. And roll they did. Two decks of live stock heading east to the big Chicago yards. Pigs also rolled down Ogden Ave in two tiered trucks, most of them squealing as they went...maybe they, too, knew their fate. Across US 34/ Ogden Ave to the North was the forest reserve and Bemis Woods that had a great toboggan slide. In 1956, steam engines, spewing smoke you could see for miles, still roared down the Burlington tracks. They were really something to see. You could hear them coming for miles. Powerful.

"Give a small boy a hammer and he will find that everything he encounters needs pounding."

— Kaplan's Law

Western Springs had one barber shop and Tony the barber on Hillgrove near Claussen Ave. knew how to cut a "flat top" as good as anyone, and better than most. Short hair was the style of the day and only "greasers" wore long hair, usually smoked, rolled up the sleeves on their tee shirts and drove "souped up" cars. There were no parking meters in downtown Western Springs and the A&P grocery store flourished at Wolf Road & Burlington Ave right next Jim Benak's Shell gas station, a landmark in Springs. Jim Benak's Shell gas station was owned and operated by an old school guy who provided quality work who stood behind that work. You could get maybe cheaper parts and labor, but not better. Something you don't see today. But, if you go to the corner of Burlington and Wolf Road today you will see Benak's Shell. Maybe old school knew something no one else knew. Maybe old school knew that if you did honest work, which you stood behind, and communicated with each individual customer, your business would flourish. Many companies never figured this out.

With two drug stores within a ½-block from each other the competition for the prescription drug and sundry business was fierce. But, Wally Sauerberg's corner drug store on Burlington was brighter and cheerier looking establishment than Schuler's, and got the lion share of the business before the Monster, Walgreens, moved in to Western Springs. It was hard to compete with Walgreen's prices, but old Walt Sauerberg made his millions before Walgreens found the friendly confines of the Queen. Timing is essential, huh Walt? Jay always remembered how nice Walt was to give out an ice cream sandwich whenever Jay visited. At both drug stores there was a soda fountain and ordering an "ice" was the thing of the day. An "ice" was a paper cup of chipped ice with soda fountain flavored syrups squirted on top. All those calories and all that sugar for only 10-cents. Sauerberg's had the best bike rack in town and most everyone congregated around the bike rack. Many mornings in the summer of 1956 were spent in front of Sauerberg's sitting on the bike rack watching the California Zephyr trains roll through Western Springs. 50-California Zephyrs per day passed through Western Springs. They all looked like they were in a hurry. Mesmerizing as they passed. Today there are two California Zephyr trains going through Western Springs everyday. At a time when our highways are getting clogged and almost impassable, our airports jammed, it is time to bring back the railroad in the form of high-speed trains, President Obama offered the State of Florida in excess of $3-billion to build a light rail system between Tampa and Orlando which would run parallel to Interstate 4. If you have ever been on Interstate 4, particularly in "season" (the winter months) as they call it in the Sunshine state, you know what I'm talking about. The traffic on I-4 would rival the traffic going from downtown Chicago to O'Hare on the Eisenhower Expressway during rush hour (there is no such thing anymore as "rush" hour, the expressways in Chicago are always packed). So what did Gov Ricky "Don't Lose That Number" Scott do? He told Obama that they didn't need the Fed's money for light rail. And no light rail has been built. Ricky don't lose that number…it is the only one you own.

But, the real gem of Western Springs was Kirschbaum's, an old school European style bakery on the south side of the Burlington tracks just slightly east of the Western Springs bank (which is now a hardware store I believe) on Burlington Ave. Kirschbaum's Bakery that had out-of-this-world sweet rolls is still in the same spot it was in 1956. If you got this far in this book, add Kirschbaum's to your list of places to go in Illinois. It is a real throw back to a more peaceful time. Just ask Alice.

They built the Garden Market in Western Springs adjacent to the South Campus high school at 47th Street & Gilbert Ave in 1957 and one of the first stores up and doing business was a new edition of the A&P grocery store. Somehow in later years the Atlantic & Pacific grocery store chain lost their customer base, business focus and went under, but back in 1957 it was a big chain. One night, returning from the Corral, we passed the A&P and noticed they had carts upon carts filled with bread and rolls. Knowing that we would be passing Roz's house (we both had a crush on Roz) we decided to grab some buns and deliver the bun (regular, hot dog, hamburger, etc) assortment and stack them high on Roz's front porch. Roz's folks could have invited all of Western Springs over for an outdoor cookout of hot dogs and burgers for all the buns they had. Neatly stacked I might add.

"City girls just seem to find out early,
How to open doors with just a smile"
— "Lyin' Eyes", The Eagles, 1975

Afternoons were spent during our youth, depending on the season, playing base-ball at the spacious Spring Rock Park, touch football on the dirt at McClure Jr High field on the south side of the junior high, ice hockey at the Old Graue Mill in Hinsdale and basketball at Brook's, Shry's, or Gilbert Park that separated LaGrange from Western Springs. We hated the steel nets at Gilbert. In August, we spent time at the Western Springs swimming pool. It was a quiet town with very few outsiders riding through. The closest I ever came to trouble was after school in my sophomore year. I had ridden the bus home and was within 1 ½-blocks of my house when a car pulled up along side me and the driver, a white mobster looking guy in his 40's or 50's, asked me if I wanted a ride. I'm probably here today because I was only 1½ block away from home and didn't accept the ride. It seemed that every time it snowed in Western Springs during my high school years it snowed 8-10". Leaves in the fall; snow in the winter.

## Trick-Or-Treat...

On the back side of the Western Springs 4-5 story water tower located in the center of town, housing Western Spring's Police Station and finest men in blue, was a walled entrance that led to a rear door. You could have driven by the walled entrance to the back door many, many times without ever really noticing it. On Halloween night in 1959, a Western Springs resident by the handle of Diego Jim, crawled on his belly about 20-yards across the grass to the rear door to deposit his trick-or-treat greeting. Diego Jim provided this greeting for the Men in Blue by laying down a short fuse, with a lit Lucky Strike cigarette attached to the wick. This provided Diego time to crawl out of the wall lined rear door and sneak back across the grass on the north side of the station toward Lawn Ave. which ran parallel to the police station about 50-yards from it. At least that was the plan. Diego Jim lit the Lucky Strike and hoped it would burn long enough to light the fuse to the Halloween trick-or-treat. We all waited for the explosion at the corner of Hillgrove and Lawn Ave. It seemed like we waited forever, but the "Triple Blockbusters" (they send a blast 3-times in a row) 1959 Halloween Trick-Or-Treat package Diego Jim bestowed upon those men in blue on that chilly Fall evening, with leaves falling to the ground, was very much worth the wait. The blast from those Blockbusters was so loud the explosion could be heard 3-blocks away. My stepmother Betty and my Father said they heard it from their front door while handing out candy to the trick-or-treaters. They were 3 ½- blocks away. I think the "Triple Blockbusters" delivered a much bigger package than Diego Jim thought they would deliver. But, to this day, the guys who were there fondly look back on Officer Tuma leading the charge out the front door of the police station. The same Officer Tuma that repeatedly stopped Diego Jim on his motor scooter and handed out tickets like they were ice cream cones. It was very sweet revenge for Diego Jim and made him a hero amongst his peer group. We were one up on the Western Springs cops.

We stood across Lawn Ave to watch the trick-or-treat fireworks display. We thought this location was far enough away from the Triple Blockbuster explosion sight to provide us with what we thought would be a good running start to get away. We also liked the location because we were still close enough to see that the cops running out the front door of the tower building. Actually too close to the scene I thought. They picked up our scent immediately and charged toward us yelling "stop where you are, stop where you are". Not that we weren't mindful of authority, but on this particular night at this particular crime scene we knew it was going to be more than a slap on the hand if we were apprehended, Some of the cops ran for their cars that were parked in front of the tower. Immediately we knew the cars presented trouble because they could block off streets with them. And, we could tell immediately they were dead serious about chasing us down. We raced to disappear behind the yards of the houses located just across from the cop station. Led by Officer Tuma, who rarely led the charge, they tried very hard to catch us. I think it was the sound of the blast that made it serious. But, there wasn't a cop in shape to chase the cross-country team members across the backyards. The other thing we had going for us was the cops didn't take too well leaving their car and running through those manicured backyards. A good chance in the dark of running into a cyclone fence that, of course, one couldn't and didn't see. Those fences always scared us too when we were running from the cops. Fortunately for us, Squatman's house was a block away and we ran for his garage. Because a lot of treat-or-treaters out that night, it didn't make it appear as if we were lone wolves running on the streets. We agreed ahead of time to head for Squatman's garage and it was the best decision we could have made. There was a lot of talk the next day at Sauerberg's bike rack and at the high school as to what guys lit the bomb that went off in the back of the police station, but no officer of the law ever knocked on any of our doors to ask questions. According to my stepmother, who had no idea I was involved, and who was a big friend of Chief of Police Officer Tuma, serious charges were going to be laid on the guilty if caught. I wonder if those charges are still pending? And I never told stepmother Betty. Oh, what a night!

And, every year since we have been meeting together, the story of Diego Jim's explosion in the rear entrance to the cop station is remembered. The cops moved out of the tower in the 1970s I believe, and the Western Springs Water Tower became a National Historical Society treasure. The engineering marvel Diego Jim pulled off that cold Halloween night will go down in the annals of Western Springs' folklore. If you weren't there, you missed a wonder. I don't think, or at least we did not hear, of any other resident of Western Springs who ever duplicated Diego Jim's event. Because the back door of the tower had 8-foot walls running out 10-feet on either side away from the door, the placement of the Triple Blockbuster close to the door created a boom that seemed to echo and reverberate for about 2-sceonds longer and much, much louder, The boom created by the Triple Blockbusters in the space sounded like a bomb, not a couple of firecrackers. It was the sound of the boom that brought the cops out the front door so quickly. The speed in which they headed out the front door of the station indicated to us that they dropped everything to race to the rear of the station to investigate.

It was very dangerous running with break-neck speed through back yards at night. As a matter of fact, returning on foot to Jay's house after a basketball game and a late trip to the youth center, violating the semi-strict Western Springs cur-few, we ran through the backyards to avoid a cop from hauling us into the cop station, and I ran into an unmarked fence. With the cop in pursuit (he must have been new) and my ankle badly sprained, Jay dragged me across the back yard into some bushes to avoid detection. The cop gave up the pursuit, but by then the entire neighborhood was awakened. We overheard one neighbor ask the cop "what is all the ruckus about". "Two kids violating curfew" was the cop's reply.

The average income in Western Springs in 1956 was $15,000. A burger at McDonald's cost 15-cents, and you could add fries to the order to complete the nutritious dinner for a dime. Western Springs was home to a lot of very success-ful corporate America businessmen. The breadwinner of the Family who lived across the street from us on Central Ave was the Editor of the Chicago branch of the Wall Street Journal. In early 1970, while driving to Columbia, MO to interview journalism students, feel asleep at the wheel of his car just west of St Charles, MO, and was never the same. His youngest son, Jack McWethy, who my brother played tennis together with on a court behind their house during their high school years, went on to fame as a television reporter on one of the major networks…"this is so and so reporting from the Pentagon". Sadly, he died in a skiing accident in Keystone, CO just after his retirement and making a new resi-dence in Boulder, CO. Perfect little town that Boulder. My brother, who moved to Aspen in 1969, heard about it soon after he died. It is easy to "catch an edge" skiing and down one goes quickly. My brother did it once on Ajax Mountain and came within 3" of having his head collide with a bolder. I broke my thumb twice skiing. Both times I hit ice on the last run down the mountain.

The neighbors who lived two houses down from us had three sons. All three of their sons went on to successful careers in business. The middle son, Dave, was in my class in high school and you would be hard pressed to find a nicer, more caring guy. So did fellow hockey player C.P. Scratchison. Chicago White sox catcher in the 1950's, Sherm Lollar, also lived in Western Springs. A fact I loved to point out when describing W. Spiggs, as we used to call it, to my col-lege buddies. Floyd Kalber, news anchorman for one of the major networks in

Chicago in the 1950s and 1960s, was often at our house playing bridge with my parents and their other buddies. Bridge was a big, big game back then, and, our dining room table was the scene of many a Friday and Saturday night card game with the special bridge-playing friends. And, they played late into the night some times. We never seemed to get into the bridge game scene.

# Chapter 5

*"Some silicon sister, with her manager mister, told me I've got what it takes""*
— *Manfred Mann's Earth Band, "Blinded By The Light"*

"Time of your life, huh kid?" — Guido in "Risky Business"

IN THE SUMMER of 1959, my parents decided to take a vacation trip out West for 2-weeks, taking my younger brother and stepsister, Cheeta as I called her, with them. This left the responsibility to my stepbrother and myself to "watch the house". We watched the house ok, and so did a lot of our friends. As soon as they left, my buddies came over to play poker in the basement, and, two days after that, everyone we knew, and many people we didn't, were partying at our house on Central Avenue. The beverage of choice was Budweiser, chased with Jim Beam. A beer and a shot were called a "boilermaker" at West Lafayette, Indiana. It was all about drinking and talking and hanging out was what brought everyone together. Quite a few of the women couldn't hold their sauce (got drunk), but we always got them sobered up with a cold shower to be "presentable" by the time they got home between 1:00-2:00am. One evening during the height of the party, I counted 4-poker games (with cigars) going in the basement and about 50-people upstairs and another 25-people outside on the huge front and back yard surrounding the house. The cars, parked along the curb, stretched a block long. We started getting rid of the beer cans, they were bagged and driven off, the night before the parents returned, and, we were very lucky they didn't come home early. Not one thing was stolen or damaged during the 2-week party.

No beer or liquor was spilled on any of the rugs. When I relate the story of the 2-week party, friends can't believe nothing was damaged or stolen. But, that is the way people were back in the 1950's…respect for other peoples property is something you learned early. My parent's front living room, off limits to the children of the family, except for special occasions, looked as clean as the day they left. No one would have known we had a party and if it hadn't been for the neighbor woman next store, the parents would have never known. I'll always think that the surprise of hearing that we had a party, when nothing bad happened to the house, threw them off guard, and voided the possible punishment. Their favorite punishment was "grounding".

My Father seemed to delight sometimes in "grounding" me for the weekend for sins I had committed during the week, most notably, missing the 6 o'clock dinner bell, coming home late, not shoveling the snow as soon as it hit the ground and other similar type reasons. What he didn't know, with my bedroom on the upstairs floor, one floor above their bedroom, was that I got very adept at using a rope and climbing out my window and heading, by foot, over to Squatman's or The Corral youth center, next to the newly built LTHS South Campus, to meet up with my buddies. I don't think I was the first guy to sneak out of their bedroom window, but I know I was one of the very few who never got caught. Squatman's Father caught him one night as he tried to sneak back into the house. Squat snuck out of his house to go get a baseball he hit on the top of his grade school. He got the ball, but he never snuck out of his house at night again. Mark Twain was right about the fact that we should get out of an experience the wisdom that is in it, and stop there.

## It was like the President of the USA himself walked into the cop station…

Of all the parents of my Western Springs friends, Squatman's Dad was the most intimidating. At 6'3', with Cary Grant looks, and an athletic body, he was one guy who could scare you. When Fred T walked into the Western Springs Cop

Station to pick up Squatman arrested for speeding on his way to church on Christmas eve, he brought with him a presence unlike I have ever seen before. When Fred proclaimed as he walked into the door of the cop station that "my son never sped in his life" even the Western Springs cops were intimidated. But Fred T had a way of doing that. And when he said to the officers, "my son never sped in his life" whether it was true or not true, it was true if it came from his mouth. While living at home, Squat used to go the opposite direction in which his Dad was going, i.e., if his Dad was coming in the front door, Squatty was going out the back door. Fred was captain of the Northwestern University (Evanston, IL) basketball team and a Ranger Captain and decorated war hero in World War II. It was his Ranger troop that was one of the first to liberate the German concentration camp Dachau. After the war he took a job as Vice-President of big Agar Chicago Packing Company in downtown Chicago. I used him as one of my references when I was looking for a job to replace my low paying high school teacher job. In those days, the pharmaceutical company I was applying to asked for, and called, 8-references. I had listed on my application I later learned that the reference checker tried and tried to catch up with Fred T to ask him questions about me, but found it very difficult. Finally, Fred took the reference checker's phone call, told the checker he didn't have time to talk. When the checker said it was a reference check on my background, Fred said "hire him" (meaning me) and hung up the phone. The last time I saw Squatman's Dad was at Squat's wedding. He died from a heart attack in his early 60's in the emergency room at Naples Community Hospital in The Naples, Florida. His son today is working on following his Father's World War II footsteps (by bicycle and car) from Normandy to Czechoslovakia The right thing to do. When Squat's Dad walked into a room you would have thought the President of the USA himself had just walked in...he commanded a presence unlike any guy I've seen since. I think to this day, as a college basketball ref, he is the only one who called a technical on the fabled basketball coach Adolph Rupp at the University of Kentucky. He didn't talk much about World War II and what he did or where he went and saw, but you just knew looking at him that he had been there and done it. A terrific basketball player in his day, the Chicago newspapers attributed him to shooting the first jump shot ever shot in a basketball game. You can just imagine what his son had to live up to.

I seem to recall the minimum wage in 1956, although we only had paper routes and weren't affected, was $0.95 or $1.00 per hour. Jay had a newspaper route and so did I. We worked out of Herbie Buck's newsstand that was on the south side of the railroad tracks between Sauerberg's Drug Store and Schlueters Drug Store. We had to be at Herbie's at 6:00am to pick up our papers.

McClure Junior was the big junior high school located on Wolf Road in Western Springs. While it was highly regarded and respected for its academic excellence, somehow our man Squatman somehow missed the academic train when it rolled through McClure. Squatman was more interested in the gym where he could practice his jump shot. I didn't attend McClure but Jay, Baldy and Squatty did.

## The LaGrange Park, Illinois years...

From 1950 to June 1956 we lived in LaGrange Park, IL that bordered LaGrange, IL to the north. The grade school I went to was a brick building with nicely placed windows to allow some light to enter. The windows were very important for a daydreamer like me. We did play McClure in basketball during 8th grade. With their front line standing at 6-feet and having a slick shooting guard by the name of Kenny Roo, we were overmatched from the start. With the exception of one of those players, all went on to be high school stars. Not that they were great athletes or better ball handlers, but they were a foot taller than the rest of us. The other Forest Road starting guard and I both stood about 5-feet tall. Neither one of us knew how to "create" a basket like Derrick Rose of the Chicago Bulls or Allen Iverson of the Philadelphia 76'ers could create a basket, and if our one-handed or two-handed set shots from the top of the key weren't dropping, we were in trouble. And, most every game found us in trouble. I could dribble, but it wasn't until later that I really learned how to shoot. I do remember taking the first shot for Forest Road in that game before I was relegated to the bench, a 20-footer that hit the rim and bounced wide.

The Village of Lagrange Park, in 1953, decided to build a baseball diamond on vacant land just north of The Village Market, and form Little League baseball teams. The Little League had a 2-day try out where the managers of the 4-teams drafted players based on the tryouts. Tryouts consisted of fielding ground balls, throwing, catching and batting. I remember missing the first two ground balls hit to me, and thinking I wouldn't even be drafted. But, I was drafted by the Village Barber Shop Team who went on to finish 2nd behind Rogers Drug Store in 1953 and 1954. Rogers Drug had a pitcher and player by the name of Dick Ruggles who was undoubtedly the best athlete ever to come out of LaGrange Park, IL. Dick went on to letter in baseball, football and basketball at Lyons Township High School. In basketball, he led the West Suburban Conference, consisting of such schools as Hinsdale, Downers Grove, Arlington Heights, Maine (Harrison Ford and Hill Clinton both attended Maine), York, Glenbard and Riverside-Brookfield (RB). The Univ of Kansas basketball team came calling and Dick ended up in Lawrence, KS. His college career was not as glamorous as his high school basketball career. At the end of each season, All-Star players were selected from the 4-Little League teams to play in the Little League World Series.

It takes a lot of wins to advance to the World Series in Williamsport, but the journey to Williamsport, for us, began with the very first game against LaGrange. By the summer of 1954, LaGrange Park had never beaten LaGrange on the ball diamond. The big game was played in August in scorching heat (for Chicago that is), and, Bert Hammerick, the coach of LaGrange Park put Dick Ruggles on the mound to face LaGrange. As you know, every dog has his day, and in that game, I batted 3rd and caught a ball at the left field fence to seal a 1-0 win for the good guys from LaGrange Park. It was a joyous occasion. 50-years later, at a high school reunion, I had dinner with Connie Pier who caught for LaGrange Park in the big game vs. LaGrange, and Bob Ferguson who played for LaGrange.

A comment about the LTHS high school coaches 50-years after graduation...

The night of the 50th high school reunion, Bob Ferguson told me the story of a bunch of his friends in their senior year of high school at Lyons Township, who never got a second look by the basketball coach Mr. Les Glick, challenging the regular Glick selected basketball team to an official refereed game. Ferguson's team beat the high school varsity basketball team. How they picked who was going to play in high school, especially basketball and baseball, was totally unfair. Ferguson and his buddies never once played a game for Lyons Township High School. And, I never made the cut to play baseball at Lyons Township. It was most likely because I was all of 5-foot 1-inch entering high school and 5'8" leaving it. But the 2nd string catcher on the LaGrange Park, IL Little League team, who beat LaGrange, played baseball for all 4-years at LTHS. Jay, who was a very good left handed hitter, never got a sniff at the LTHS baseball try outs, and, later said the reason he made it as a star track "miler" is because the coach gave everyone a good look. The reason he got a "look" in track was simply because there weren't too many guys to look at. You didn't have a line of guys wanting to run the mile and be on the track team. There were no politics or "reputation" involved, if you could run, and wanted to run everyday, you made the team. To this day, I think the LTHS coaches selected who was going to play long before we were freshmen in high school and no one gave Jay or me a second look during baseball tryouts. I also think Jay could have been a baseball star because I saw him hit rocket line drives in our "stickball" games in the tennis court at Spring Rock Park hitting a tennis ball thrown as hard as I could throw from 30-35 feet. The ball I threw at that distance was much harder to hit than a high school pitcher's fastball.

In the championship 16" softball game between Don Brooks' Sox and the Senior Class played during the spring of our junior year in high school, Jay hit a rocket down the right field line for a double. Jay later described his double in the high school newspaper as "a rope ripped down the right field line". But all the bullshit was thrown to the wind when Jay stepped out on the track. He wasn't a sprinter, but he could do the distance routes. And he was determined to win. I've never seen a guy who ran so hard that he collapsed at the end of every race.

# Chapter 6

*"Everyone has a plan until they get hit"*
*— Mike Tyson, boxer*

## Western Springs, Illinois…affluent, quiet and boring

WHEN I MOVED to Western Springs I thought it was neat to have a downtown area, a big park and a big community swimming pool. My Father loved the hardware store because it was close by, but I got hives every time I walked into a hardware store. True to this day. The park, called Spring Rock, was located on the south side of the railroad tracks and stretched from the tracks all the way to 47th street. It had two major baseball diamonds but no outfield fences. And there was no Pony League, Colt League or American Legion baseball. As a matter of fact, there wasn't any Little League either. What did Steve Stelmack really do anyway as Park Director? Even at a young age, we ourselves could answer that question. It had 3-tennis courts that needed re-surfacing and a big tennis wooden backboard that we used to play stickball up against. No one played tennis. Bobby Riggs v Billie Jean King changed all of that but that came after our stickball days on the tennis courts at Spring Rock Park. From 1960-1964 no one was playing tennis in the morning at Spring Rock Park. On the south side of the park along 47th street every year the circus came to town and we all went simply because there wasn't much else to do during the evening in Springs.

On the north side of the railroad tracks was the Western Springs community swimming pool managed by the best cross-country coach LTHS ever had,

Max A. Max had an eagle eye for staffing with some of the best looking female lifeguards headed up by lovely SB who later went on to high school cheerleading prominence. And for young guys like us, the thrill of the day was to wait until she hopped into the pool to cool off and hopped out again with her sheer, no padded cups racing suit on which revealed every curve. Jay and his friend Chuck Duck would stand outside along the fence to view the daily show and had it timed when to be there. Lucky for me I was a good enough swimmer to make the Western Springs swim team and got to watch SB at swim meets. I always finished 2nd in free style to a 6'0" 8th grader, but who cared when SB was hopping in and out of the pool.

1956, we all agreed, was a perfect time...and Western Springs, IL in 1956 was a perfect town. And, it was close to Chicago by train or by car. They built the Eisenhower and Kennedy expressways in Chicago in 1958 so running downtown to the bright lights of the Big Onion from the western and northwestern suburbs was a breeze. In those days it took 30-minutes to drive from O'Hare downtown. With 16-million autos sold every year in the USA, it didn't take long for it to take a lot longer from downtown to the big one, O'Hare. While we were running to Chicago, our peer group in Bloomington-Normal. IL was driving from the Normal, IL Steak-N-Shake to the Bloomington, IL Steak-N-Shake. It was years after that I learned that the Normal, IL Steak-N-Shake, the first of their restaurants built in the USA, was torn down and left as another vacant lot. Who in the upper circles of corporate Steak-N-Shake could possibly make the decision to tear down their very first restaurant ever built?

By the start of school the day after Labor Day in September 1956, I had met the Western Springs guys---Squatman. Baldy and Jay. I also met a character by the name of Denny Bo who went on to do great things with the American Legion. In our Junior Year we met John "BS", Buck and Willie The Wop. I met the Western Springs guys in downtown Springs at the bike rack in front of Sauerberg's Drug Store. All characters in their own right and no one at the time would have known, or thought to have known then, that we would become so close as to have a reunion with the same group of guys from our high school 35th reunion in 1995 every year until 2015. But I'm getting ahead of the story.

Western Springs, as I remember it, in addition to a non-existent crime rate, was also a perfect Republican voting town, with two gas stations, Odegaard's 3-fingered laundry, a bakery, a news stand, a bank, two drug stores, a post office, a library and a train station to get you down town Chicago on the Burlington in 30-minutes. The only excitement Police Officer Tuma's men had seemed to be chasing down people speeding on Hillgrove. A town where you could leave your bike unlocked uptown in the bike rack next to Sauerberg's all week and come and pick it up a week later with no parts missing. A town where all the kids were programmed to go to college and it became big status symbol in our senior year of high school to announce you were going to DePauw, Carlton, Dennison, Miami of Ohio, Univ of Denver or the likes…it meant you were going to be a big success. My Father told me I could go to any university in Illinois as long as it was a public school. He would pick up the tuition that amounted to $25 per semester because of a teacher's scholarship I received from the State of Illinois and room and board. I was responsible for paying for everything else. Prior to making a selection between Western Illinois U in Macomb, IL, Northern Illinois Univ in DeKalb, IL and Illinois State Normal Univ in Normal, Illinois, I visited all 3-schools. Macomb, Illinois looked like the Wild West and Northern Illinois was, at the time, a commuter school. That left one school to go to that was located in the middle of the cornfields in Bloomington-Normal, Illinois. It was one of my best decisions I made in my life.

To this day I couldn't tell you what I liked specifically about Illinois State Normal Univ, but I could tell you what I didn't like about Western Illinois University in Macomb, IL & Northern Illinois University in DeKalb, IL at the time. Jay was off to the big Univ of Illinois in Champaign-Urbana, Illinois to pursue a degree in journalism, and one of the tragedies of my life was seeing him never get the chance to be the Sports Editor of a major newspaper…he would have been the best.

For the most part, the good citizens of Western Springs all thought alike, all dressed alike and all played bridge together on Saturday night. And, I feel confident in saying that like my Father told their children not to grow up to be a truck driver. Long before the computer and Internet arrived, our summers and time during high school were spent playing baseball at Spring Rock Park, football on the grass at McClure junior high school and basketball at various outdoor courts around town. We shoveled snow to play basketball and we played tackle football in the snow at the LTHS South Campus high school field. If it was 40-degrees or above the basketball bounced. If it was colder or there was too much snow we played "no-dribble" basketball which some of the high school basketball coaches could have learned from. We played stickball in the tennis courts at Spring Rock Park with a bat and tennis ball. The batter stands in the corner of the tennis court, where the two fences join, and the pitcher stands about 30-35-feet away. At that distance, when the ball hits you, you can feel it. We played hockey on Salt Creek without pads on and to this day I have a scar on my left shin from getting hit by a high rising slap shot. I once fell through the ice into Salt Creek by the old Graue Mill. My pants were like frozen cardboard before I stepped foot into the warm confines of Central Avenue and home. At night, after an 8-12" snow, when the wind stopped howling and it started to get cold, the 4000 block of Central Ave looked beautiful decorated in white. And when it got so cold the snow made a crunching noise under your feet and your nose started to freeze up, it was good to be alive.

## Cross-Country and Coach Max...

Looking back on it now, some fifty-plus years later, I think there were several major reasons that year that formed the bond for this group of guys to still be hanging together for those so many years later. The first was, that we all, with the exception of Jay, BS, Buck and Dutchy, went out for cross-country in the fall of 1958. Jay and Buck worked after school on the school newspaper and that took up a lot of their time. Journalist they were...I don't think anyone wrote better than Jay and Buck. At least Time magazine thought so as they hired Buck to be their White Hose correspondent. At least one of Jay's journalism professors at the University of Illinois thought so because he confiscated and never returned one of Jay's papers. While the fall season in Chicago is the best weather wise, cross-country, under the direction of Coach Max, wasn't as great. Not that Coach Max had anything to do with it, we were all slow, and, 95% of our cross-country time was spent racing down the final stretch of the course so as not to finish last. Guys that bitch together, and there was plenty to bitch about during cross-country runs, stay together. And, it was worth running cross country just to hear Max, at the start of every race, either home or away meets, shout out as the gun went off, "get up there Burman". Lennie The Loon" Burman, as we called him then, had great potential, but like the rest of us found running, at the speed he was running, a lot of work. So Max brought out the cattle prod at every race to make sure he didn't drift at the start, With a tall thin body and a long stride, The Loon was built for speed. But in cross-country you didn't have to be the fastest runner, although it helped, you had to be a fast runner at a persistent pace.

Jay started running cross-country in our senior year…just as Baldy, Squatman and I decided cross-country to be a good jog ruined, and a good walk in the park was easier. Jay became an excellent cross-country runner and switched to running track after cross-country season ended. He ran a 4:10 mile in the Spring of 1960 finishing 10th in the State of Illinois in the mile, often times beating out present LTHS high school board member, and area, John T. To the day of his death, I know Jay relished every minute beating Poly. Jay used to run so hard that two guys had to catch him at the finish line for fear he would collapse. At 6'2" and 160-pounds he looked like a runner. Track teammate, and ¼-miler Lucky Lou, called him "Physical" because of his appearance, I always thought that cross country season in our junior year brought us all together. When you ran like we did, it was a long run, and sometimes suffering together brings you closer together. It did for us.

BG Wimpy restaurant…

In the fall of 1959 Jay and I started work part time after school and on weekends with the newly built BG Wimpy's restaurant at US 34 (Ogden Avenue) and US

45 (LaGrange Road). I never like the intersection because the big cattle trucks traveling East on US 34 carried cattle stuffed in the vans so tightly the cattle were pressed side-to-side against each other stopped at the traffic light. In the winter, you could see the cattle's breathe coming out from the thin slates on the side of the trucks. A very tough scene for me.

As bad as busing tables and washing mounds of pots and pans can be, Jay and I had a good time working at BG Wimpy for the then minimum wage of $0.90 per hour. Cigs were 20-cents and so was gasoline per gallon, and less if there was a "gas war" as they were called…one gas station lowering the price of gas versus their competitors. We learned at BG Wimpy, that above all, it wasn't the quality of the product going out to the customer that was important, it was the speed in which it got there so make sure you flip those burgers on time. We learned how important it was to keep smiling even when a rude customer was chewing your ass for not cleaning off their table immediately after they woofed down their burger and French fries. BG Wimpy's did make semi-great burgers. Not as good, or close to comparing with out favorite, White Castle, but worth eating. If you have never eaten a White Castle hamburger, put it immediately on your "to do" list. Especially after midnight on New Year's with a couple of beers under your belt. We also learned that we didn't want to "bus" tables again, but we did a couple of summers later at the famous Lilac Lodge located on the corner of 31st Street and Wolf Road in Hillside, Illinois. We did so because during the hiring process the manager, Andy V., talked to us. Andy ended up being one of the best managers we ever had.

The spring of 1959 brought with it great weather and intramural high school 16" softball at Gilbert Park in LaGrange, IL. I know of no other major city outside of Chicago that plays 16" softball. It is not so much a game of homeruns, like 12" is, but well hit and placed line drives line drives that fall in front of or between the fielders. With a "short center" fielder, who can roam wherever he wants, the ball needs to be hit perfectly. There are few Texas Leaguers. Most of the balls are hit to the outfield so a team needed a good left and a fleet center fielder in particular. Guys who could get a good jump on the ball; Guys playing the left side of the infield had it rough trying to field a 16" ball off a hot grounder on playing field that were not manicured like Wrigley. The pitcher was important, too, not only for balls and strikes, which were called, but also for keeping the ball out of the batter's "wheelhouse" where he could hit a line drive or real "jack one". We fielded a very good team our junior year...Chuck Duck, Landy, Curt B and the Ex man. DG was the Captain. "Captain, Third Base, Leadoff man DG" as Jay used to call him. We went into the championship game against a team from the senior class and won 9-8 when our third basemen, Curt B., gunned down a runner from third trying to score. It was a pivotal, but controversial play, because the players on the other team insisted that catcher, Jay, had juggled the ball and didn't have full possession at the time of the tag. The ump didn't see it that way. Because Jay was Sports Editor of the high school newspaper we got our pictures taken and it appeared in the "The Lion", the high school newspaper. One of the few clippings I still have from high school. It was a long intramural baseball season and we played in several very close games...the team brought us together, and, I always thought that championship game, long talked about for many years following it, was another reason we came together in school year 1958-1959.

# Chapter 7

*"Wipe it off. This is the Big 10"*
*— Jay Crawford*

THE ONLY REAL place to go following a high school basketball game in the fall and winter (November through March) was the high school youth center called "The Corral". The Corral had a dance floor in the center, served physical education teacher Bert K style hamburgers, with booths for talking and ping-pong tables by the front door. The top girl clique always seemed to be at the Corral on Friday night not that they had anything to do with the likes of our group, but they did improve the scenery. One or two of the clique girls actually talked to us by the time we were seniors, but it was seldom and fleeting. You had to be a "jock" to have airtime with the top group of girls who formed their own special clique. As the song went "you have to be a football hero". We weren't on the bottom of the social ladder in high school, but we were a long ways from the top also. If I had to give a grade to our popularity with the best looking and most popular women in the class, the homecoming queen and court if you will, we would have received a grade of "C-". And maybe part of the reason why I am writing this story is by the time of the 35th reunion our little group of guys had improved their collective grade to an "A" with the best looking girls in our class.

The building housing The Corral was located on the high school South Campus property after being on Calendar Ave in downtown LaGrange for many years. In 1956, our class of almost 850-students was too large to go directly to the main high school built in the late 1880's and stood at Cosset and Brainerd.

So "South Campus" was built at 47$^{th}$ and Gilbert and because they had a lot of land used it to build a sprawling one-level building with a lot of hallways and distance between wings.

> "People get ready there's a train comin'
> You don't need no baggage, you just get on board
> All you need is faith to hear the diesels hummin'
> You don't need no ticket, you just thank the lord"
> — Impressions, "People Get Ready", 1965

## On to the story of the "burley express"...

By the time basketball season got started in 1959, we had made a couple of trips to what we called the "burleys" in 1959, and called the "peeler" bars in 2000, (burley and peeler---our language for burlesque theaters and strip joints), on South State Street and felt like we were veteran observers of what the Follies and the Rialto Burlesque Theatres had to offer. It has always amazed me in this life what I remembered from years past and what I didn't remember. One thing I did remember, and will always remember, came out of Buck's mouth on a Saturday night after a basketball game in December 1959. I remember standing by the ping-pong tables, near the front entrance of the Corral, when Buck came by and yelled out to me over the crowd noise the words for this group that will go down in infamy and became the name of this book, "First Call for the Burley Express!" Priceless.

"First Call" became "the call" for the 8-guys who bonded together in high school and who went on to meet together to this day. And every one of them took a different road upon high school graduation. But in December 1959 when we left the Corral and got in the Buck's Burley Express 1953 Ford station wagon for the evening run down Congress Street expressway (it really was an express-way back in the day) we were just good friends heading downtown for fun at the Follies to watch the striptease on a weekend night. There are some moments in this life that seem to last forever, and the trip from Western Springs to the

Follies burlesque theatre on South State are etched in my mind 50+ years later. No question about it...the Burleys became a bond for the 8-of us. As Guido the Killer Pimp said to Tom Cruise in "Risky Business", "time of your life, huh kid".

The Follies Theatre, and its sister theatre the Rialto a block south of the Follies on South State, looked on the outside like the LaGrange movie theatre. The photo on the cover of this book is an actual picture of The Follies theatre taken in 1960. Even in full bloom, however, the Rialto was strictly second banana to the Follies. Site of the legendary "Midnight Shambles---Bring The Ladies", the Follies showcased such talent as the immortal Evelyn "$50,000 Treasure Chest" (as insured by Lloyd's of London) West, Tura Satana "Miss Japan America", Lady Zorro and Star Markee, "the White Indian Princess", while the Rialto had "Linda Love" and other lesser talent. You purchased your ticket from the lady working the front enclosed glass ticket counter, With ticket in hand you entered one of the most iconic theatres in my life time, proceeded down the center aisle to find a seat on the left side or the right side. I don't remember how many people could fit in the theatre, but on Friday and Saturday night it was always packed, especially on Saturday night for what was advertised as the "midnight shambles, bring the ladies". You were hard pressed to find too many women in the audience, but I always felt attendance by the co-eds of Lyons Township High School would have been an excellent learning experience for all of them.

Of all the women burlesque stars we saw at the Follies and Rialto Theatres in our high school years, I think our two favorites were Linda Love and Tura Satana. Not only did they both have great bodies and shapely breasts but seemed to have fun taking off their clothes and occasionally interacting with the audience in front of them. We first saw Tura in 1959. 50-years later Jay flew out to Las Vegas to attend the annual Strippers Convention and interviewed Tura. Tura and Jay speculated together in Vegas as to whether her meows had provided the catalyst for me to shout out during one of her performances, "come on down and scratch my bird" moment of immortality, but Tura was unwilling to either confirm or deny participation. "Sounds like something I could have done," said Tura. The former Miss Japan Beautiful also advised our humble reporter Jay that Scurvy Miller was "a good family man". To this day we can't understand why Jay didn't take the time to write up Tura's thoughts and publish his notes from the interview. Tura died shortly after the Vegas convention and her obituary appeared in Time Magazine on February 10, 2011. We all thought that it was so classy of Time Magazine to post her passing. We knew that Buck, former Time Magazine White House correspondent, definitely had something to do with it. We also thought that the Harold Washington library, where the Follies Theatre formerly stood, should have lowered their flag at half-mast in respect. Squatty thought, too, that Time Magazine should have had a photo of Tura on the front cover. And, the boys thought that Daley should have made it a Chicago day of mourning. Anyway, the guys who went to see Tura perform on South State Street on some of those very cold nights in January 1959 will always remember her. She was the show.

The routine each night at the Follies went something like this...following each stripper, who took off their clothes down as far as "pasties" (little cups that covered their nipples) and panties, "the Pitchman" selling orange juice ("fresh squeezed") and other "goodies" came on stage. Buck had memorized "The Pitchman's" sales routine lines word for word. Jay called him the "intermission entrepreneur". He said the orange juice was fresh from Florida and when he rubbed his magic dice together fifty million Frenchmen couldn't be wrong. He was usually followed by "Scurvy" Miller a comedian who told the same jokes for months but was one of our favorites just because of the way he dressed, spoke and the corny jokes he told. Tommy "Scurvy" Miller never seemed to tire of the whole thing. The repetition---if he'd done a skit once, he done it 10,000-times---didn't dampen the man's professionalism. Having sat through two Follies shows, and 4-5 women strippers per show, more than once, we all knew that Scurvy was seeking an elusive perfection. If he died with "...I could drive a tank in there" at 9:30 pm, he might well try "I could drive a Mack truck in there" two hours later. We all wanted to sit down and talk to Scurvy, but never did.

Intermission time brought forth the music from a 3-piece all black ensemble, always dressed in black, sitting at the same level as the audience on the left side of the stage as you faced it. The trio's rendition of "Night Train" and "My Heart Belongs To Daddy" were as good as it gets. The crowd was, for the most part, made up of old men who had been there and seen the likes of strippers, in our opinion, many times. You didn't see many Glencoe, IL or Winnetka, IL businessmen in suits, but then we never attended a matinee. On Friday and Saturday night the place rocked around 11pm and it was especially flavorful when the stripper interacted with the audience. I didn't see many Glencoe or Winnetka businessmen on Friday or Saturday night either.

Buck, on the other hand, was a veteran of mocking the pitchman, shouting out the pitchman's lines ahead of him to the delight of those around him.

One night "The Pitchman" became so irritated with Buck's continued mocking of his lines that the pitchman said, as he pointed at Buck, "you again, always causing trouble; bring Smitty down here". The thought of Smitty coming down to throw you out of the theatre was something none of us wanted to experience because Smitty was not only well built and big, but had the appearance of as tough ass bouncer that none of us wanted to cross. Smitty! Great name for a bouncer we thought. Though only occasionally in view, Smitty possessed the appearance of a force to be opposed at extreme peril. A muscular black man invariably attired in shiny midnight blue-to-black suit of dubious background. He would cruise the aisle of the Follies with an ominous dignity. On the far Southside of Chicago there was Bad, Bad Leroy Brown and on the near south side; Smitty the Bouncer at the Follies. And, as Jim Croce told us, you didn't spit into the wind nor bring Smitty down the aisle. Buck apologized to Smitty, promised to let the pitchman sell his wares, and peace resumed. Watching Smitty walking down the center aisle at the Follies instantly brought back the memory of Bobby Hull of the Chicago Blackhawks coming down center ice in the old Chicago Stadium, and Dick "Skull" Barnett of the NY Kicks coming down center court, stopping at the top of the key, shooting that one-of-a-kind jump shot which resembled no one else's, and yelling "fall back, baby" because he knew the ball was going into the hoop. When Barnett shot his jump shot he resembled a guy struggling to climb up to the top of a pole as far as he could go, and then letting go of the basketball with the flick of the wrist and hands following through. We never saw another jump shot like it. You knew you were seeing greatness. Like Dick Barnett and Bobby Hull, Smitty's appearance was magic. It was the only time we ever saw Smitty come down the center aisle, and, for it, Buck would forever live in the memory of those great, great nights at the Follies.

On another trip to the Follies, Jay attracted attention to himself when using his parents baroque opera glasses to magnify his view, caught the attention of Linda Cotton "The Sweet Southern Belle" who yelled out to Jay, "Hey you with the binoculars, what are you looking for, fleas"? The crowd roared, all of us yelled out "way to go Jay" and till the day he died Jay remembered the "binos" (binoculars) at the Follies. Rightfully so. To have Linda Cotton direct her attention to the 300 or so sitting in the audience on a Friday night was, to us, a big deal.

The Follies format was quaintly traditional and surely rather staid by today's pornographic standards; there were no simulated sex acts or actual nudity, nothing, in fact, as lascivious as, say, American Bandstand. Genuine wickedness---B-girls, brothels, or whatever---was obtained else where in locations like Calumet City ("Cal City" in the day) or Braidwood. I can't recall ever seeing more than two or three civilian females in all of our nights at the Follies, even the "legendary" shambles, which was basically more of the same. I often think back to those nights at The Follies and can almost hear the 3-piece ensemble, dressed in black, hitting the first notes to Night Train and watching Tura come out to center stage. Moments like that never go away. It wasn't just her looks and great breasts with those tassels affixed swinging to and fro, but the way she came out from behind the curtain with style. You just can't buy class and style. Tura had both. To this day, every time I hear "Night Train" I think of her. Star Markee, Tura, the pitchman, and Scurvy Miller are all gone now, of course, possibly reuniting for an eternal matinee somewhere, but the "scratch my bird", Smitty coming down the center aisle and the "bino" stories will always live on.

Whoever picked the sight of the Harold Washington library on South State in Chicago, which now stands on top of the old Follies Theatre, knew exactly what they were doing and, in our minds, should have been commended for doing so. After all, the Follies strip joint was a place of learning just like the Harold Washington library. One institution was a place of book learning, the other a place of street learning. In our opinion, looking back 50-years, you need both. The City should have placed a plaque in the sidewalk at the corner of State and Congress commemorating the great Follies theatre, Scurvy Miller and our favorite burlesque queen Tura Satana.

**This is the email Jay wrote to the high school class on 2011 when it was announced that Tura Satana died:**

February 8, 2011

"The Braidwood Bunch team flag lowered to half mast today following the transition of the immortal Tura Satana to greener pastures. According to the Chicago Sun-Times obituary, Ms Satana died of heart failure at 72, which would have put her at the age of 22 back in those magical nights when she was wowing future Bunchers and other art patrons at the fables Follies circa 1959 as "Miss Japan Beautiful" inspired among other things the birth of the "Burley Express". Fifty years later, I interviewed Ms Satana at the 50th annual Exotic Dancers convention in Las Vegas, where she accepted the award as Icon of the Year. The still dynamic Tura recalled the Chicago days with some fondness, having come up on the mean streets of the Big Onion the hard way as a "gangstress", an identity she later extended Internationally with the Russ Meyer cult classic, "Faster Pussycat, Kill Kill". She was disappointed at what she perceived to be a tragic deterioration of burlesque and all it stood for, observing scornfully, 'anybody can screw a pole' I retain her personally autographed photo, thoughtfully inscribed "in your dreams". RIP Tura Satana."

## "My kind of town and my kind of people too..." — Frank Sinatra

Chicago in the late 1950's and early 1960's was more than a toddling town. It was a town you could go almost anywhere in if (i) you knew where you were going and (ii) you kept everything in front of you, i.e., you didn't go out of your way to piss anyone off. My favorite description of Chicago came from some author who I don't remember the name of, who said, "Chicago---is a no bull shit town". From Al Capone's north side to the ChiSox and Comiskey and the Regal Theatre on the south, we went where we pleased during those high school and early college days and never got into a situation we couldn't handle. None of us would have ever traded the experience and education learned by growing up in Chicago.

While I never got to go with them, Squat and Jay always talked about how much they enjoyed going to the Regal Theatre at 47th and Grand Ave on the south side of Chicago. At the Regal, with plush carpet and velvet drapes, they listened to live performances by the Miracles, Mary Wells, Barbara George, Little Anthony and the Imperials, the Supremes and the Crystals. Jay and Squatty loved their Motown music and WVON Chicago radio disk jockey Herb Kent, nicknamed "the cool gent". The Regal was demolished in 1973, and like he did when the Hotel Lexington that was Al Capone's hang out was leveled, Jay got a brick from the Regal Theatre. Sweet Home Chicago.

On one of our many trips downtown to the Follies, because I looked 12-years old when I was 16, the ticket seller at the front door asked for my ID showing I was 18. When I told her I left it in the car, she told me she was sorry but could not sell me a ticket. I walked two blocks to a parking garage where I asked a guy working all night at the garage if I could borrow his driver's license to get into the Follies theatre. He loaned it to me; I returned it after the show. That is how people were back then. Chicago was our kind of town and our kind of people too. And, to tell you the truth, to paraphrase Frank Snotty, to this day, "each time I roam, Chicago is calling me home".

To this day, it is almost impossible to visit Chicago without eating an Italian beef sandwich at Al's and Chicago style hotdog featuring mustard, relish, onions, a sliced tomato and slice of pickle. Some people, including Jay Leno, preferred Mr. Beef on Orleans Street downtown, but we liked Al's better. If you put ketch-up on your hot dog, you aren't from Chicago. We always thought Parky's on Roosevelt had the best hotdogs and fries…both put in a brown bag for 25-cents with the fries loaded to the top of the brown bag Gold Coast in the Food Court at Midway Airport, surprisingly, has an excellent char-dog and an even better sign about the wrong doings of putting ketchup on your dog. Vienna Hot Dogs hate ketchup, and Vienna is the dog of preference in the Windy City. For some unexplained reason we always bought our hotdogs outside the park from a street vendor before going into Wrigley. A tradition started long ago. I think maybe the tomatoes and pickles were better.

"A little bit of Monica in my life
A little bit of Erica by my side
A little bit of Rita is all I need
A little bit of Tina is what I see
A little bit of Sandra in the sun
A little bit of Mary all night long
A little bit of Jessica here I am
A little bit of you makes me your man"
    — "Mambo No. 5", Lou Bega, 1999

## The one and only Maxwell Street.

If you wanted to learn the Art of Selling and The Art of Dickering and The Art of Negotiating in the late 1950's and early 1960's, Maxwell Street, the "open air" market on the near south side of Chicago was your place. The vendors knew how to arrange the merchandise on hangers, close the sale, and, more impor-tantly knew how to size up a customer. This knowledge enabled them to sell a customer who bought one piece of clothing, a second piece of clothing. They knew how to probe without sounding like a "quiz show director". The other thing I noticed about the vendors, the guys doing the selling, was their keen art of listening carefully to the customer, almost waiting too long to say anything after the customer finished. I always thought the pause put them in the driver seat because then the customer had his ear trained to what the vendor was going to say. Years later, I saw Ray Biggs, owner of Biggs Marathon gas station in Springfield, Illinois, do the same thing, i.e., pause a little longer than normal after a customer said something prior to speaking himself. Like there was a lot of thought going into what they were about to say.

You could buy almost anything on Maxwell Street, although they mainly featured clothing. What always impressed me about the place was that the guys doing the selling, in my opinion, had seen and heard it all. You could tell just by the way they weren't intimidated by anyone or anything. And, they knew their merchandise and how much the same shirt would cost you at Marshall Fields or Wiebold's where some people thought it came from in the first place. On one trip down to Maxwell Street a vendor told Jay & Buck to "get loose". Meaning get your money out of your pockets and buy something. That was an example of the minimum amount of sales pressure they fired at the customer. Jay liked the saying so much he ran around high school telling everyone to "get loose". If you wanted to learn how to sell, you could of hung around Maxwell Street and those guys would teach you in a hurry. Very, very few people who bought one item left only buying one item...they were that good. They might have been scruffy looking, but they could sell. I think a part of the soul of Chicago passed when Maxwell Street, in the name of progress, was closed.

# Chapter 8

*"It is hallowed ground you know"*
*— in reference to Wrigley Field as said by old man in Sec 209,*
*circa 1961*

## Wrigley Field...Home of the Chicago Cubs

IN THE EARLY 60's during Spring Break we didn't have the money to fly to Fort Lauderdale or Daytona Beach or Cancun like the college students of today, so we attended as many baseball games at Wrigley or Comiskey as we could squeeze in. It was usually Hank, Jay and I who went to the baseball game. We always entered the park at the main entrance of Clark and Addison and the sight of green grass and green ivy on the walls will be etched in our minds forever. This is the entrance you want to go through if you are making your first trip to this special place. The grass always reminded me of the famous quote by Dick Allen when he played for the Phillies said, "if a horse can't eat it, I don't want to play on it" in reference to the many parks which had gone the astro turf route. What I remember most about Wrigley Field in the spring of 1960 is that a big crowd then consisted of 5,000 fans. There might have been only 5,000-fans attending, but make no mistake, they were Cub fans. Mostly made up of old men who would sit in the grandstand and bring their newspaper and little brown bag with their lunch in it and watch batting practice and then the opposing team beat the Cubs. What was great about Wrigley then was you could sneak down to the box seats behind home plate or the Cubs or visitors dugout. We preferred the visitor's dugout because there were far fewer people sitting there. We became experts at sneaking down to the boxes...timing was essential. We would sit in the Grandstand during batting practice and the first two innings watching which seats in the Club Box section (we liked Club Box section 31) remained unoccupied. Just at the start of the 3rd inning intermission, we made our move from the Grandstand to the Club Boxes acting, once we reached Club Box level, we portrayed guys who knew where we going and were in a hurry to get there. The guy in front of the procession down from the Grandstand to the Club Box's held two ticket stubs in his hand prominently in view in case one of Andy Frain's finest (the ushers) were watching. While it was very hard for us to believe, there we sat, 5-10 feet away from the likes of Roberto Clemente. Willie Mays, and Pete Rose.

It would be very difficult today to sneak down from the Grandstand to the Club Box seats for a couple of reasons...(i) 95% of the seats are taken and (ii) the Cubs security, sitting in folding chairs, guarded the entrance to every entrance row to the Club Boxes. We did sneak down once under the new security system but it was after the 5th inning. However, I feel confident that it could be done today if you followed our 1960's rules...watch for vacant seats for 2-innings, make your move during intermission at the start of the 3rd inning and go individually, not together as it draws suspicion. And act like you know where you are going and belong there. But don't talk to the people next to you unless they start acting funny. The seats you are sitting in most likely belong to season ticket holders. Those people sitting next to you may be season ticket holders also and know the people who normally sit there. And, they know you do not belong in those box seats. I think, at last count, there is a waiting list of >100,000 people waiting for a chance to buy a season ticket. In 1960, Wrigley couldn't find anyone but perhaps a small handful of fans that would buy a season ticket. We always felt the 1960 fan was the true, most loyal fan on the planet and if the Cubs ever made it to the World Series again, those fans should get first crack at the seats. Or so we thought. We usually parked south from the field on School Street near Sheffield and after the game, if the Cubbies won, we saw the white "W" flag go up next to the centerfield scoreboard. The white flag with a blue "W" on it was put up in the 1940s to notify the people coming home from work driving down Sheffield or Waveland whether or not the Cubs won that day. Today after every

Cub victory you can see hundreds of people in the stands waving a small replica of the "W" flag. I think it will now become a tradition to last a long, long time. Go Cubs!

While the Cubs had the great Ernie Banks, sweet swinging Billy Williams and a few very good players, the great players we saw, and I mean the absolute best, were on opposing teams---Roberto Clemente with the Pirates, Willie Mays and Willie McCovey with the SF Giants, Eddie Mathews and Hank Aaron with the Milwaukee Braves, Ted Kluszewski and Pete Rose and Frank Robinson with the Cincinnati Redlegs, Sandy Koufax and Don Drysdale with the LA Dodgers, Stan Musial with the St Louie Cardinals, and the Cubs own, for a time, Lou Brock. To this day Cubs fans don't talk about the trade that sent Ernie Brolio to Chicago for Lou Brock. I'd often asked the old men prior to the start of the game, sitting in the Grandstand with their brown bag lunch, who was the greatest Chicago baseball player they saw in their day, and many said that was an easy question...Shoeless Joe Jackson of the Chicago White Sox.

We were lucky to watch the Dodgers especially when big Don Drysdale was on the mound. Not only did he have stuff, he had no problem throwing the ball inside to prevent the hitter from digging in. The old timers told us that Sal "The Barber" Maglie, sporting a 5 o'clock shadow look, was a master at brushing the batter back. It was said that Don Drysdale credits Sal Maglie with teaching him the art of brushing batters back. Today you see the homerun hitters digging in at the plate waiting for their pitch with little worry of getting brushed back. Not so with Drysdale. He would pin the ears back on homerun hitters.

The biggest and longest homerun we ever saw in Wrigley, still rising as it rocketed over the bleachers in left center, was hit by Roberto Clemente of the Pittsburgh Pirates It looked like a F-14 taking off and still lifting as it reached the left center bleachers. And, one sunny spring afternoon, I saw the Cubs bring in Marcelino Solis, fresh off the Mexican League circuit, in from the bullpen to pitch to big George Crowe of the Cincinnati Redlegs. I don't know how many triples big George hit in his career, but it couldn't have been many because his running style resembled a 16-wheeler starting from a green light. But on this afternoon, George hit a Solis fast ball so high it almost went out of sight, hit the top of the wall in right field and bounce 50-feet in the air back toward the playing field while big George continued to roam the bases ending at third. So long to Marcelino Solis. I often wondered what Pat Piper was thinking seeing all this Cub mediocrity.

But Wrigley was Wrigley and that made up for a lot of Cubbie ineptitude. The 8th Wonder of the World we called it. Search the baseball parks the world over and you will find nothing remotely close to Wrigley. The green grass, the Boston ivy on the outfield walls, the close proximity from the stands to the ball diamond, the neighborhood surrounding the ball park, the huge green non-electronic scoreboard with the clock in the center rising up in centerfield to be seen in each of the ~40,000-seats, Pat Piper on the public address system...it was perfect. The old men in the Grandstand carrying their lunches in brown bags told us it was hallowed ground. If you haven't seen Wrigley, to really do the trip to ballpark right, start from downtown Chicago, catch the Howard Red Line El going north and ride with the Cub fans to Wrigley. Get off the train at Addison, walk down the steps from the El platform to the street, walk ½-block toward the west and you will be at Addison and Sheffield. Walk another block in the same direction and you will find yourself in front of Wrigley at Clark and Addison. Many, many die-hard Cub fans stood on the corner of Clark and Addison. Never been to Spain, but I've been to Wrigley Field. Back in the day in 1969, the left-field bleachers became famous because of the "Bleacher Bums". Their signature move was to throw the opponent's home run back on the field to show them that the ball didn't belong in the left field bleachers. We always wanted to know where those so-called "Bleacher Bums" were in 1962 when the Cubs weren't winning. You didn't need season tickets in 1962 because there was never a sellout. We had Wrigley all to ourselves in 1962, and, the funny thing about it, we just knew it was a gift. We had box seats in the greatest ballpark in America. And that is the truth.

We always got our hotdogs outside of Wrigley before entering…they were just better. I don't think they sell hot dogs outside of Wrigley anymore. I would be hard pressed to explain why a Chicago hotdog was the best, but it just was. Maybe one of the reasons why the Cubs haven't gone to another World Series since 1945; someone put ketchup on a hotdog during the last game of the Series with Detroit. Every time I hear Shirley & The Shirelles "Will You Love Me Tomorrow", their smash hit of 1960, I can see myself in Squatman's 1953 Ford sedan listening to the AM radio running down Congress Expressway on the way to Wrigley.

The games always started at 1:05 in the afternoon with Jack "Hey Hey" Brickhouse and Vince Lloyd doing the TV and the Hamm's bear dancing from The Land of Sky Blue Waters on the commercials. The Hamm's beer bear commercials were classics. We never stopped for a cold one after the game because there were no bars close to Wrigley. In a city that features a neighborhood bar on every corner back in the day there were only a few bars close to the park. The entire ballpark was surrounded by residential homes and apartment buildings. Today from the ballpark on Clark as you make your way toward the City, there is one bar after another bar. And Cub fans hang out in them long after the game is over. If we caught a foul ball and wanted to get the ball autographed we headed for Waveland where the Cub players exited the park. In those days the player's clubhouse was entered down the left field line past the bullpen. Ron Santo, Cub third basement, used to click his heels in the air following a Cub win as he walked along the left field foul line to the clubhouse. That was 1969.

It has been a long time since the Cubbies made it to the World Series. If you were a Cub fan in the 1960s you learned early that losing was part of the game. And you dreamed that one day you would be sitting in the left field grandstand about 20-rows up in Section 209 to watch the Cubs make it to the World Series. But in the 1960s it was always "just wait till next year". "Just wait till next year" came to a brief stop in 1969 when the Cubs led their division by 16-games in August only to go on to lose at the end of the season to the NY Mets. The Mets were called the "Miracle Mets". These were the same Mets who went on to win the World Series from the Baltimore Borioles (as in "boring"). With the Mets and the Cubs within 2-3 games of each other toward the end of the season, as I recall, in a crucial play at home plate in a crucial series in New York the call went against the Cubs. Cub catcher Randy Hundley, years later, said the "safe" call made on the close play at the plate was "not correct". Had there been an instant replay, like they use today, the entire series could have turned around. But we were Cub fans and knew how to suffer the defeat. The losing quit bothering us after a time.

A wandering group of musicians walked around the ballpark playing music between innings. And it was great talking to the old men who had watched the Cubs in the 1930's when they had great teams. Great stories. Great players. Jay, and a good friend of all of ours, Jeff "Tazie" Taylor, snuck into the first row box seats right behind home plate to watch big Don Cardwell in May of 1960 pitch his no-hitter. Cardwell had a good fast ball, but impressed Jay, as he watched behind the plate, was the way he moved the ball up and down/in and out. We learned a lot about baseball strategy from those old men, and we delighted especially in listening to them talk about the 1945 Cubs and the Cub teams of the 1930s. They talked about Clem Labine's curve ball that they said was unhittable ("it was like the ball dropped off a table"). It was always rumored that if you wanted to bet on the game, whether or not the next pitch would be a ball or a strike, whether or not the hitter would get a hit, the place to do it was under the scoreboard in center field. We never made it out there, but there were a lot of rumors. They talked about the long high drives Hank Sauer hit to left field. The 1958 Cubs were our favorites and Milwaukee Braves outfielder Andy Pafko, who once played for the Cubs, broke our hearts on July 4th when he went into the left field vines to make an unbelievable catch off a ball hit by Bobby Thompson... the same Bobby Thompson of Giant fame and The Shot Heard Round The World when the Giants beat the Dodgers for the National League pennant. They never recovered after Andy Pafko's catch. Jay cried. That was 1958. So for all of the long time suffering Cub fans, especially those who supported the team in the 1950s and early 1960s, for all of what you have been through, this Bud's for you. For all the long suffering Cub fans who were there in the 1950s and 1960s when no one else attended, this Bud's a for you. For all the old men sitting in the grandstand in the early 1960s, who taught us so much and made us proud to be Cub fans even thought they were losing, this Bud is for you.

> "Don't let anyone say it is just a game
> For I've seen other teams and it's never the same
> When your born in Chicago your blessed and you're healed
> The first time you walk into Wrigley Field
> Our heroes wear pinstripes
> Heroes in blue
> Give us the chance to be heroes too
> Forever we'll win and if we should lose
> We knew someday we'll go all the way
> Yeah!
> Someday we'll go all the way"
> — "Go All The Way", Eddie Vetter

Comiskey Park on Chicago's Southside, while it didn't have ivy on the outfield walls, saw more fans attending simply because the Sox had a good teams in the late 50s and early 60s. However, we still managed to slip down into those boxes too. At Comiskey, we saw some of the great Yankee teams and players---Mantle, Berra, Skowron and Ford. We hated the Yankees and that is why the Go-Go Sox, who won the American League pennant in 1959, will forever be in our hearts. Minnie Minoso in left, Luis Apariso at short, Nellie Fox at second base. Billy Pierce on the mound. And Western Spring's own Sherm Lollar catching behind the plate. They electrified the City of Chicago in 1959. People who never knew how to read a box score, learned in 1959. They were an exciting team and one that didn't overpower the opposition but made contact with the baseball. The Kansas City Royal, who won it all in 2015, were like the go-go ChiSox of 1959...put the ball in play and good things happen. I heard the crack of the bat against the baseball from the box seat level at both Wrigley and Comiskey Park, and of all the cracks I heard when ball hit bat, McCovey, big Joe Adcock, Teddy Kluszewski, George Crowe, Harmon Killebrew, Hank Aaron, et. al, there was nothing that compared with the sound of the ball hitting bat like it did when 5' 11" Dick Allen, with the Phillies, Chi White Sox and other teams, hit a homerun. It sounded like a canon went off in the stadium. The sound was one you would never forget. The old timers said only the ball coming off The Babe's bat sounded like the ball coming off of Dick Allen's bat. I never heard that sound again until one recent day in Wrigley when I heard the sound of the ball coming off the bat of young Kyle Schwarber of the Cubs. Watching Dick Allen hit was Just like being in the box seats at Wrigley (ground level) and watching Clem Labine with the Brooklyn Dodgers throw a curve ball...it looked like the dropped 3-feet by the time it got to the batter's box. We got to see all those players, including one of our all time favorites, Ed Charles playing 3rd base for the Kansas City Athletics. The Kansas City Royals came later. Time of your life, huh kid?

Comiskey had a beauty all of its own, and we thought it was a sin to tear it down in 1991. The site of the old Comiskey was turned into a parking lot and that bothered Squatman for 10-years. Some old ballparks seem to deteriorate as they aged, but Comiskey took on a life of its own with the Bill Veeck exploding scoreboard and the most notorious grounds keeping home field advantage of all time. Chicago always knows how to work the tables to their advantage. Comiskey Park, we all agreed, had soul; and, it too was in its own neighborhood. Didn't the owners know that Joe DiMaggio, Al Kaline, Vic Power, Ted Williams, The Babe, Rocky Colavito and Shoeless Joe Jackson all played there? But there is big money in those corporate boxes so all that is left of Comiskey is home plate that sits out in front of Cellular Field and with it all those memories of our youth. To this very day, and probably to the day we all die, we will always call the ballpark at 333 West 35th Street, Chicago, Illinois, Comiskey Park in remembrance to all those great Chi Sox players of our youth. You never seem to forget certain things in life and when I think of Comiskey I will always remember the excitement generated by the 1959 go-go Chi Sox team. The seasons came and went after 1959, but that was the season we will always remember. We had Tura Satana on South State at the Follies, we had box seats in Wrigley and the

White Sox taking the extra base, laying down the perfect bunt, stealing a base at Comiskey…where did all the 1959 Chi Sox go, long time passing.

In our day, we learned from Ernie Banks that it is important to display a positive attitude…every time he said "Let's play two" the people of Chicago, Cub and White Sox fans, admired his positive attitude. Back in the day, a Negro ballplayer, who never received the accolades for his playing ability as he should have, by the name of Leroy "Satchel" Paige told us, "don't look over your shoulder, someone might be gaining on you". Today in 2016, a Boston Red Sox first baseman by the nickname "Big Papi" offered us some sound advise about life:

- Smile…make a good first impression
- Be a great friend
- Dress for success
- Give the best hugs
- Awaken your latent psychic power---tap into the kinetic energy of the universe long enough to sense what is coming next
- How to express your feelings---emotional speech after the Boston Marathon bombing that immediately became iconic
- How to hit monster homeruns---you have to go on the journey yourself, but he can teach you how to appreciate them

Jay and I played semi-pro hardball in the summer of 1960 against Wheaton, North Chicago and the likes. We hated the coach who was also a "teacher" at LTHS, and was a complete idiot and a guy who constantly belittled us. The end for me came in the 4th or 5th game when the coach complained that I miss timed a jump for a ball playing 2nd base. For Jay, the end came when he staggered trying to catch a high fly in left field at a game played at Spring Rock Park in Western Springs, IL only to see the ball fall to the ground almost 10-feet from him. The crowd had a good laugh and the opponents did as well of his well orchestrated stagger. But the coach didn't particularly care for it and Jay didn't play again. Our time was better spent playing whiffle ball then putting up with the crap the coach dished.

I was always very proud of the fact that I was born and raised in Chicago. Ernie Banks. Ted Kluszewski. Al Capone. Dick Butkus, Mayor Daley. And, I have always been very proud to say that Ernie Hemingway and I were born in the same hospital that stands to this day in West suburban Chicago. While a suffering Cub fan through and through, I always pulled for the White Sox when they weren't playing the Cubs. Just like we always pulled for Milwaukee when they played the hated St Louis Redbirds. Wrigley will take your breath completely away. Many people say it is right behind the Taj in splendor. The experience of watching the best of the best play was, as they say today, priceless. We used to stop and think how many great ball players played in Wrigley. Babe Ruth played there. So did Stan Hack, Gabby Hartnett, Joe DiMaggio, Hank Sauer, Frankie Baumholtz, Dee Fondy, Handsome Ranson Jackson, Ralph Kiner, Al Dark, Al Heist, Sad Sam Jones, Marcelino Solis, Gene Baker, Ken Hobbs, Ryan Sandberg, Ernie Banks, Randy Hundley, Dave Kingman, Mark Grace, Ron Santo and Phil Cavaretta. They were worth more than the price of admission.

Pat Piper, the public address announcer, always broadcast the starting line ups with his signature phrase before the start of every game…"attention (sounded like tension)… attention please! Have your pencil… and scorecards ready…and I'll give you…the correct lineup…for today's game" "Leading off for Cincinnati 12 [never number 12, just 12] Don Blasingame, second base". We were free in those early years in the 60's…only grades in school and finding a summer job to worry about. Of the two, finding a summer job was the toughest. I have to this day been proud of the fact that I am a Cub fan. While "just wait till next year" talk on opening day pissed us all off, the 8th wonder of the world, Wrigley Field, the old men sitting in the grandstand watching batting practice, who had seen the winning days, the hot dog vendors at Addison & Sheffield and sneaking down to our beloved box seats made it all worthwhile. And then I don't think there were better ball players assembled like we saw in the early 1960's…I mean the National League All Star team had Hank Aaron in left, Willie Mays in center and Roberto Clemente in right field. It just didn't get any better.

We always thought if you missed Mays catch a ball in centerfield, with his basket style catching form, you missed the best of the best. McCovey, Jim Ray Hart and Mays, the Giants had power. Willie Mays could hit, hit with power, run and make impossible plays in the outfield. Years later, when you could no longer sneak down to the boxes in Wrigley and the price of box seats cost a week's salary, we became the old men sitting in the grandstand answering questions as to what it was like in 1962 when 3,000-fans showed up for a game. We are now the old Cub fans, and should they win it all in 2016 or 2017, we experienced the 1962 Cubs, and I wouldn't trade that experience and those spring days at Wrigley for anything. Those days were the best of the best. Even better than Fort Lauderdale and Daytona Beach combined we thought. And sitting there one afternoon behind the visitor's dugout I had a feeling that they were going to be the best. There was plenty of room to spread out; plenty of seats available. Memories…Stan The Man's 3,000th hit was in Wrigley, a line drive (did he ever hit anything else) to left field off of Mo Drabowsky. 25-years later in a parking lot in St Louis, MO I had a chance to talk to Stan in person as he was doing some benefit. He said he could always hit Drabowsky. What Stan didn't say was that he could always hit everyone and, in our opinion, Stan "The Man" Musial of "here comes that Man again" fame, was as good a hitter as you will ever see… right up there with Ted Williams, Rod Carew and Tony Gwynn. Stan retired from baseball with a .331 batting average in a time when the old timers thought the pitching was better. Here comes that Man again, and "The Man" killed the Cubs for many, many years. While the Milwaukee Braves, and later the Brewers, played 90-miles to the north of Chicago, it was the St Louis Redbirds, when they played the Cubs, who brought the fans out in both Wrigley Field and Busch Stadium. There was no victory in Wrigley like a victory over the hated Redbirds. I thought the Cubs had a good team in 1968, but Redbird pitcher Bob Gibson was unhittable, and it was just another year watching the Redbirds go all the way.

A brief comment about Spring Break back in the day… first, we could have saved for a year and still not afforded an airline ticket from O'Hare (The Big One) International Airport to Fort Lauderdale. Second, we couldn't have afforded a hotel room and 4-guys sleeping in a car gets a little old. Further, it was 1800 miles from Chicago to Fort Lauderdale. Even if you punished the car we were driving, there were no interstate roads back then and US 41 through Georgia saw you run through a lot of small towns, a lot of speed traps hungry for dollars that were set up by Georgia cops. The "briar patch" as it was called up North. Then you had to go through the upcoming, congested Coca-Cola town of Atlanta on Hwy US 41. Once you got through Atlanta you had approximately 600-miles to go before you reached the tropical paradise of Fort Lauderdale, where the girls were in 1960.

So Wrigley Field became our "beach" during those Spring Breaks, and, we were the better and the wiser because of it. Ernie Banks was not hitting home runs in Fort Lauderdale or Daytona Beach or Boynton Beach for that matter. You wouldn't have seen Clemente's home run over the left center field bleachers and on over Waveland Ave if you had been sitting on South Beach in Miami. There is only one Wrigley. We knew it then and we know it now. One day they will win the World Series and on that day everyone will be a Cub fan. One thing is for certain, no matter what team they play against when they get to the World Series, the baseball fans of America, with the exception of the American League team they are playing against, will be pulling for the Chicago Cubs. After all, it has been a long time between World Series conquests. And when they do win it all, all of those old Cub fans that missed being there to see them win the World Series can finally rest in peace. I remember the great Cub pitcher, Rick Sutcliffe, who is presently a damn good TV baseball analyst, mention what he remembered most driving from the hotel to San Diego's baseball stadium during the 1984 playoffs was that the street on the route to the stadium was lined with old Cub fans who wore old Cub hats from years gone by cheering from the curb as the Cubs passed on the bus. To this day, game # 5 in San Diego still haunts the Cubs and it probably always will.

But the worm will turn one day. And when it does, the ghosts of a sure-fielding Leon Durham who saw a sharp groundball roll through his legs in Game 5 in1984 that lead San Diego on to beating the Cubs, the ghosts of 2003 with Dusty We Trusty and Bartman, who interfered with a foul ball preventing

Moises Alou from catching the ball, and the ghosts of Al Heist's dropping fly ball in center field in 1969 in a crucial game against the Mets, will all be gone. Chief Hosa's ghost will come down from the foothills of the great Rocky Mountains just outside of Denver, Colorado and will do a little dance in the left field bleachers to remember Ralph Kiner, Dave Kingman and Hank Sauer and all the greats who played in the outfield for the Cubs. Then Chief Hosa's ghost will touch all the bases and Alex Gonzales' error on a routine groundball at shortstop in 2003, which to this day bothers him, will be erased from memory. The Chief's ghost will take the mound and dance in recognition of pitcher Claude Passau who did everything he could in 1945 to have the Cubs beat Detroit in the World Series. 1945 was the last World Series appearance for the Cubs. While standing on the pitcher's mound, the Ghost of Chief Hosa will recognize the names of three great Cub pitchers in the modern era---Fergie Jenkins, Rick Sutcliffe and Greg Maddux.

Life will go on, but those old Cubs will never be forgotten. It will be a passage in time and gone forever will be the days of talking to the old men with their sandwiches who sat in the grandstand section above the Cubs dugout. We learned and we listened. The old men sitting in the grandstand never seemed to be too high when the Cubs won a game nor too low when the Cubs lost. We knew we would never forget it, but we didn't know how really perfect it was. For there we were in the front row box seats in not just any ballpark, but Wrigley Field...if you liked baseball, as we did, this was as good as it could possibly get.

# Chapter 9

*"The lion and the tiger may be more powerful, but the wolf does not perform in the circus"*
*— Anonymous*

## The Call of the Wild...a bouncing basketball

By the late 1950s and through most of the 1960s, we headed downtown to the old Chicago Stadium on Madison Street to watch college basketball triple-headers on the weekends. From November to March, basketball for us was everything. There was no place on earth that compared to watching a basketball or hockey game at the old Chicago Stadium. It looked big from the outside and even bigger when you got in. While the temperature outside may have been below zero, inside the joint was rocking to the tune of double and triple-headers pitting some of the best teams in the country against one another. You could smoke inside in those days and by the time the 2$^{nd}$ or 3$^{rd}$ basketball game rolled around it looked like a fog had developed at the upper deck seating level because of the smoke. A local kid would "watch" our car for $3 as we parked on a street nearby the Stadium. If you didn't pay the local kid, chances were good you lost a headlight or your rear view mirror. Business is business. We saw some great, great games at the Stadium. I remember one night when Branch McCracken led the Hurrying Hoosiers of Indiana in to play featuring the Van Arsdale twins and big Walt Bellamy who was the closest dominating player we saw in person who compared to Wilt Chamberlain. A special moment for us was sneaking down to courtside and watching Red Holtzman's National Basketball Association

New York Knicks play...whoever had the hot hand, got the ball. There was very little dribbling around and a lot of passing the ball quickly. At courtside you could hear it all and the communication the Knicks had with one another was something to hear. As the number of great basketball players to come out of the high schools in Illinois and particularly Chicago---starting in the 50's with Ted Caiazza of LaGrange, Paxton Lumpkin and Charlie Brown from DuSable, who were screwed by one corrupt referee in the championship game, George Wilson of Marshall, Cazzie Russell/Carver moving all the way into the 2000's with Derrick Rose from Simeon.

Our favorite clutch performance in all of the Illinois high school basketball games we watched over the many years was watching Anthony Smedley a 5'7" sophomore yanked off the bench to provide defensive pressure, drill a 17-foot baseline corner shot to give Carver High School in Chicago a one point victory over Centralia, IL in the Illinois High School Association basketball championship game in Champaign-Urbana, IL at the old Huff Gym. From that point forward, it was always Smedley from the corner when we practiced shooting jump shots from the side. We always pulled for Chicago teams particularly against those from southern Illinois.

From 1952 to present, many people in Chicago that know anything about basketball in the State of Illinois think that DuSable High School Panther's great team of 1952 was the best that ever played and didn't win the big one in Champaign-Urbana, IL thanks to a racist ref who made it impossible for them to do so. I didn't see the game and I've never seen a video of the game, but those in attendance screamed "foul" long and very loud. And then the very next year, the 1953 Lyons Township High School, LaGrange, IL, Lions, fielded a team many thought was the greatest high school basketball team ever assembled in Illinois. With Ted Caiazza at center who was 6'8", Leon and Joel McCrae at the forwards and two slick ball handlers by the name of Chuck Sedgwick and Nate Smith at guard, the Lions not only went undefeated to win the State of Illinois High School basketball championship in Champaign, IL; now played in Peoria, IL), but average 89-points per game in 1953. The 1953 LaGrange High School

Lions scored 89-points per game without a 3-point line or a shot clock. Sitting in the Fort Myers, FL airport in October of 2010 waiting for a flight to Midway and Chicago I overheard this couple talking about LaGrange and going back for a reunion. It was none other than Chuck Sedgwick the playmaking guard on the 1953 LaGrange, IL Illinois High School Association championship basketball team. Chuck mainly talked about how good Ted Caiazza was at center. "Unstoppable" said Sedgwick.

> "You never drink all day unless you start in the morning"
> — Phil The Plumber

I can't remember once in the 1960s, whether at Normal or hitch hiking up and down Route US 66, that when someone asked me where I was from or where I went to high school and I said in LaGrange, IL, if they knew anything about high school basketball, and even if the didn't, always asked about Ted Caiazza. Ted was elected to the Illinois High School Association top 100 high school athletes of all time. Yet, for reasons totally unclear to me, and my friends, the great Ted Caiazza was never appointed to the Lyons Township High School Hall of Fame. The "Hall" has doctors who treated otitis media, but if you were the most well known basketball player in the State of Illinois in the mid-1950s, in a State where a bouncing basketball is the Call of the Wild, you just didn't make the cut. So LTHS can keep Ted Caiazza out of their Hall, but if you were hitching up and down US Route 66 in the 1960s you just knew that Ted put LaGrange on the map.

The 1963 Loyola of Chicago Ramblers, to this day, are still the only university team in the State of Illinois to win a NCAA basketball championship. Down by 15-points in the first half (without a 3-point shot line or a 30-second time shot clock) to a heavily favored Cincinnati Bearcat team, they came back to win in overtime with Vic Roesch putting a missed shot by Les Hunter back in for the victory. After the game, Vic was asked how he happened to be in the right place at the right time to rebound Les Hunter's missed shot and put the ball back into the basket. Vic responded by saying, "I've played basketball with Les hunter since 5th grade...when he misses I know where the ball is going". We

70

followed Loyola very closely in 1963 seeing them play Santa Clara in the Chicago Stadium on a very, very cold January night in Chicago. Loyola finished 25-2 in 1963 after beating Cincinnati in the finals at Freedom Hall in Louisville, KY. Jerry Harkness, Loyola's All-American brought them back single handedly.

The Ramblers started 4-black players and a hard-knocking white guard by the name of Johnny Eagan. They played Mississippi State in the quarterfinals, an all white team, in East Lansing, MI and the Governor of Mississippi refused to let the team play Loyola. But that didn't stop Mississippi State. The team and coaches voted to sneak out of the State of Mississippi anyway to play the game and the picture of Jerry Harkness and Joe Don Gold, the Mississippi State's center meeting at center court and shaking hands prior to the tip off, is immortalized to this very day. Two years later, Texas Western Miners started 5-blacks and went on to win the NCAA basketball tournament. The movie "Glory Road" commemorated the team. The fact that the Ramblers were from Chicago, the fact that we watched them play during the year and the fact that they were heavy underdogs made their victory the greatest of all time for us.

I went back to the old Loyola gym on the north side of Chicago in 2009 just to see it again. Squatman's Dad, as Captain of Northwestern's basketball team, played in that gym. So did the great Larry Bird. And so did that storybook 1963 team. Just to look at the Rambler's championship trophy in the Loyola gym trophy case 46-years later brought tears to my eyes and great memories of that team. I never thought that Loyola Rambler team received the recognition they truly deserved. To come back that far in the second half when there was no shot clock and no 3-point shot should gone down as the single greatest feat in the history of NCAA basketball. But, instead, Christian Laettner's shot at the buzzer is always touted as the great play of NCAA basketball. But if one was watching Loyola's come back and victory in overtime there would be no doubt in your mind that Loyola's comeback, not Duke and Laettner, was the greatest moment in all of NCAA basketball. Jerry Harkness elevated his game in that second half against a tough, well disciplined, defensively minded Cincinnati Bearcat team like no one we have ever seen since. We only wish ESPN would recognize the 1963

Ramblers of Loyola in a 30/30 segment or during the "Road To The Final Four". And we have never liked the whining Coach K who almost brought basketball to a complete stop with his "flopping" style of play. An assistant Duke white coach today by the name of Jon Scheyer was the best of the floppers, and if the call went against him, and it rarely did, Coach K would crunch his face together to look like a rodent and scream bloody murder. Is Coach K the greatest? You would have a lot of "yes's" and a lot of "no's". Personally, we always thought that Coach John Wooden of UCLA was the best and the second best was Al McGuire at Marquette, hands down. In the NBA, what Coach Jerry Sloan and Coach Red Holtzman did with both good and bad teams put them on top of our coaching list. We rarely watch the NBA during the regular season, but wait for the finals when every shot is contested and defense is played.

When we cashed a 65/1 ticket on the Connecticut Huskies in 2013, the clerk at the Sports Book window at Red Rock Casino in Las Vegas asked how we happened to pack a 65 to 1 shot to win it…we replied, "we have watched a lot of games". Jay, when he worked as Sports Editor of the Milwaukee Star newspaper, learned from coach Al McGuire, the famous basketball coach at Marquette in Milwaukee, how to pick a winning team. If you plan to bet the "Final Four" make sure the team you are betting has a guard who can penetrate, a shooter with 40% or better accuracy from the 3-point line and an aircraft carrier in the middle. By aircraft carrier McGuire meant a 6' 10" or taller center who could clear the boards and put in the rebounded shots. One thing about Chicago high school basketball that we discovered in the 1960's, they learn early to go to the basket. Very few players knew how to drive to the basket and the flopping that occurred which led to a charge being called on the offensive player by the referee made it almost impossible to do so. But, if you have a player that can drive and create and one that can shoot, you have the makings of a very successful basketball team. One of the best all time was Allen Iverson when he played for Philadelphia. He was quick and he could drive to the basket. Iverson would be a starting guard on my all time best basketball team. "Be quick, but don't hurry" as Coach John Wooden said. One thing on Wooden. He had accepted a position at the University of Minnesota and on the night the Gophers were supposed to call and confirm his appointment as their new head coach there was a snow-storm in Minneapolis and the telephone lines were down. UCLA called and offered him a job, which he accepted. Minnesota called the next day but by then Wooden had accepted with UCLA. So a snowstorm in Minneapolis gave UCLA and Los Angeles the best college basketball coach ever. One thing on Wooden… his UCLA Bruins didn't "flop" like Duke.

The beauty of being a sport fan in Chicago, whether you pulled for Loyola, Northwestern, The Cubs, the Bears or the Chi Sox, the fact that they won the big one so infrequently meant that when they did win the big one it was, and still is, a big deal. A deal so big you remembered the names of the players on the team. Ask any guy today that watched that 1963 final between The Loyola Ramblers and the Cincinnati Bearcats who was the Ramblers All-American, and they will be able to tell you. But Loyola's come back in the final without a 3-point line is etched in my mind forever. Never seen one like it since. Loyola, our beloved Ramblers, was a heavy underdog to the Cincinnati Bearcats. I didn't know what the odds on the game were because we didn't have money to bet anyway, but I'll bet they were in the 40 to 50 to 1 range. When Vic Roesch put in that missed Les Hunter shot in overtime, we jumped for joy in Jay's basement like we were teenagers all over again. We didn't even know the broadcast was delayed by two hours. The fact that the broadcast of the game was in 1963, tells you just how far NCAA basketball has come with the American viewing public. We paid close to $1,000 per man to watch the Sweet 16 in Omaha in March of 2015. Only to have the rude Wichita State boosters (better yet, idiots) in a row of seats placed just for them next to the floor, stand for the entire game, thus blocking our view. We wrote the President of Wichita State to let him know the Wichita State Shockers' coach's son was a rude, snot-nosed kid who had no respect for adults, and Mrs. Coach was a first class, card-carrying rude woman with malice toward everyone who asked her to sit down. They never did. But, we sold our tickets for the next day's games, at a profit, and called Stub Hub to complain that we were supposed to be seated "courtside". Stub Hub saw it our way and paid us back for the misunderstanding. And Wichita State lost which made us feel even better. Had those Wichita State fans pulled that "blocking the-view-trick" at the old Chicago Stadium, they would have ended up in the upper deck with their head in their hands. As the man said, "Chicago is a no bull shit town". In all our years of attending and watching basketball games what the Wichita State people pulled by refusing to sit down so people behind them could also see the game was just bullshit.

> "I'm not a girl that could linger
> But I feel like a butterfinger
> I wanna do it again"
> — The Staple Singers, 1975

The 2012 NCAA basketball "Final Four" tournament saw us take the Amtrak from Chicago to St Louis, Missouri. We decided to stay at the Marriott Hotel at the old St Louis railroad station because it was close to where the Amtrak stopped and it was a beautiful hotel, and if you like trains as we did, even nicer. The Ohio University Bobcats were also staying in the hotel and their fan support was good to see and good to hear…"let's go Bobcats". As memory recalls, the Bobcats lost to the University of North Carolina and the coach of the Bobcats left to the University of Illinois the next year. Of all the "Final Four" tournaments we have been to, St Louis was the most fun. We walked to the basketball arena and we ate at some excellent Italian restaurants on The Hill in St Louis. But, the best dinner of all was in a little hamburger place just outside the basketball center because we were joined for dinner that night by TV commentator, Craig Sager. We couldn't begin to tell you what a nice guy Craig Sager is and a real asset to college basketball. He has interviewed all the big names in college and professional basketball and is a genuinely humble guy who loves the game. Here he was sitting down with us having dinner and talking basketball. He took time to autograph stuff from people passing by our table as he ate dinner. It greatly saddened all of us to learn that Craig had developed cancer and we all wish him nothing but the best. We only hope that other announcers learn how to interview like Craig Sager does.

One of our favorite players from that era of basketball was a 6' 2" skinny guard out of Kokomo, Indiana by the name of Jimmy Rayl who played for Indiana University. I think he still holds the single-game Indiana scoring record to this day. He had the "green light" to cut loose from half-court and it seemed like his shots soared to the rafters and then hit nothing but net. The arch he had shooting the ball was even more than Steph Curry's with the Golden State Warriors, and that is saying something.

# Chapter 10

*"When the tennis ball is on your side of the court, the opponent can't do a thing with it"*
*— Vic Braden, "Tennis For The Future", 1977*

## Graduation means good-bye...where did all the good guys go, long time passing

ON JUNE 15, 1960 we graduated from LTHS and all said good-bye to our high school days, and with each going his separate way. Our playing days were over we thought leaving the graduation ceremony held at Vaughn Gym. I can't say I learned a lot in high school, nor did I open many books. I can't say I was motivated by many of my teachers although I didn't put too much energy into studying. We did make some long lasting friends and that is worth all the tea in China. To have one long lasting friend is amazing, but to have seven lifelong buddies is unheard of. I didn't finish in the top 100 academically or make the National Honor Society, like Buck did. I didn't have a burning desire to do so. The four years in high school passed by rather quickly and if I could bring them all back, I would have gotten more involved in making better grades.

I got a summer job at the Fred Harvey restaurant on the Tri-State Toll way in Hinsdale, IL busing tables. The Tri-State ran from Wisconsin to Illinois to Indiana. While I knew of her in high school, I didn't know her exactly, but KS, and I started dating that summer. She, too, worked at Fred Harvey's as a waitress, and we had time to meet and talk after work. In the fall, she headed to Jacksonville, IL and MacMurray College. A pricey little co-ed school nestled among the trees and old dorm houses on campus. One weekend, Jay had come to Normal and we, and the Duke of Kankakee decided to hitch hike over from Normal to Jacksonville for me to spend some time with KS and build a base, and for them to be fixed up with dates by KS. We went to see the romantic movie Moon River together on Sunday night instead of heading back to Normal, Illinois for Monday classes. So at the crack of dawn, knowing that hitching from Jacksonville to Springfield, Illinois could be tough, we "borrowed" three big tire bikes and headed out to US 36. US 36 was a 2-lane federal highway that ran from Jacksonville direct to Springfield. A tough 30-mile trip that took up to 1 ½ hours to get to New Berlin, just half the way to Springfield. Like most US highways of its day, it didn't have a shoulder and we took our lives in our hands trying to keep the big tired bike up right biking along the side of the road when a car or a truck passed at 70-mph. We would have been off the bike had the tires been of the skinny variety as they are today. I wouldn't trade that bike ride past the cornfields in central Illinois for "Ride-The-Rockies" the annual Colorado bike race up and over mountain passes from Grand Junction to Boulder, CO. or The Tour De France. We parked the bikes next to US 66 and proceeded north to Normal by thumb. One thing you could count on traveling through Illinois---flat roads. KS and I went out together during New Years Eve, and once again, it wasn't my best performance. Shortly after that, sitting with her on the sofa in her living room one night in the winter of 1961, she got up unannounced, left for the kitchen and I never saw her again. Her Father came into the living room asking me to leave immediately, I walked from her house in LaGrange Park back to Western Springs in a blinding snow storm swearing never again to get romantically involved. I had plenty of time to think about it as the walk was 7-miles. Some they do; some they don't. My heart wasn't broken but what a way for her to say good-bye. She ended up marrying some "stem" she knew from high school and never attended a reunion, I ran into her brother in a bar in Chicago having dinner with Squatman and Jay around 1995, gave him my business card to give to her, but never heard from her. I think she died 3-years after that, divorced from the stem.

Squatty, after high school graduation, headed West to the cornfields of Iowa and Parsons College in Fairfield, Iowa where to this day his transcript shows that he was valedictorian of his class and captain of the basketball team, Before heading West to Parsons, after a card game one summer evening, I remember all of us going to Eddie Doucette's Pancake Plantation at 47th and Gilbert right down the street from LTHS South Campus. . They made the best banana waffle. The waitress' name was Dot. She was in her early 40's, somewhat attractive with a good personality. Why this question came out of Squatman's mouth I'll never know, but to the day Jay died he always asked Squatman the same question Squat asked Dot that night she was serving us. Here is the question…."Dot, do you know what I'm thinking? Dot said, "No Squat, what are you thinking"? To which Squatty replied, "I'm thinking I would like to take you to bed". The screech Dot let loose could have been heard in the restaurant parking lot and completely startled the customers in the restaurant. She was insulted and pissed. We gulfed down our waffles and made a quick exit. For me, it was my last trip into Eddie Doucette's place. From that day forward, Jay always asked Squat, "Senor, do you know what I'm thinking"?

Squatty drove back and forth from Parson in Fairfield, IA to home in Western Springs with important stops along the way, with a favorite being Quincy, IL. Quincy, IL is famous for the Lincoln-Douglas debates in the 1858 and Jackie's House of Ill Repute, where there was spacious parking in the back, overstuffed couches, candy dishes in the living room. On special occasions, it was said that Jackie served fried chicken. After making your selection at Jackie's, the question always asked once you made your way up the stairs to the bedrooms above was "Honey, what kind of party do you want"? More times than not the "half and half" party was ordered and the women at Jackie's turned party on. Prior to getting to Jackie's it was necessary to stop at a little town called Ursa, IL where one of Squat's friends would siphon gas from a semi-truck into a gas can they always carried. It was also necessary to stop at The Broasted Chicken Inn where they greased very hard. And, Quincy, IL had great donuts. Standing by the Mississippi River in Quincy you could almost see Tom & Huck floating by. Sadly, most of Squatman's college buddies from his beloved Parsons have all passed...characters all. To this day, I don't think our boy Squatman could tell you what Lincoln and Douglas were debating in Quincy, IL. But it didn't matter.

## "It will put a little pep in the gumbo" — Jay Crawford

John 'BS" also ventured into Quincy and called Jackie's "The den of iniquity along the Mississippi River" that offered free samples of the gift that keeps on giving. BS later reported that it took his doctor 3-shots in his ass to kill the bug. Quite a town that Quincy. Actually famous for its high school basketball coach, Sherrill Hanks, who developed a full court basketball zone press that was deadly. If you are a new basketball coach reading this Google up Sherrill Hanks' of Quincy, IL High School and his zone press. I don't know how many games Hanks won with the press but it had to be a lot. Few teams ever beat it. But in triple overtime in 1967, big Dave Robisch and the Springfield, IL Senators beat the Quincy Blue Devils in triple overtime. People who attended the game said it was one of the greatest games ever played in high school basketball. In later years, Hanks had a Quincy Blue Devil team that was often compared to the top high school basketball team ever in Illinois, the Lions of Lyons Township High School and LaGrange, Illinois.

Willie The Wop headed off to Valpo in Indiana and we all knew he was headed for success in corporate America. And, we were correct. He had the style and the temperament perfectly suited for the back-stabbers of corporate America. He presented well and had excellent manners and seemed to hold up well under fire. He had a keen eye for good-looking women and is presently married to an attractive younger woman. Further, Mike was a good listener who cared about what you were saying. While I admired President Ronald Reagan for hanging a framed picture on the wall in his office with the following inscription----"*There Is No Limit To How Far A Man Can Go Or What He Can Do If He Doesn't Mind Who Gets The Credit*"---it didn't hold any water in corporate America. But more on corporate America later on down the line.

Buck headed north to college and later became a writer for a well-known national magazine. From there he moved on to be a Press Secretary of a President of the USA. He interviewed and met prominent world leaders on trips he made all over the world, including Muammar Gaddafi. And early one evening, in the Tulsa, OK airport, obtaining word that my flight out was delayed, I went to the bar to have a beer. I took my first drink and looked up at the television screen on the wall in front of me in time to just catch our boy Buck, asking the President of the United States a question. "Your question, Buck?", asked President Ronald Reagan. A long ways I thought from the Follies and "The Pitchman" calling Smitty to come down center aisle to throw Buck out of the theatre. Buck is a classic example, I think, of how far one can go if he applies himself. In 1959, "The Pitchman" at the Follies Theatre on South State Street is calling Smitty to have Buck kicked out and 25-years later the same guy is asking the President of the US a question…it just doesn't get any better. Buck made us all look good. We were all very proud of Buck's success, and like Jay, John BS, Squatman, Willie The Wop, Buck was a character in his own right. Jay and I argued with Buck for years about the value of Food Stamps. Buck loved his college basketball and years later we met in St Louis, San Antonio and Omaha to see "The Road To The Final Four" games. Put NCAA "Road To The Final Four" basketball Sweet 16 tickets on your Bucket List for certain if you like basketball. Even if you aren't a big basketball fan, the roar of the crowd and the intensity and determination shown by the players is something to see. It is a great weekend.

On June 15, 1960 I thought the last place I would ever end up in would be corporate America. I knew I would miss the basketball games we played at night under dismal lighting conditions our senior year at DG's house in Western Springs in 40-degree weather. The only cement on the "court", to enable your ball to get a good bounce, were two thin strips about 3-feet wide that ran vertical to the basket. In between the two strips of cement was grass and dirt. Dribbling was rather tricky. Below 40-degrees and the ball doesn't bounce well. But the game was so physical we played in tee shirts and didn't even feel the cold. And, the basketball games at Gilbert that we played sometimes had so much snow on the court that you couldn't even dribble

Sitting there at the graduation ceremony in the Vaughn gym I very well knew I would miss meeting lovely Lenore at lunch. I knew I would also miss the intramural sports, especially basketball and 16" softball. And, I knew, as Jay knew, that our playing days were over. No more Big League Manager (BLM) baseball game in the basement on the ping-pong table at Jay's. When Jay died, he still had the records he kept from BLM days.

## The Lilac Lodge Restaurant, Hillside, Illinois...

The first order of business on June 16, 1960, to get Lester "The Pester" (my Father) off my back, was to find a summer job that paid over the minimum wage of $1.00 an hour, was close enough to Western Springs and didn't take away all of our evenings. Pickings were slim in the summer of 1960. But stepmother Betty and Lester the Pester kept your nose to the grindstone looking for a job. They were relentless We searched for jobs but the only experience Jay and I had was busing tables and flipping burgers at BG Wimpy's, I don't remember how we got the job, probably just going in and applying for a busboy job, and we both landed a job busing tables at night at the Lilac Lodge at Wolf Road and 22nd Street in Hillside, Illinois. Sometimes in life you just fall into it, and the Lilac Lodge job was one of those summer jobs we just luckily fell into. Andy V, the manager, made us feel like we were wanted, needed and part of the team. Can you imagine, a manager who actually communicated with and appreciated a busboy? A manager that wasn't looking for something we did wrong. A manager who wanted to give us his help and teach us how to deal with disgruntled customers. It was rather funny, for some reason customers at the Lilac Lodge, if the customers thought they were waiting too long, always complained to us (the busboys) first. Little did they know we were last on the totem pole to know where their order was, but Andy taught us how to handle a customer in distress We quickly realized how important our job was and why Andy paid attention to our every need. On our past jobs no one cared about how well we were doing or anything about us. Andy actually communicated with us.

As I recall, the classy Lilac Lodge restaurant seated about 250-people and on a Friday and a Saturday night the place was packed to the max with a long waiting line even for those who had reservations. It was critical for us to get each table "bussed" immediately after the guests had departed as to not keep the customers waiting any longer than necessary. Jay and I covered the entire dining room together and from 6:00pm till 11:00pm on the weekend nights we were slammed. The waitresses paid us a percentage of their tips on top of the $1.00 minimum wage we were making so it turned out to be a job that put some money in our pockets. Money that was sorely needed as it always seems to be. And thanks to Mr. Andy V we had dinner prior to starting the job each night prepared by some outstanding chef's who often commented that the food they served "put a little lead in the pencil". Years later, when I was promoted to District Sales Manager managing 12-Reps, I remembered how Andy treated us when we started, and how much it meant to me and I adopted what Andy demonstrated, Look for what people are doing right and let them know. The more they do right the more they are going to want to do right. Teach, but don't lecture. Ask for feedback and provide help wherever and whenever it is needed. And, make yourself available and don't get upset if someone offers a suggestion to change things. Listen to it; and adopt it if it is good. Andy V. was our kind of guy…in our kind of town. We made a lot of money that summer busing tables for Andy. One other thing about Andy V, he always dressed for success. He dressed like he was the manager. Years later, when a fresh out of college drug sales rep was hired for a job calling on providers in Cape Girardeau and Poplar Bluff, MO, not close to Wall Street, he bought a couple of new suits with vests. When he asked his manager if the suits and vest were too much for rural Missouri, his manager said, "no you want to dress like you are the most successful guy out there". If you are going into corporate America this is worth remembering. Dress like you are making a million dollars because people want to do business with successful people.

One of the last things we did as a group before we headed to our respective colleges and universities---Squatty, Jay, Dutchy, BS, Willie the Wop, Buck and Admiral Dan---and until we all got together again in Las Vegas for golf and handicapping horses in the Fall of 1996, occurred in the summer of 1960 when we all went to Comiskey Park at 35th and Shields, to watch the go-go White Sox play the NY Yankees. We hated the Yankees. On this Sunday afternoon for the Yankee game we sat in the upper deck in right field. Even though it was the Yankees we had plenty of room. I can remember buying a beer for everyone who was there. We had a good time; spirits were up for what lie ahead. A lot different than Wrigley, Comiskey had a history and a soul all of its own. After all, the Babe stood at home plate many times at Comiskey. So did Joe DiMaggio and Mickey Mantle and Yogi Berra. One of the best hitters the game has ever seen played for the White Sox...Joe Jackson, who went down in history as Shoeless Joe Jackson and was involved in the 1919 Black Sox scandal, played with a flair never seen again in Comiskey. The old men sitting in the grandstand eating their lunches from a paper bag used to talk to us at Wrigley before the start of the game, all sang the praises of Shoeless Joe as a hitter. "A deadly line drive hitter", one old man told us. "Better hitter than Stan Musial" another old guy thought. In 2008, after watching the Colorado Rockies play the Cubs, Squat and I walked west on Addison to this little house that sold some of the best base-ball memorabilia on this planet. We rummaged around for over an hour, and I found a picture taken of Shoeless Joe at the plate at Comiskey for $60. Priceless. The picture hangs proudly in my office. If you are looking for old pictures of your favorite ball players, this little house/store on West Addison, 2-blocks west on Addison from Wrigley, is your Fort Knox. And, as much as I didn't like the Cardinals and Musial for always beating the Cubs, Stan "The Man" Musial was one of the greatest hitters I ever saw. Like an unsung hero by the name of Forest "Smokey" Burgess who played for the Cincinnati Redlegs, it was said that both Stan "The Man" and Smoky could hit a line drive in a blizzard in January.

John BS indicated in the senior high school class yearbook that he was headed to the Air Force Academy in Colorado Springs, CO to study aeronautical engineering, but instead went down to the Univ of Illinois with Jay only to flunk out immediately the first year and end up the following year to attend Lyons Township Junior College. A long way we thought from aeronautical engineering at the Air Force Academy. We all thought that might come later, but John didn't get the nickname "BS" for nothing. I often thought BS left Champaign because Jay used to torment him when they all lived together by calling him BS. BS hated the name BS and would get pissed off and say there was "nobody here by that name". In 1960 you could get admission into the University of Illinois, but 50% flunked out in freshman year. "One and done" as Jay would later call it, mainly pertaining to my play in US Tennis Association tennis matches I played in. Everyone has an opinion. In later years John BS signed off on his emails with his signature closing…"don't let your meatloaf". A true Mensa, he always had difficulty relating to management until his later years when, instead of having the opportunity to retire, he worked at Home Depot in the tool department. BS and tools went hand in hand. First called the "Maximum Leader" by Buck, BS worked at Home Depot in Hawaii for one reason…to make enough money to make at least four runs each year to Las Vegas and the slot machines as he lived to do. There wasn't a slot in Vegas he didn't like and most likely pulled at one time or another. Don't let your meatloaf BS.

After Jay's funeral we had pizza dinner in Skokie, IL arranged by Huey. Following pizza that we each individually paid for, I got a ride with John BS back to the O'Hare Marriott a short ride by car. Almost true to form with BS driving, we ended up heading north instead of west until I happened to notice this big lake out of my passenger side window that looked exactly like Lake Michigan, We were in Winnetka, IL north of Chicago. The big wind from Winnetka. I remember BS telling the story about a "one time" visit to see a high school buddy and walking on the sidewalk at dusk heading to the EL station when a Chicago police squad car rolled along side. The fuzz yelled out his window to tell BS to come over to their squad car. When BS arrived at the squad car, the officer asked BS, "are you nuts". The cops didn't like to stop too much around Cabrini because of an occasional gunshot coming from the Cabrini windows and here our Max Leader was walking through. Much like Jay, John BS was a one-of-a-kind-guy. How many guys do you know who bring their pillow with them when they come to visit? Two pickets to Titsburgh were also always on John's menu and I think his past loves and wives cost him a lot of money. He never said. I went to visit him once in the San Francisco Bay area while he was living on the east Bay side. Every room in his house had a stepladder in it because every room was under construction. And, his driveway was loaded with rolling stock. Unlike Jay, BS loved his automobiles. John BS never ceased to amaze us...we just never knew what was next. It must have been 30-years out of high school when one of our classmates, John Shanks, came up with the grand idea to start a website devoted exclusively to our high school classmates with the idea to exchange information about what each classmate was doing. Seizing the opportunity to re-new old high school acquaintances and perform, what he thought, an educated and valuable service, John BS writes his class mates and encourages them to contribute $1,000 to a high school stock club he was putting together. Unfortunately, none of the classmates checked out BS' previous stock club, "The New Kids On The Stock" and how it ended in failure. Getting his stock tips from perfect strangers in bars, John BS preceded to select stocks for the Club that went belly up, most in less than 6-months. It didn't take too many of these stocks, and stocks that lost 50%, for the Club to go broke. High School Classmates, who couldn't afford to lose $1K, quickly did lose it all. BS quickly changed his email address and rode off into the sunset never to be heard from again. He shut The Club down and that was that. Probably looking for another Bollinger Band. It was reported that classmate Carlton T, who had moved to Germany, was ready to kill the old BS'er. The chance of four characters like BS'er, Jay, Buck and Squatman being in the same close-knit group of 8-high school buddies was astonishing. As Jay always said, "keep it tight".

The 3<sup>rd</sup> true character in our group was a guy we called "Squatty". He loved his Amos and Andy re-runs, his beloved Chicago White Sox and, in his youth, the peeler bars in Chicago. He was a big, big fan of Motown. Chicago was his kind of town and he would defend it to the end from any outsider trying to put it down. He loved his 16" softball and was an excellent left fielder that could handle line drives; most couldn't, because of his big hands. He entered high school at 5-feet and left close to 6-feet. Next to baseball, his other true love was basketball. For a white guy, he had an extraordinary ability to jump and his "jump" shot was very difficult to block because he got the ball so far back over his head. No telling how good he could have been in high school had he only been 6-feet when he entered like the guys who played. He made the varsity b'ball team in his senior year and I remember sitting in the stands on a Friday night home game in the home bleacher section and seeing his Dad enter Vaughn gym to sit in the visitor side of the court. It had to make Squat nervous. In high school he wasn't concerned about his grade point average as most of his fellow classmates were. After all, DePauw Univ in Greencastle, Indiana didn't accept just anyone.

# Chapter II

*"It is an old Indian game, Chief. Just put the ball in the basket."*
— R.P. McMurphy, *"One Flew Over The Coocoo's Nest"*

## DePauw in Greencastle, Indiana...our kind of place?

Ah, DePauw University in Greencastle, IN.  In the Fall of 1963 Jay asked me if I would ride down to Greencastle with him to see his only real true love, Diane N., who had been going to school there for 3-years. We were just going to drop in on Diane. The first minute when I walked into the DePauw University Student Union to get something to eat shortly after we arrived I knew we were out of place.  After finding a table I began eating and looked around the place to see if we could spot Diane in the crowd.  Sure enough, Diane appeared and was shocked to see us for two reasons, first we were unannounced and second she was dating this frat guy who she ended up marrying.  As soon as Diane introduced him to us, I could tell he was a first class asshole. Jay was devastated but later recovered. We met Diane again 32-years later at the 35th LTHS high school reunion, the only one ever held downtown.  The asshole had divorced her just as we imagined he would do. The only good thing to happen out of that trip was when I was waiting to pick me up at a gas station the owner sold me a 1955 Chevy for $50 which I picked up upon return from Greencastle. I named the car Matt Snortin'.

Back to Squatman...the thing you had to like about the guy were his sense of adventure and his love of baseball and basketball. He had season tickets to the

White Sox, and still does, and season tickets to Northwestern basketball which he has followed for many years He stood by the 'Cats in good times and bad, and mainly bad. In the early 60's we used to go down to the old Amphitheatre in downtown Chicago to watch the Red and Blue Division Chicago high school playoffs. Squatty loved his basketball and devoured the Chicago Tribune sport section every morning to study the baseball box scores. Later in life, he improved his writing skills, which he missed learning in grade school and high school, by attending Northwestern Univ (Evanston, IL) writing classes. He worked for All State insurance company as an auto accident investigator and the years taught him much about bogus and staged accidents. After retirement, he worked in homeless shelters in Chicago and in one of the very large animal shelters. He investigated animal abuse and got several citizens arrested for abusing helpless animals that could not defend themselves. This came as a surprise to all of us because he never showed this side of his face to us growing up in high school. But he was relentless when it came to tracking down people who abused animals. And he traveled in some very tough Chicago neighborhoods to do this. He was appointed Deacon at his church in Park Ridge, IL and you really never ever knew what he was doing to do next. He took Jay's death extremely hard and stood up at Jay's funeral that June day in Skokie in 2016 and delivered a heart rendering speech about his life long friend. I think he watched what his Dad went through long enough to convince him that corporate America was not his bag. He loved to talk to strangers at the ballpark, particularly old men who had no reason to try to impress. He loved the old men in the grand stand at Wrigley Field when we went during Spring Break in the early 1960's. "They weren't trying to impress you", Squatman recalled.

What Jay loved about Squat was simple…he did things without trying to impress anyone. For whatever reason it really was, he missed attending one of our yearly get together in Vegas, blaming it on some plumbing issues he was having at home. Jay immediately called him Roto-Rooter and the nickname and story stayed with him for the past 15-years. We never did really get a detailed explanation of the plumbing incident. Another routine that Jay loved to talk about when it came to Squatman was that he claimed on every

Friday night he and his wife would go out for pizza. Pizza in Park Ridge before he headed to LaGrange to Poly's "Polyfeed" held every 2nd Friday of the month at a restaurant in downtown LaGrange. All LTHS Class of 1960 grads invited to attend. Few did, but the few who did enjoyed it. Including our man Squat who had pizza before arriving. There was one more thing about Squat that drove Jay absolutely crazy and a perfect example of why Squatman was Squatman. Squat once told us that his wife allocated to him so much money per month for gasoline, lunch, incidentals, etc. He was placed on a budget. When Squat's Father died, Squat inherited a lot of money that his wife took control over as she did with his All State Insurance Company pension. One night, out of the blue, Squatman challenged his wife on his monthly allowance, she got mad, and out of her mouth came her reason for being the banker and dolling out money that "killed" Jay till the day he died. Her reason, and Jay told this story better that I could write it, was due to the fact that as Squat's wife, when pressured for allowance stipend, ranted on and on about how she patiently fixed Squat years of nutrious and healthy meals, morning, noon and night. Unfortunately, we did not get copies of her recipes or the menus. "Years of nutrious and healthy meals" is what tickled Jay.

Another friend. Shorty, of the Western Springs Police Station Tower fame (aka Diego Jim) packed up his stuff and headed to Colorado State in Ft Collins, CO madly in love with a young lady from LaGrange a couple of years younger. No sooner had he arrived in Ft Collins then he learned that the girl had found another guy. Diego Jim raced back to Western Springs to try to win her back, but it was too late. As the song said, "many a tear has to fall but it is all in the game". Our friend never recovered after the split and he ended up on an island in the US Virgin Islands the rest of his life, only once attending one of our reunion meetings as I remember around 1998 or 1999. I could never see getting that depressed over a woman to have it destroy your life, but then again, I wasn't in his relationship. Better to have loved and lost we all thought. I did think, when he was heavily dating her that he might be over his head, but one never knows. But he sure dropped out after she dismissed him. But, everyone has an opinion as to why he did drop out.

While understanding his pain, the Braidwood Bunch to this day couldn't understand why it took him so far down. After all, when the beautiful SP from Rockford, IL broke up with me in the summer of 1961, my Father's comment as I had my head bowed reading Sally's final letter to me while I was slaving away raking leaves in the backyard was that there were "plenty of fish in the sea". And plenty of leaves to rake so get over it.

Baldy went into the Navy and had a very successful career. A nicer guy you would be hard pressed to find. After retirement, he didn't see a golf course he didn't like and often played with Willie and Dutchy during our yearly reunions in Vegas. While slow at golf, Baldy was just a good caring guy

Because he was an excellent writer, and was successful as Sports Editor of the Lyons Township high school newspaper, Jay headed off to Journalism School at the University of Illinois in Champaign-Urbana, IL attending many of the same classes as Ebert of Siskel and Ebert, well known movie critics and Taylor Bell of Chicago sports newspaper fame. Dutchy Van also left with Jay and BS to attend the University of Illinois, but he too flunked out his freshmen year, returned home, and headed to the Marines. Dutchy joining the Marines prompted Mama Dutch to ask Squat when he too was going to join. To his credit, Dutchy Van returned to school, this time Northern Illinois Univ in DeKalb, IL, and received a degree in accounting. I always silently tipped my hat to Dutchy for bouncing back after he got de-selected at the University of Illinois. Dutch became a successful CPA in the western suburbs of Chicago. Dutchy and I go back as far as 3rd grade together at Forest Road elementary, and next to my brother, has known me longer than anyone on this planet.

In September of 1960, none of us would have realized what was going to happen next to all of us. An event that to this day I called the trip of a lifetime in a lifetime of trips. A trip that is talked about every time we get together. And, each year the stories get better. Out of the trip came the quote of the lifetime in a lifetime of listening to Jay quote stuff, and out of it was, at the time, perhaps the best education we could get…"here's to you, Mrs. Robinson." 50-years later we are still known to our LTHS classmates, the ones we cared about anyway, as The Braidwood Boys.

"This time I'm in it for love, This time I'm in it to win"
— Player, 1978

## The road to Illinois State Normal Univ…go you birdies

For some reason, and at the time I really couldn't say why, I thought I wanted to be a high school teacher after graduating from college and elected to go to Illinois State Normal University (ISNU) Redbirds now called Illinois State Univ in Normal, Il, to get a degree in teaching. Normal was half of what was called the Twin Cities of Bloomington and Normal where Route US 66, a 4-lane highway running from Chicago to Los Angeles, CA, intersected with US 51 a 2-lane highway running from Rockford, IL on the north to Cairo, IL on the south. Bloomington, IL in the heart of McLean County, fielded the richest farmland in the world and the corn and tomatoes grown in the black dirt of the fields were unsurpassed for flavor. I've never had a tomato or an ear of corn half as good as the ones I have eaten in Illinois, especially McLean and Sangamon Counties. Coming from Chicago and seeing the tractors drive down Main Street in Bloomington was an eye-opener when I first got to town. I can remember sitting there on US 51, Main Street, right across the courthouse in the center of town wondering what Normal was going to be like…would it be normal? Bloomington at that time had a population of around 50,000 and most everyone was employed in agriculture or the big State Farm insurance long before State Farm Insurance was doing any double checking in their khaki pants as they would have everyone believe today on their TV commercials. Bloomington, IL the hometown of double-check.

I didn't see much of Baldy after high school graduation until we all started getting together for reunions in Vegas following our 35th high school reunion. Squat and I would see each other during school breaks back in Western Springs.

BS, Dutchy and Willie the Wop I would see occasionally at parties and one big Braidwood trip we were involved in together in March of 1961. Jay I saw almost every weekend. He would hitch from Champaign to Bloomington or I would hitch to Champaign. I still remember those central Illinois town along Illinois highway 150 connecting Champaign with Bloomington…Downs, Leroy, Farmer City and Mahomet. Cornfields were on both sides of the road as far as one could see. There was a truck stop at US 150 and US 66 called Brandtville…great lumberjack breakfast and a great hamburger stand in Leroy. My favorite burger joint in 1960 was Mr. Quick in Normal, IL. Ray Kroc, back in 1960, was just getting started with McDonald…burgers were 25-cents and a bag of fries were a dime. About all we could afford back then especially if you lost your money in a card game. The "Green Door" at Illinois State Normal Univ served all-you-could-eat-spaghetti for 40-cents on Thursday nights. We used to sneak the spaghetti out of the restaurant after eating dinner and put it on our windowsill to freeze so we could eat it later when we got hungry. That is an example of what little money we had in those days, particularly if you had a losing streak in the nightly poker games in the basement at the Green Gables. Freezing spaghetti outside the window in the wintertime took some doing.

Jay had an intramural softball team at the U of Illinois in the Spring of 1964, and, he invited me over to Champaign one afternoon to play on his team while I was visiting just down the road in Bloomington, Luckily I caught a ride from Bloomington to Champaign with a Catholic priest who drove me all the way to the baseball field just in time to borrow a glove and play right field. The good Father lectured me all the way about the importance of college and avoiding hitchhiking. Shortly after his lecture I bought my first car a 1953 Chevy that burned more oil then gasoline and the good people of Minonk, IL probably thought I was the mosquito abatement truck when I pulled through. The smoke coming out of the rear end of that car could be seen for miles. However, the '55 Chevy was better than my 2ⁿᵈ car I purchased for $50, a 1958 white Ford station wagon. As soon as I got it a block from the guy I bought it from, the brakes failed and I ran right through a stop sign on 47ᵗʰ street. In LaGrange, IL. We learn by doing. "Everything runs on the car", the guy who sold it to me said. What he didn't say is that the brakes didn't work. Brake work would have cost more than the Ford itself so I got $10 bucks from the junk year dog and off it went. Down $40.

After years and years of playing baseball from Little League to Pony League to American Legion to semi-pro, the hardest ball I ever hit in my life occurred in that intramural game at the University of Illinois A good reminder not to burn your bridges because you do not know who you will run into later in life…in this case for Jay and the 2nd basemen it was 51-years later on a tennis court in Las Vegas. The second time up in the game, 12" slow pitch, I hit a shot, and I do mean a shot, about chest high right past the third basemen into left field. The 2nd basemen on that team went on to star in a television series. In a Cat II United States Tennis Association tennis tournament in October of 2014 at Darling Tennis Center in Las Vegas in which I participated and Jay watched, playing on the court next to me was the same 2nd baseman on Jay's softball team, The Brave Bulls, in the Spring of 1964. Jay said they both had tears in their eyes after meeting after all those years. A couple of years earlier on the Soldiers and Sailors Home in Normal, IL (the Home and ball diamond are there to this day) ball diamond, in a money hard ball game arranged by this friend from Kankakee, IL at 7:30 in the morning, I hit a ball that was rising as it cleared the shortstop's head by 3-feet and went all the way to the wall for a triple. It was a good thing we won because I didn't have the $10 to pay the other team if we lost.

> "A thumb goes up, a car goes by, It's nearly one A.M., and here am I Hitching' a ride, hitchin' a ride, Gotta get me home by the morning light"
> — Vanity Fair, "Hitchin' A Ride", 1969

Off to Normal, Illinois I went in September of 1960 with one suitcase in hand. With no car, and train service (Chicago, Burlington & Quincy) often 4-8 hours late, which you had to catch in downtown Chicago Union Station and dropped you off in Bloomington, Il 10-miles from ISNU's campus, and

US 66 close at hand, my parents drove me out to Wolf Road and Route US Route 66 to allow me to hitchhike to Bloomington-Normal, 120-miles south.

## You can "Get Your Kicks on Route 66"...

Route US 66, "The Mother Road" as it was called, built in 1926, running from Chicago to Los Angeles, probably had more written about it then any of the original highways built in the history of the US. It was appropriately recognized in pop culture by both the hit song "Get Your Kicks On Route 66" and the Route 66 TV show. Heading north on Route US 66 in Illinois, after passing through the Chicago suburbs, US Route 66 entered Chicago itself, where it terminated at Lake Shore Drive. To me Route US 66 was a lifesaver traveling to and from Western Springs to Bloomington-Normal, Illinois. The more time I spent hitchhiking on it, the more I appreciated the scenery along the way---corn, more corn, soybeans, barns, cows, pigs brownish-red colored snow fences, and the well positioned traffic lights in towns like Lexington, Chenoa and Pontiac. Compared to the interstate highways of today, the road was a lot thinner, had no on/off ramps or over passes and a lot of cross roads crossing it for farm machinery to pass over it. With a speed limit of 70 mph it made it as tricky a drive as any highway you could have possibly traveled. As you approached a farm tractor on the side of the road, there was no way to know if it was going to attempt to cross the highway or not. Looking at US 66 from the Amtrak that travels from Chicago to St Louis 50-years after my hitchhiking days ended, I could not believe how frail 66 looked. I also could not believe how many little cross roads there were. But, by 2016, Route US 66 was 90-years old and had served the nation very well and deserved the right to look old and tired. Route 66 sure did a lot for me and I would not have traded the hitchhiking experiences or enduring the wind, cold driving rain and blowing snow on The Mother Road for a free pass on the Amtrak which began service to Normal, Illinois long after my college days had ended. On a couple of occasions, I got picked up by two guys heading to California to find their fortune, who invited me to go along with them if I chose to do so. I thought about it one time but decided not to go.

# Chapter 12

*"Oh, Jimmy Mack...when are you coming back"*
— *Martha and the Van Dellas, 1967*

THERE WAS SO much traffic on 66 that, unless it was dark outside, it was pretty easy for the car driver to hopefully notice that I was a college kid heading or coming from school and stop and offer me a ride even though they sometimes were doing 80 mph. It got real tricky when you got dropped off on a north/south road without a traffic light or an intersection like where the Manor Hotel at US 6 was located. No traffic light meant the drivers had little time to check you out to see if you were a college student. I started turning down rides once I knew where every traffic light was between Chicago and Normal. Cold rain, the kind you get around Thanksgiving, was always the worst particularly if the rain was coming directly in your face. Snow you could brush off of you, but that rain soaked in. At 35-degrees, with wet pants and socks, and any wind at all, it didn't take long out there to start bitching. Without overpasses there was no place to run for cover, and several times I was drenched to the bone. No fun in 35-degree weather and if your shoes got wet you were cold until you could take them off. The shoe attire for me in those days was Converse All-Stars that coat $8. You wore them until the backs of the shoe split open or fell apart. No socks. Black Levi jeans, that cost $4 a pair, and either a parka or a windbreaker depending on the season. The shirt brand we wore was Gant Hugger. You weren't the Duke of Earl unless you had on a Gant Hugger. I think Gene Chandler brought the "Duke of Earl", a great song, to our attention in 1963.

I entered college in Sept 1960 at 6-feet and 175-pounds having grown 4-inches the summer after my senior year. And, I walked into Barton Hall, the men's dormitory, room # 204 the day after Labor Day with my Gant Hugger on. Chuckles Duck was my roommate. He was a rather quiet guy and a math major. Down the hall from us was Seaman with an "E" as Jay called him. Two floors down in the basement were Vinnie P and Harry Grass. The card playing Feeney also lived in the basement and he played all night, every night, smoking menthol cigs and playing bridge. He lasted two years before the grades caught up with him.

I lived in the dorm for 2=years before moving off campus into the palace known as the Green Gables…10-other guys resided at the Green Gables, an old 3-story fire trap of a house right across the street from Milner Library. The rent was $5 per month for me because I cleaned out everyone's waste paper baskets every Saturday. The Green Gables never made the ISNU Administration's non-cut list and was demolished by 1967 to make room for another new co-ed dormitory fashioned after its earlier cousins Hamilton and Whitten. My roommate at the Green Gables was a guy by the name of Joel Bates. Above his desk he had one picture. It wasn't a picture inside the frame, but a quote…"this to shall pass". Neither one of us will have an ISNU dormitory named after us, but we can sure live with it. We weren't the dormitory resident types back then. A good guy that Joel.

Snow always scared me hitchhiking on US 66 because drivers from California were not experienced driving on it and with so much cross traffic on US 66 causing periodic quick stops, off the road you could go quickly. If the car wasn't damaged from hitting a culvert (a structure that allowed water to flow under Route 66) it still took a long time to get a tow truck to pull you out. And there was no cell phones to call a tower directly so we had to rely on a passer by to tell the garage in the next town to send a truck out. Luckily, in all that hitchhiking was I in a car that slid off the road and that was just south of Pontiac. The driver tried to pass another vehicle, for some reason gunned it in the snow-packed lane, and the rear end slid and then the front of the car and then we quickly and luckily found the median, Fortunately, the driver got out of the car turned, scooped the apples out of his pants and we got back on the snow-packed highway heading North with just a dented fender to remind him not to accelerate on snow..

I think the longest I ever had to wait for a ride was hitching north from Bloomington to DeKalb on US 51 in the spring of 1964. I got a late start getting on the road and it must have been 11:00pm before I started. I got a ride right away and the guy was going to Rockford. He said he would go all the way to Rockford, that is, if I stayed awake and talked to him. For the first time ever, just north of El Paso, I fell asleep, it was still cold outside and the driver had the heat blasting. The next thing I remember is his pulling off the road at LaSalle-Peru-Oglesby (LPO) to find a hotel room for the night. I was out in the middle of nowhere just south of LPO. From approximately 12:30am to sunrise I walked north on US 51. Maybe a dozen cars went by in that time. None of them stopped. It was 8:30am when I rolled into DeKalb. It took 8 ½ hours to go 120-miles. And walking along Illinois Hwy 51 at 3am is an experience everyone should have. It was the first and last time I fell asleep on a hitch.

The most memorable ride of my hitchhiking career, and if you are a beer drinker you will like this, also occurred on US 51 in the same little town of LaSalle-Peru-Oglesby (LPO). The Illinois River runs through LPO and US 51 that crosses the bridge narrows a little at the bridge. A 2-laner as the truckers called it. To get to the bridge via the north or south side of US 51, one had to traverse a long, steep hill that ran straight down to the river and the bridge. One evening, heading once again from Bloomington to DeKalb, I caught a ride from a Budweiser beer truck hauling a heavy load of beer north to Madison, Wisconsin for a football weekend. To this day I remember that big wheeler beer truck hitting the top of the south peak of US 51 headed north and down straight to the bridge. As we got to the top of the hill, bouncing in our seats, I looked over at the speedometer and we were doing about 60-mph. As we rolled down that hill on US 51 I watched the speedometer rise and by the time we hit that bridge the speedometer registered 110-mph. Three-fourths of the way down the hill, as we were gaining speed, the truck driver looked over at me with a grin on his face and said "we are really hauling the beer now, baby". Yes we were. If my Father told me once when I was growing up, he told me a thousand times that I didn't want to grow up to be a truck driver. And here I was bouncing down the highway in the biggest semi made hauling beer to the Wisconsin state capitol. I didn't see anything wrong with being a truck driver. Every trucker who picked me up in those hitchhiking days seemed to take pride in their work, appeared happy and loved to talk. I listened to their stories about places they had been and the good places to eat along the way. Every driver who ever brought up the subject of restaurants on the highway always said the Dixie Truck Stop in McLean, IL on US 66 was one of their favorites. Dixie specialized in blue-plate specials as they fondly called them. But I never got a blue plate special on a blue plate and never at a student discount price. A few years later I stopped at Dixie just to see for myself. The truckers were right…huge place, big parking lot and great mashed potatoes and gravy. While I didn't give it a try, the truckers raved about Dixie's fried chicken.

I became adept at determining if I wanted to get in a car even if they did stop. One rule of thumb was 3-guys already in the car…I always passed on those rides. Two people in a car made me nervous. If they were young or had a hotrod I would usually accept the ride, but two 40-50 year old guys was different, and I usually passed by telling them I was going further then they were. I always asked them how far they were going to give me an "out" if I didn't like the looks of the guys. I once rode in the back in the wheel well of a car transport truck that was heading north on 66 in mid-March with my shirt off to get a suntan. If the truck had to stop quickly I would have flown at least 50-yards in the air. Truck drivers in those days used to pick me up and I got rides heading north from a big diesel rig carrying tomatoes and a Bud Bowman milk truck heading to Chicago. If you haven't ridden in one of those big trucks, put it on your list of things to do. You will be surprised how much you bounce up and down. What always amazed me was how outgoing and funny the truckers who picked me up where. Sometimes I thought they picked me up just to have an audience, but the were always genuinely, I thought, interested in my well-being. They knew how to drive and time after time each driver would tell me to watch the car in front of the car in front of you. That way you would have more time if there was a sudden stop that had to be made. Tailgating with the professional truck drivers was taboo.

Dwight, IL was halfway home and a crucial stop because there were very few traffic lights between Dwight and Wolf Road in Western Springs. For me, or anyone hitchhiking at that time, it was a hammock green if you will. Illinois Highway 17 met US 66 in Dwight and headed East to Kankakee. As in Arlo Guthrie's "City of New Orleans"---"all along the southbound odyssey, the train pulls out of Kankakee". I always liked the gas stations in Dwight. Dwight had friendly people always willing to help. Just ask grade school friend Bobby Repel B. who got a speeding ticket on US 66 driving Judy Chimes home from Normal, IL. They were friendly enough to drive Bobby, who got his nickname repel for the mountains in Colorado he was going to climb, to the Dwight courthouse. And bill him $25. Robert Dean "Bobby Repel" became most famous with all of us for the response he gave at The Corral one night in our senior year when we asked if he wanted to join us for a trip to The Follies. Robert Dean said "no", but the reason he gave for not going went down in infamy…he was "going to a private party on the North side". 50-years later when someone wanted to joke about where they were going, the response used was the famous one issued in January 1960 by Bobby Repel, "a private party of the north side." Jay quoted the Bobby Repel quote often.

Getting caught out there by the Manor Hotel and US 6, 40-miles Southwest from Wolf Road and US 66 where I headed north on Wolf Road into Western Springs, was no fun. The problem was cars went by so fast at night. It was the night time hitching that scared me the most. The people in the Manor Inn were always pleasant if you got dropped off there. There was always plenty of coffee and restroom facilities were clean. To pass the time once while hitching, Jay pulled a football out of his bag and we played catch right along US 66. Drivers stopped just to see if we were o.k.

The other problem at night sometimes could be the wind because on Route 66 in the 1960's there was very little to block the win. Cornfields do very little to block the wind and it can be very uncomfortable out there at night with no iPOD or iPhone and usually under dressed for major shifts in weather...wind especially. But we adapted and survived. And, remember, people were more friendly and less guarded back then going out of their way to make you more comfortable. If you hitchhiked as much as we did, you never forget that cold wind and the cold driving rain. Paying the Piper.

It was almost 50-years later that I drove by car back to US 6 & US 66 and the field where Jay and I threw the football along side of US 66 was still there. It was like hallowed ground. I remembered how happy Jay was then particularly if he was playing touch football or pitching the whiffle ball. After 50-years, the field looked exactly the same. The Manor Hotel, on the east side of the US 66 and US 6 junction also looked identical to what it did in 1960. Heading north on US 66 you knew you were getting close to Western Springs and Wolf Road. There was no stop light at US 66 and US 6 and the first light was at Wolf Road just east of the Tri-State toll way back in the day. If you got dropped off south of Naperville, Illinois you saw a lot of cornfields, and ran the risk of someone stopping for you. Naperville was a little town in 1960...there were more cornfields than people.

Of all the times I hitch hiked on US Route 66, I only saw a hand-full of hitchhikers. If the guy was heading in our direction, and was there first, we waited in the closest gas station till he caught a ride. Looking back on it, there must have been more danger to hitchhiking then I thought or more people would have been on the road. But, during those days, at least when it came to hitchhiking, I thought I knew exactly what I was doing. I pondered that line of thinking many times over in my later years. And, looking back on all the many, many guys who picked me up, I know how lucky I was that no serious trouble ever happened. When you accept the ride, and get into that car, you have committed and they are behind the wheel and have all of the control. In a situation and tight space like the inside an automobile things can happen very quickly. By the summer of 1964 even my parents got worried about my hitchhiking, and "The Pester" sent my stepmother, Betty, up to DeKalb, IL to pick me up. Maybe too, they felt they should do something for me because younger step-brother, I called Running Bare, got Betty's door-to-door limo service to the University of Wisconsin in Madison, Wisconsin With one "family" member being driven, and the other hitchhiking on of all roads, US Route 66, how did that sound over a bridge game with the neighbors or the who's who of Western Springs? And, if I had been killed out there, how would they explained to their friends what really happened to me. He was sodomized, shot and dumped on US Route 66 north of Coal City? Even my parent's bridge playing friends would have swallowed hard at that.

Hitchhiking on US Route 66 from Chicago to Bloomington, without a doubt, taught me a lot. It also saved me time and money versus taking the train, money that was desperately needed for food and incidentals while at Normal. Hitchhiking also gave me confidence to meet any situation involving people. Because of US Route 66, I thought I could have walked into the White House and started up a conversation with President Kennedy. Route 66 taught me how to be a good listener and how to carry on a conversation with someone I had just met. It taught me to allow the guy who picked me up do the talking, and I became a better listener. And it taught me how to stay awake no matter how tired I was after pulling two all nighters prior to getting on the highway because of exams. And, I certainly met some interesting characters along the way. Some guys picked you up to be able to talk; others picked you up to help out a college kid making his way to and from school. Most started talking as soon as you got in the car. There were many, many questions from the out-of-state drivers too about Chicago, so many I thought sometimes I was the Chicago Chamber of Commerce. They started building Interstate 55 in 1967. I have a picture hanging on my office wall of US Route 66 next to the newly constructed I-55 just north of Dwight, Illinois and south of Coal City, Illinois. By 1970 both directions of I-55 were completed. For Jay and me, it was a sad day. We knew our hitchhiking days were over and so were our playing days.

The conversation along the way hitchhiking somehow always drifted back to college. What was Illinois State Normal like? How many kids go there? Is it a good school? Why do you want to teach? Aren't you worried about getting into trouble out here hitchhiking on US 66? What are you majoring in? What do you plan to do when you graduate? "Let me give you some advice", they said... and I got tons of advice from every driver who stopped to pick me up. People love to talk about their own successes, and in a million years I couldn't begin to tell you all of the things I learned on the road. In talking about themselves, particularly if they were a college grad it was good to hear of their college experiences. I also got to hear many woeful tales of those who didn't finish college. What they could have done with their lives had only they finished? Why didn't they go back to finish later I always wondered, but didn't ask. How much more money they could have made if the just finished college. For many, the lure of making immediate money was too much. I related to that because in those days I couldn't rub two nickels together myself, had few clothes, and treasured my trusty Converse All-Stars, low-cuts of course. One thing for sure, come hell or high water, and whether or not the Cubs got out of the National League cellar, I was going to finish college.

# Chapter 13

*"Because when I go up to the plate,*
*I want one guy in the ball park pulling for me"*
*— Milwaukee Braves shortstop, Johnny Logan, when asked why he*
*gave the batboy 25-cents for each hit he got, circa 1958*

THE FIRST 3-YEARS I spent at Ill State Normal Univ were perhaps the best days of my life. A very small school in 1960 with no fraternities, a group of guys led by Bud Harry Grass from Maine High in Park Ridge, IL, decided to form a group called the Menkins. How Bud got the name is unknown, but there were about 20-members who wore sweatshirts around campus with the name Menkin on it. The best of all during my first 3-years at Normal was the Saturday morning touch football in the Quad. Jay came over from Champaign on many weekends and loved the football games. Chuck Duck, Seaman with an "E", Sonny from Melrose Park, IL, the speedy Harry Grass, who burned me more than once on the down and out, and others all got up early to play football. The games were always competitive. My roommate the first year, Chuck Duck, always played football. We kept wondering why Chuck never showed up for the high school reunions and later learned from a high school buddy, that Chuck had early dementia. So sad. My sophomore year I roomed with Seaman with an "E", a farm boy from Roanoke, IL. Because he was in Navy ROTC, Jay called him Seaman, but it was always Seaman with an "E". Seaman went on to a distinguished career in the Navy. Another one of those good guys I met along the way that enjoyed life and took it one day at a time.

I learned quickly at ISNU to raise my hand in class and talk to the teacher when class was over so the teacher saw my interest in their class and got to know my name. If I was having trouble in a very large class >100, I would set up an appointment to meet with the professor. Failing Freshmen English, I had Jay write a paper for me that counted for something, I recall, like 40% of my final grade. He wrote the identical story he wrote in a journalism class at the University of Illinois and received a grade of "A". I received a grade of "C-" on the exact same paper, but it saved me from having to repeat freshmen English.

"Oh, what a night, Late December, back in '63, what a special time for me, as I remember, what a night"
— Frankie Valli, The Four Seasons, 1975

## Oh, what a night...

On a hot August night in the summer of 1961 without much fore thought I called up a high school classmate, who in the opinion of the guys I ran around with back in the day, the absolute most beautiful girl in our high school graduating class, to see how she was doing and see if she wanted to go swimming in the nun's convent outdoor pool on Ogden Avenue close to her house. It was a very hot August evening in LaGrange-Western Springs. The grounds in which the Nun's house and pool were situated were expansive. A winding road came toward the house from the north side of the property. Through trees and bushes the road must have been 3/8th's of a mile long. It was the only road into the property. We entered from the south with no road but a lot of grass between the pool and us.

I remember picking her up about 8 pm and we walked together west down Ogden Ave (US 34) until we came to the convent. The pool was about a block from Ogden and we got there by walking across the nun's well-manicured lawn and around the many trees. To this day I still can't believe how it happened, but no sooner did we get our clothes off (we were wearing our suits) then I see two cars coming from the north into the property going at a pretty good clip. Thinking that the cars weren't coming for us because we were a long ways from the road, and it was getting very dark, we started to get in the pool together, she in a white bikini. I can't recall much in this world, but to the day I die I will always see her in the white bikini. Stunning. As luck would have it, the two cars continued toward us, by passing the road to the convent, and I knew it was cops. Four of LaGrange Park's finest hopped out of their cars to put the flashlights on us and mainly on her They continued to shine the flashlights on her while she was putting her clothes on and only when I got in between her and the flashlights did they stop shinning the lights at her. The trip to the LaGrange Park police station followed and we held hands all the way to the station in the back seat of the squad car. The cops put us in separate rooms and called our parents. I could hear her crying as her Dad came in to pick her up. Just as they were leaving my Father arrived and by the tone of his voice when he asked, "where is he?" I knew it was going to be a long ride home. The only punishment either of us received was that I was barred for life from LaGrange Park. Had they forgotten 7-years earlier I batted 3rd and played left field for the LaGrange Park All Star Little League Team which beat LaGrange for the first time? Barred for life! I thought of calling Lenore many, many times but couldn't get up the courage knowing how devastated her parents probably were with their daughter facing a possible trespassing offense. It was at the 25th high school reunion that I had a chance to see and talk to Lenore again. She said she told the night at the convent story to all of her friends and it turned out to be one of the most exciting events in her life, and that she heard her parents laughing about it two weeks after with friends they had invited over for bridge. Never the luck I thought…and, as I learned later in life, you make your own bounces. I just didn't have the confidence. But, to this very day I remember it to the tune of Frankie Valli and The Four Seasons said in their hit, "oh, what a night". At the 25th LTHS high school reunion, my Nun's convent swimming pool date was easily voted the best looking woman attending, and, as they were announcing her victory, I thought back on what could have been. If only.

## Ryerson Steel Co…the best reason to finish college

In the summer of 1962, Squatty, Jay and I got grave yard shift jobs at Ryerson Steel Company in Melrose Park, IL where we labored from 7:30pm to 7:30am

5-nights a week. For the most part, we got the shit jobs with the exception of Hank who had it made dipping steel edging in the paint shop for use in gardens as an edge along walks. Picture yourself inside a huge factory with steel beams all over the place and different machines, beam splitter, shot blaster, welders, blast furnace etc located in different areas of the factory. There were some areas to hide but if Old Bucket Erickson, the foreman on the night shift caught you, it was curtains. Hank was particularly adept at squatting around the different machines to catch a wink. To this day we still call him Squatty or Squatman. Jay and I were relegated to the job that did more to get me to finish college then anything before or after and that being grinding burrs off of the huge I-beams being shipped off to be installed in the many new buildings going up in the Big Onion. The grinder, developed to smooth burrs off of steel I-beams, looked like a big upside down crock pot with handles out to the side on the bottom and a rotating disc with something like sandpaper on the bottom. You can imagine how strong the sandpaper had to be to file down an I-beam. We didn't know the RPM's on the grinder, but the grinder spun fast enough to take your leg off if you lost concentration and it happened to slip. Try holding on to a 15-lb grinder at 3am as it whirled around on a 30-foot I-beam for fun sometime. Occasionally we would stop in one of my all time favorite bars, the "Come Back Inn" in Melrose Park, IL, to have a cold one before starting work. I think that was our all-time favorite name for a bar.

After work, Jay and I would always stop at the Western Springs Spring Rock park tennis courts to take off our soiled Ryerson shirts and play stickball with our big heavy black boots on with steel in the toe. We never had to worry about the "diamond" being available because the only guys I knew playing tennis in Western Springs in 1962 were Jack McWethy, later of ABC News, and my brother DK who went on to Northern Illinois Univ to star in tennis. But for us in 1961, it was one less thing we needed to worry about. A baseball bat and a tennis ball was all we needed. As we could both throw pretty hard, a direct hit by the ball in your back with no shirt on, woke you up in a hurry. A homerun was over the tennis court fence heading in the direction of east as the plate was in the northwest corner of the tennis courts. By the way, the tennis courts are still there till this day. And that is a good thing. The single, double and triple lines were all marked off. The right field fence was much closer than the left, but neither one of us was adept at hitting to right field even though the tennis balls were coming in very, very fast. Different than whiffle ball, the game we called stickball, was very tough. An occasional half-assed curve was thrown but mainly high hard ones that caused a lot of strikeouts. We would play for about an hour and then by around 10:30am it was off to bed, no air conditioning in our house, except for my parent's bedroom, and trying to sleep in the heat of summer was tough. But Jay, Squat and I enjoyed that summer a lot...parents were off our backs to find a job, making $2.80 an hour and, for me, only having to do yard work on Sundays, aka raking those leaves. Who could ask for more? I thanked Ryerson a lot for the education they game me. How to get along with guys you worked with and how important it was to get an education so you wouldn't be grinding burrs off of steel I-beams at two in the morning. There was one thing you did learn grinding burrs...how to concentrate and not fall asleep.

The workers at Ryerson, most eastern Europeans, were characters in their own right. "Where are you going on vacation"? I asked one of them at our night-ly dinner in the company cafeteria. "California" he replied. "Oh, Los Angeles or San Francisco"? I asked. "No, California Avenue in Chicago...I'm going to drive up and down". Willie Calhoun worked the shot blaster machine and we had many a long talk waiting for the steel beam to run through the blaster machine. The air was filled with smoke and dust and I often told Willie that breathing all of this shit wasn't good. I hope he led a good life. A good man, and just happy to have a job. To get some sleep, guys would head for the toilet stalls where some of the greatest artwork in Chicago appeared on the walls. But, old Bucket Erickson, the night foreman, knew that trick and would periodically check the washroom and peer under the stall door. One night at dinner in the cafeteria (we brought our own lunches) one of the eastern Europeans, Gorko we called him, sat across from us and proclaimed "Ah, the future of America" as he looked across at Jay and me. Little did Gorko know that we were flying by the seat of our pants in those days. My parents, who would scream about my getting a summer job the day that school was out, never said a word when I worked at Ryerson. The sight of me walking in the door at 9:00am with those big, black steel-toed boots on, and grime on my hands and face, convinced them that I was actually working. It is worth repeating that no job prior to JT Ryerson convinced me more of the value of a college degree. Summer jobs like that aren't available to college kids anymore. We were wiser for the experience. And all the lectures in the world about the importance of staying in school didn't come close to one summer on the "grinder" at JT Ryerson Steel Fabricating Co. You can take that to the bank as Jay said.

# Chapter 14

*"— Nothing you can't handle nothing you ain't got*
*Put the money on the table and drive it off the lot"*
*_____ Boz Skaggs, "Lowdown", 1976*

## "Paradise By The Dashboard Light"...The fabled trip to Braidwood, Illinois

To this day I don't remember where we were when we decided to head to Braidwood, IL one night during Spring Break in late March 1961. I do know that BS was driving and the objective was to find this house of ill repute somewhere in Braidwood, With sketchy directions in hand, and no GPS system to guide us, we got on US Route 66 and headed south to Braidwood about 40-miles southwest of Chicago right on US Route 66. When we first got to town we stopped at a gas station for directions to the house. I vividly remember pulling up to this farm style house out in the middle of the corn fields on this very dark night, getting out of the car, and walking into this joint to see 6-8 women lined up in panties and bra. I particularly remember this one with red panties and a red bra on who was old enough to be my Mother. While she wasn't very attractive, I guess I thought, and had in my mind's eye, that the women would be a little bit younger. Dutchy didn't participate that evening because he said he didn't have "to pay for it". With both guns blazing, and without breaking stride, Squatty picked out his new friend and headed off to the bedroom The sexual activity called "around-the-world" in those days cost $10 which was more than a day's pay for us working at minimum wage. It looked a little too businesslike to me and women my

Mother's age, at that time, didn't appeal to me. Later, I thought nothing was more attractive than an attractive looking older woman, but on that night in Braidwood the stark reality of it all was too much. BS and Squat participated, Jay and I returned to the car to wait for our friends. The quote of a lifetime came from Squatman's trip to the bedroom when, Squat recalling his deed with the rest of us in BS' car on the trip home said the woman told him when he first entered, what he described as the "promised land," you've got to move, honey". "Paradise By The Dashboard Light" is how Meat Loaf described it. Fifty years later "you've got to move honey" is mentioned every time the trip to Braidwood comes up at one of our reunions. Anyway, word got out to the members of our high school class, and the women in the class particularly wanted to know all the details of the trip. We then became known as the Braidwood Boys. There was some mystique to Braidwood as allegedly it was associated with the Chicago mafia. A group you didn't want to get involved with.

## "Betty is that you?" — Jay Crawford

1961 was also the year that I was dating Trudy from Western Springs. The story that Jay loved to tell the most about me involved a visit I made on my bike (I didn't own a car) to see Trudy late one afternoon at her house about 3-miles south of where I lived. Making sure that Trudy didn't see Brown Betty, the name I gave my bike, I ditched Brown Betty in the weeds in a vacant lot about 1-block from her house and walked the rest of the way. After being in her house talking for about 15-minutes, we heard this car honking in front. Trudy's Mother went to the door and quickly turned to me and said "Ron, is that your bike in the driveway? My husband wants to get in the garage". I hopped up went to the front door to look out to see Brown Betty lying across the driveway blocking Dad's entrance to the garage. When I went out to move the bike off the driveway I could hear Jay, and his buddy Jeff T, laughing their collective ass off from the spot I parked Brown Betty originally. Embellishing the story over the years, Jay added that I said "Betty is that you?" when I first looked out the front door. I don't think Jay missed many opportunities to re-tell that story particularly when he were "double dating" in those days. It was his all time favorite story. People who didn't even know me heard him tell the story. And no one could craft a story quite like Jay. Jay was a wordsmith artist.

On New Years Eve in 1961, the Pester gave permission for me to use his Chevy II for the evening and Trudy and I triple dated with Jay and Squatman, who also had dates. We decided to drive to downtown Chicago to Rush Street and party down there. A classy thing to do, I thought. Jay was supposed to meet his date at a designated bar, the Scotch Mist. Rush Street was the place to be in Chicago on New Years in 1961. All the big name entertainment was there and it was what made Chicago the "toddling" town Frank Snotty sang about in "My Kind Of Town". The evening for Trudy and myself was going fine, but by close to midnight Jay's date decided to split and we decided to change locations to have a drink before heading back to the suburbs at the Edgewater Beach Hotel. I think it might have been Jay's idea. The Edgewater was packed and we got separated from Jay who stood close to the bar. Before he surfaced from the crowd, in approximately 30-minutes more or less, he had drowned his sorrows with 5-Manhattans. Around 1:00 am we decided to hit the road for home before Jay got into a fight with other people at the bar. It had snowed about 3-days prior to New Years and the cold, which always follows the snow, paid a visit to the tune of about zero degrees that night. On the way home, heading south on the Tri-State Toll way, with Squatman, his date and Jay in the back seat, Jay got sick. Squatman rolled down the window so he could barf, but Jay, too drunk to know if he was hanging out the window or not, got a little bit out the window and let go. Some of the vomit reached the back shelf (the space between the rear window and the rear seat) and the remainder went out the window. It started to smell so bad, and with the likelihood of him throwing up again, I pulled off the toll way and on to the parking strip to let jay out. Squatman threw him out of the car and he went head first into the snow. He lay there while we tried to get some snow wash the wash the vomit off the ledge in back of the car. After 15-min or so we got it cleaned enough to be tolerable to drive with the windows up and the heat on. We then tried to get Jay back into the car. At 6' 2" and approximately 160-pounds Jay was no lightweight. But on this eventful night he was dead weight and we tried and tried to stuff him back into the car. Squatman, getting madder by the minute, proclaimed, "leave the son-of-a-bitch here". Finally, with Squat's date getting in the front seat with Trudy we had enough room to get Jay back into the car. By the time we got back to Jay's house on Woodland Ave in Western Springs, he had sobered a little and when we tried to get him out of the car and help him to his house he got as mad as hell at us. Imagine that. He's pissed. He learned to take the offensive if he knowingly was at fault. His parents woke up to let Jay in the door. They were accustomed to his rolling into their driveway with special things happening. One time, returning to his house after a date in his Dad's car, he accidently flipped a cigarette out the front driver's side window that landed on the seat behind him and started a fire in the back seat. He pulled into the driveway with the back seat smoking so bad he could hardly see out. His parents came running out to the driveway with pans containing water to dump on the back seat to put out the fire. It was the last date I ever had with Trudy. Cute girl. Trudy was smart and friendly. She learned how to roll with the punches New Years Eve back in 1961, and was the wiser for it. Jay, I think, learned a lesson that night and developed a softer more conversational approach with the women.

When I told Squatman that I would carry the torch and write this book of our adventures, he wanted me to be sure to include the party we had at little Jimmy Pooper's house when both Jimmy and his parents were off to visit relatives in Tennessee. It was the summer of 1962, I recall, and it was a Sunday night. Pooper's folks had a nice little bungalow in LaGrange Highlands. It was a single story house. I don't know how we met Darlene and her buddies, all Western Springs girls one year behind us in high school, that night but we ended up actually taking a screen off one of Pooper's back windows and sneaking in to his house. We didn't call him to ask him if it was ok because we knew the answer before we called on the phone. We did have them in those days. We put Mrs. Pooper's best glasses in the freezer section of her refrigerator to have extra cold beers. Darlene and her buddies were a class behind us and always had the reputation of never seeing a party they didn't want to attend. All very attractive, all college bound and all in good shape, especially Darlene who had a body built for speed "with points on her own standing way up firm and high" as Bob Seger sang in his big hit song "Night Moves". The dance called "the bump" had just come into its own and Darlene got me out on the make shift dance floor to learn how to "bump". It was a dance worth learning, sexier and easier than Chubby Checker's popular twist of the day. It had the two dance partners "bumping" up against each other hip-to-hip and butt-to-butt. We all agreed that Darlene had the best butt in Western Springs and there I was on Popper's "dance floor" bumping the night away. Oh, what a night. To this very day the Squatman still talks about Darlene. Olive skin, of Greek heritage, Darlene had, what Curtis Mayfield sang about in his classic "Gypsy woman". John BS attended the Pooper party that night with a date on his arm. He claimed later that he and his lovely date had sex in the bed in the master bedroom that evening. If little Pooper had found out BS had sex in Pooper's father's bed he would have lost it. I don't think BS told him when he thanked him for letting Pooper use his house that night. Upon returning to LaGrange following vacation, Pooper and his parents were livid with our entertaining in their house in their absence. And looking back on it all, who could blame them. A church going guy, Jimmy Pooper just wouldn't understand the attraction of "The Bump" with Darlene. Squatman, to his credit, never forgot it. Rightfully so Squatman…hope this was a good little trip down memory lane for you. Little Pooper became a starting guard on the Lyons Township High School basketball team our senior year but was too small to make it past high school ball.

He attended a college in Tennessee and dropped out of our sight never to be heard from again. While BS made contact with Pooper, he never attended a high school reunion. Some guys and girls are like that. Particularly the girls who gained a lot of weight as early adults and were too embarrassed by their "looks" to attend even the 10th high school reunion. The two most popular reunions for the Class of 1960 were the 25th and the 50th. At the 50th you might as well been walking into a room of perfect strangers because without name tags, no one recognized anyone.

## My transfer to Northern Illinois Univ., DeKalb, IL

Why I decided in the summer of 1963 to transfer to Northern Illinois Univ in DeKalb, IL where I didn't know anyone was, to this day, a mystery even to me. I guess I wanted to grow up and be a businessman and a degree in Business Admin from Northern would get me there faster that a teaching degree from Normal. Or so I thought. Everything was different…for one I didn't know anyone and while it was closer to home than Normal it took longer to get home because there was no 66 to hop on. From DeKalb to Western Springs by thumb took you through the growing metropolis of Hinckley, IL

I hitchhiked home for Thanksgiving that year at Northern Illinois U in 1963 and my first ride dropped me off at the western edge of this little town called Hinckley, IL. Back then, and I'm sure it holds true to today, the small towns wouldn't allow hitchhiking within the city limit. It set a poor example for their youth. Anyway, as soon as I got out of the car to begin my walk through Hinckley it started to rain. I dashed for cover under the entrance of this nearby brick building to try to weather the storm so to speak. After I cleaned off my glasses so I could see, I saw this little plaque in the ground next to the building entrance that had inscribed on it, "The Harlem Globetrotters played their first game here January 7, 1927". I thought I was Christopher Columbus and had just discovered America. How many people knew that about the Globetrotters or even saw the plaque commemorating their very first game in the ground in the flower garden next to the front door of this non-descriptive building in Hinckley, IL? They were originally made up of players from Wendell Phillips High School on the south side of Chicago. Wilt Chamberlin said Meadowlark Lemon with The Trotters was the greatest basketball player he ever saw. One of LaGrange's high school basketball stars, Joel McCrae, from the famous LTHS team of 1953, played for the Trotters right out of high school. Meadowlark Lemon, the most famous of all the Globetrotters, was something to see.

I lived off campus on The Lincoln Highway at Northern close to downtown DeKalb, Illinois in September 1963 with about 10-other guys. 3-of the guys living in this 3-bedroom house were card-carrying assholes from Schaumberg, a suburb of Chicago. The 1963 Chicago Bears practiced in DeKalb, IL that year and went on to win the National Championship when outside linebacker Larry Morris, knocked Y.A. Tittle out of the game. What a great defensive team the Bears had in 1963 under the leadership of Papa Bear himself, George Halas and defensive coordinator George Allen [later of Washington Redskin fame]. A linebacker trio as good as there ever was with Bill George, Larry Morris and our favorite, Joe Fortunato. If ever there was a name for a football linebacker we though Joe Fortunato was it. They also had a great defensive backfield with a safety as tough as they came, Vic Zucco from Michigan State weighing in at 185-pounds. Jim Taylor of the hated Green Bay Packers said he delighted in running right at Zucco, not around him.

As I returned back to the house I was renting on The Lincoln Highway, with 8-other guys, after taking my last final exam to pack for home there were 4 or 5-police squad cars right across the street walking in and out of the house directly across the highway from us. I stopped to ask one cop what was going on and he said, "you didn't know this was a house of ill repute"? For nine months we lived directly across the street from a whorehouse and didn't know it. The women of the night were college girls working their way through Northern Illinois Univ. Good for them. Nothing like a hard-working college girl I thought. I learned to be more observant of my surroundings. We always thought that three things in life didn't come back, but in 1963, saying farewell to DeKalb, IL, I learned there was a fourth thing that didn't come back…a co-ed across the street. I think it was Peter Lynch who said, in reference to picking winning stocks, that "you can't kiss all the girls". All that free time we had with the University closed for a week in November 1963 after President Kennedy was shot in Dallas. Almost Forty-five-years after 1963, following a dinner speaker program in downtown Dallas, I walked from the restaurant to the Grassy Knoll to take a look. Eerie. A lot smaller than I remembered seeing it on TV in November 1963.

# Chapter 15

*"If you can keep your head when all about you others are losing theirs, maybe you just don't understand the situation"*
*— Navy Law*

MY FORK IN the road came in early 1964 when during semester break I hitched down to Normal to see old buddies and called up, on a lark, Barbara J, who lived in Bloomington, IL with her parents, to ask her out. Never in a million years thinking that a beautiful girl like her would go out with a guy like me, I was stunned when she accepted my offer to go to Ted Caboose, a bar by the CB&Q railroad tracks, for a beer or two. At 5'9" and movie star looks, Barbara, stopped traffic when we walked in together at the Caboose Bar & Grill. I could just hear the peanut gallery, "what is a beautiful women like that going out with a chump like him". How right they were…how was he? Must have been the black Levi pants, the Gant Hugger shirt and the Converse All-Star lo-cuts with the back of the shoe practically out that cemented things for me. You just never know with women. I thought the first date was that she was very bored over the break and would have gone out with just about anyone to get out of the house. Living at home with her parents while attending Illinois State Normal Univ (ISNU). Took a lot of patience. As it sometimes is the case in life, I leave one town and find myself hitchhiking down US 51 to go back to the same town I left, every week-end to see Barbara. US 51 from DeKalb to Bloomington took you through such towns as Mendota, Minonk, LaSalle-Peru-Oglesby, Wenona, Rutland, Panola and El Paso. US 51 was the main north-south 2-lane highway in the great State of Illinois stretching from Rockford on the north to the poor people in Cairo, IL on the south. Between Mendota and Bloomington you passed through some of the best farmland in the world and row after row of cornfields planted as straight as an arrow. How they planted row after row of corn that straight was always amazement to me, the black dirt in those fields was as black as you will see anywhere and farmers said it was the richest land in the world. The cornfields stretched as far as the eye could see and I wondered where was all that corn going? I particularly liked Minonk, IL as the stores and bars were right next to US 51 when you drove through.

**Never had a beer in Minonk, but the bar patrons seemed to always be having fun as I walked past.**

I dropped out of Northern Illinois Univ in June 1964…they didn't like my grades and I didn't like theirs. I did get a "C" in Marketing from the only professor and class I enjoyed at Northern. That summer was spent finding a job and getting married to a lovely woman, in that order. Jay had dropped out of the University of Illinois and took a job at the Western Springs Post Office as a mail carrier. To save money, he stayed with his parents. Harley Hewitt, the Postmaster, a career postal employee, once called Jay a "foul ball" so you can only imagine how long Jay lasted on the job. Hank continued his "studies" at Parsons College in Fairfield, IA in 1964. BS got married and worked in LaGrange. Buck and Willie the Wop were headed for their senior year and future stardom. Dutchy Van was in the Army and Baldy was in the Navy. Barbara and I got married in 1964 and for me, a brief stint at Reynolds Metals in LaGrange paid very little money so I started interviewing for a better job. My Father told me I was "on my own" so if I was ever going to get back to Illinois State Normal University, a full time job that paid was the first order of business. Short on cash, I knew it had to be done quickly.

"It ain't nothing till I call it"
— Bill Klemm, former American League baseball umpire

## The California Zephyr...

It wasn't easy finding a full time job in 1964 for a college drop out like me, but probably not as hard as it is today. After many unsuccessful interviews and interview trips to downtown Chicago I landed a job at the Burlington Railroad counting California Zephyr cars leaving Union Station in Chicago heading west to California. 50-trains a day departed Union Station heading west in 1964. My job was to check the car numbers as the trained slowly pulled out of Union Station. The train engineers were supposed to pull out slowly but when they saw me on the platform, clipboard in hand, they speeded up and laughed their ass off as they went by. In 1964 Union Station was the hub of transportation. O'Hare International was built in 1958 but it was very expensive to fly by plane. Three months on the job with the Burlington Railroad (Warren Buffett owns this railroad today) and LTHS classmate Dougie O made a career out of working for the Burlington, I received a call from the LaGrange, IL Post Office inquiring if I wanted a job. Having worked one semester break over Christmas in the Western Springs, Illinois post office a couple of years earlier, I was very much aware of the physical attributes needed to carry mail.

I often think back to why I left the Burlington. Great guys. Little stress and out door work with no one on your back, to take a job with the post office. But, when it got right down to it, the post office paid the same and offered over time if you wished to stay at night and throw parcel post bags. United Parcel and Fed-Ex did not exist in those days. And if I wanted to see ISNU again before I was 40 years of age I needed to work over time. The Burlington guys were very sad to see me go. Sometimes I wish I had stayed, but I think my life would have been a lot different in so many ways. My fork in the road. But, as the great baseball pitcher Satchel Paige said, "don't look over you shoulder, someone might be gaining on you".

## "We Deliver For You".... the US Post Office, LaGrange, Illinois

As Rod Stewart said in his hit song Maggie May, "it's late September and I really should be back in school". Yet for the first time in many years, I was out of school in September and starting work in the Post Office. I learned a lot from the job itself and from the guys I worked with. I always hated when people laughed about "going postal" because the best group of guys I ever worked with were at the LaGrange, IL 60525 post office. The job itself required discipline from the standpoint that you had to clock in at 5:30am to begin to "case" (arrange mail for each house---each house had a slot in the case), and, while your day ended from mail carrying at 2:30pm unless you stayed, I always did, for parcel post bag throwing or getting the evening mail sorted and on the truck to Chicago. Parcel post throwing meant throwing canvas bags filled with packages out of the trucks into gurneys for sorting and routing inside the PO. Heavy bags and dusty conditions on an often times cold outside dock wasn't a lot of fun, But it was overtime pay and it got me that much closer to ISNU. It took me 6-months before I got my own mail route. When I first started my time was spent carrying different mail routes, handling the 5pm mailbox mail pickups in the red, white and blue mailboxes located around town and delivery of Special Delivery ("Special D" as Elvis Presley called them) letters at 7am. One particular Special D stands out because one early morning I personally delivered George Blanda his Houston Oilers 1964 contract. He was happy to see me as he signed off and took the letter from me. Nice guy, George.

The LaGrange Post Office had its own cast of characters. The guy who had the case (a large box with 2-wings with slots big enough to hold envelopes in and used to sort mail or "the office" as we called it; each house on your route had a slot) with the route to the left of my case was a guy by the name of Bob V. Months after getting to know him better, at Thanksgiving 1965, I invited him over for Thanksgiving dinner to our little one bedroom one living room flat next to the Belt Line railroad tracks on East Maple in LaGrange. During the dinner conversation I asked Bob why he was a mailman and he said he had walked across Europe in World War II and when he got home, he just decided to keep walking. After driving a Higgins boat (I had no idea what that was until later) to Omaha Beach on D-Day, Bob walked across Western Europe ending up in Czechoslovakia when the war ended. There isn't much he hadn't seen and carrying mail suited his style. He made me promise him that I would go to Normandy and the sight of Omaha Beach and go down to the water and look up to see what he saw that June day in 1944. Hard working and without fanfare...I missed the LaGrange PO guys when I got to corporate America.

Prior to getting my own route, one of the jobs I had was parcel post driver for the north side of LaGrange. The south side driver was a new employee by the name of Charlie. I guessed Charlie to be in his mid-50s when I first met him, and by looking at his haircut, he had corporate America written all over him. Sure enough, when we broke bread one sunny lunch hour in the back of my parcel post truck on a postcard day I asked Charlie what he did prior to the post office. "A job in the loop", he said. "A job in the Loop" translated meant a well-paid white-collar office position in downtown Chicago. Downtown got its name "The Loop" from the "El" train that completed a loop around the city. It is something to see...get on the Brown El Line and take the "loop" on the El train around downtown Chicago. As we were leaving lunch that day to go out to our separate routes, I asked Charlie why he left what I suspected to be a big, well paying job in downtown Chicago to become a parcel post truck driver in the LaGrange Post Office. "One day you will know" is all he said. And on my last day in corporate America, 46-years later, I remembered what Charlie said in the back of that parcel post truck. He was right. 46-years later, I knew.

Back in 1964, the mailmen didn't drive big fancy automatic drive trucks to deliver the mail; you had to walk your route. In good weather you had a wheeled cart, but with the snow in winter, you could not push a cart so you carried the mail in a leather bag on your back, You started out of the post office with whatever mail you had to deliver before you got to the first green relay box. You loaded up your bag again at the green relay box and began walking until you came to the next green relay box where you re-loaded and moved forward. During Christmas, and remember in those days there was no electronic mail, and because most people exchanged Christmas cards, your bag was so full you had mail strapped to the outside of your bag too. The bag easily weighed 30-pounds (a lot more during Christmas time) and pounding through the snow and deep drifts after a new snow was perhaps the best workout one could get. We averaged walking about 15-20-miles per day and my thighs got so big my postal pants would split down the seam. Of all the mail we carried Readers Digest was the worst. Too small to put into your bag and too big to hold in your hand with the letters, in the Post Office Readers Digest was called Readers Disgust. . Life and Look magazines also weighed your bag down considerably. Everyone on my route seemed to like Life magazine. My route stretched down Hillgrove past the car dealerships to the high school at 100 S. Brainard, covered the two blocks west of the high school before returning to Stone avenue and heading north to 47th street. Tree lined streets made the route a delight in the summer. A dog attacked me only one time. Some dogs just hate the sight of someone carrying a bag, and I had to scramble up the backside of a car trunk to get away, grabbing for my mace as I scrambled. A snout full of mace sent the dog running and rubbing his eyes. To this day I felt bad that I did that. But I'm sure the dog was ok.

From the day I carried mail in LaGrange to this day, I always make it a point to tip my mailman at least $50 during the holiday season. They don't make a lot of money and have huge routes with a lot of stops and driving every day. In recent years, I've made it a point to also tip my garbage man. You would be surprised at the favors he can do for you.

We walked and carried in 20-below zero weather and 8" snow falls were the norm it seemed in 1964-1965. "Neither rain, sleet, snow nor gloom of night shall stay these carriers from their appointed rounds" were words the PO lived by. My case was located in the dead center of the office. To my right, mailman John G worked the case and the route just east of mine. John was a great guy and a career carrier. His route always got the most mail and he worked very hard to get everything sorted in time to get out the door by 8:30am. During 1965 his daughter was dating the rock-n-roll singer Major Lance whose biggest hit was "Monkey Time". With no cell phones, and with the Major not getting off work singing in a local club until 3 or 4 in the morning, when he called John's residence to talk to his daughter, it woke up the entire household. On many a morning John came in to work threatening to kill the good Major if he ever got his hand on him. As the Major said in his song "you feel a groove coming on".

"Holding you this way, begging you to stay"
— "Any Day Now", Chuck Jackson

My route case was right under the big music speaker on the wall overhead and the songs of those days were as good as it gets...the 4-Tops with "I Can't Help Myself" (Sugar Pie Honey Bunch"), "It is The Same Old Song", and "Baby I Need Your Loving". Petula Clark with "Downtown", The Tams "What Kind Of Fool" (Do You Think I Am), "Tracks Of My Tears" by The Miracles, "You've Lost That Loving Feeling" by the Righteous Brothers, "Yes, I'm Ready" by Barbara Lewis and Roy Orbison's "Oh, Pretty Woman" to name just a few which allowed us to toe tap to the music while sorting the mail and "casing our routes". At 5:30am when we started, what could be better?

We listened to AM radio in those days and our two most popular stations to listen to the "hits" (and then kept on coming in 1964-65) was WLS and WVON, two Chicago stations. I can still hear Jay in the back of Squat's mother's Chevy Impala convertible singing along with Chuck Jackson in his smash hit, "Any Day Now". When Chuck got to "holding you this way, begging you to stay", you could have heard Jay screaming like Chuck did on the word "holding". You have to listen to "Any Day Now" by Chuck Jackson to appreciate why Jay belted out the words. WVON (The Voice of the Negro) always played "Any Day Now" twice. We always listened to it twice.

The LaGrange PO guys in late 1965, led by an experienced letter carrier by the name of Orville P, formed a stock investment club. If you were a member, you met bi-monthly to review possible stocks to buy or press (buy more shares of the same stock). As I was leaving the PO to return to ISNU, they were really getting their act together and really learning how to analyze a stock. I later learned that all the members of the LaGrange PO made some serious money on their stock club investments. Good for them because Uncle Sam paid very little for the work they had to do. But if there was one job back then that would get you in shape, and keep you in shape, and make you stay in shape, it was carrying mail for the US Postal Service LaGrange, IL 60525 through all kinds of weather. Later, the Post Office's motto was "we deliver for you". We delivered without trucks. That was back in the day...when a smoke was a smoke, grooving was grooving and Coke only came in bottles.

If there is one regret I have in this life it is not learning how to invest my money earlier in life. The earlier one learns how to invest his money and do his own tax return, the better. Just look at the fortune Warren Buffett amassed just by being patient, picking good companies and not getting too spread out. If you haven't read the book, *"One Up On Wall Street"* by Peter Lynch, do so as soon as you can. Lynch was a very successful investor at Fidelity and ran the Magellan Fund. The book is loaded with investment knowledge and is easy to follow and understand. I know Jay and Squat would say the same thing to this day. Even if you can't afford to pay a broker like Charles Schwab one can go online to www.computershare.com where there are many, many stocks one can buy directly from an individual company. The best part is you can add more to your individual stock investment only when you have money to do so. Instead of buying clothes you really don't need, or buying a new car that may be the worst investment in America, spend the money buying a stock or pressing a stock you already own. Most every stock pays the holder of that stock a dividend. Don't take the money you make from a dividend payment. Instead invest the dividend money to buy more stock, Nothing on earth compares to the theory of compound interest, that is, money, making money, and by re-investing your dividends to buy you more stock, the more you will make in the long run. What stocks to buy? Stand out in front of a grocery store and ask yourself what do people come in here looking for? People will always need food. Do you buy food companies or the machines farmer's buy to produce the food? People need heat in the winter... what electric utility company is the best? What about products that people have to use routinely...laundry soap, cleaners, etc. We know the population is aging, what drug companies look good? Think and project out over the next 10-years as to what will be needed by people living in America. Banks will still be there.

Security will still be a concern as will national defense. People have to eat. They will need to wash their clothes and brush their teeth. To get excellent, non-biased, up-to-date information on a stock and how the company is projected to do over the next 3-5 years go to the reference section of a library and find a copy of the stock reference book called "Value Line".

I don't know how much money it will take to live comfortably at retirement 30-years from now, but a number thrown out there is $2-million in the bank. If social security tanks, like many people think it will, how will you survive if you haven't saved money for retirement. Instead of spending $50 a month on lotto tickets you can invest it in a good company like PepsiCo. Then every time you go to the grocery store and buy Quaker Oats oatmeal, you are buying a product from a company in which you are a shareholder. People used to ask me years ago why I was buying stock in the Canadian Pacific Railroad. My response was always the same. When I went to bed at night it was comforting to know that I had 35,000 guys in Canada working for me. By the way, the Canadian Pacific Railroad was perhaps one of the best investments I ever made. Of all the things I've seen in my lifetime, the one that is far and away the worst sight of all is seeing a 60-year old homeless bag lady on the streets of Chicago pushing a grocery cart full of her stuff. Their faces almost turn from white to black because of the grime, dust and dirt in the air. A sight in later years that Squatman saw only too often. He volunteered his time (and still does) at the homeless centers in downtown Chicago.

So wherever LaGrange Letter Carrier Williams, who I had breakfast with everyday before we started our routes at this little hole in the wall restaurant on Calendar Ave in LaGrange (right down from the first location of the LTHS Corral) is today, I hope he found his own beach. The same goes for Bob, George and John. The owner of the little hole in the wall restaurant, who made great breakfasts, was an ex-Navy man. He told me the same thing every morning, especially when it snowed, as I was leaving his establishment and heading out the door to begin my route…"short steps" he would say, "short steps". Words to live by in almost every endeavor in life. Short steps and "don't go off half-cocked" my Father always said stuck with me throughout life.

I had some very attractive housewives on my mail route, in an age when women stayed at home, but never sampled while on duty. What would the neighbors think if I hauled my mail cart into a house next to them? Getting an oil and lube change? Risky business I thought. One in particular, a lovely 40-year old, living in a luxury 3-story apartment by the Hillgrove side of the railroad tracks always came down in her afternoon lingerie to meet me as I was filling the apartment pullout mailbox with letters and magazines (*flats" they were called in the PO). One day she would have on a robe opened to the waist, breast in three quarter view and the next day she would have on a see through blouse with breasts in full view. 34C I imagined. We always exchanged pleasantries, but I never asked. The mailman never rings twice. It isn't the things in this life that you did that you will remember; it is the things in life that you didn't do.

"Now some they do, and some they don't, and some you just can't tell,
And, some they will and some they won't, With some it's just as well"
— Super Tramp, "Good Bye Stranger", August 1979

# Chapter 16

*"Don't insult the 'gators until after you have crossed the river"*
*— Gen Wm Westmoreland*

## The train pulls out of Champaign-Urbana, Illinois...

BECAUSE THEY ALWAYS wanted to do it, Squat and Jay, following Jay's graduation from the University of Illinois School of Journalism, decided to hop a freight train and ride the rails all the way to New Orleans, stop and see The Big Easy, and ride back. It was the summer of 1965. They left from Champaign-Urbana, Illinois. I wasn't there so I'm going by the accounts Jay and Squat described of their journey. The journey became very dangerous on the way home hitchhiking through Mississippi.

From their stories, we learned that they caught a freight train that was traveling south out of Urbana, IL and rode in an empty coal car, defiantly waving their arms to cars passing on the highway along the tracks. As night fell, Jay said the freight took them to an open yard miles from civilization somewhere they thought outside of Memphis, TN. They had no compass and no earthly idea of where they were or which direction to head off in. It was pitch black out outside. Wandering through a field they quickly learned that they were not alone as there were two large bulls fenced in with them. A quick exit off the top of the fence to avoid the bulls saw Squatman land in a pool of water up to his neck. Jay laughed so hard he pissed his pants. Their first job was to avoid the train detectives, and to do that they caught a second train south of the yard so as not to be detected.

Getting caught by railroad dicks for riding the rails was a very serious offense then and now, and they hid in boxcars to avoid detection. They rode through Bill Bradley's (former NBA star with the NY Knicks and US Senator) of Crystal City, MO and casting all pretenses aside as they continued their journey, and, at the same time, waving to people on the highway running parallel to the train tracks. They were so close to the highway they could hear a little boy saying, "Hey Mom, look bums". Somehow they made it to the Big Easy. Jay said later that you could smell the cooking as far away as the outskirts of town. I wasn't sure about that, but having made many trips to New Orleans while working later for Johnson & Johnson, we both agreed on one thing, and that was if you didn't see New Orleans before Katrina, you missed New Orleans.

In the late spring of 1965 there wasn't much New Orleans didn't offer to our two wayward sons out of Western Springs. But, it was the trip home that they always talked about down to the small details. Running very low on money, our boys decided to hitchhike back to Champaign-Urbana, Illinois and then home to Western Springs. They left New Orleans and hitched up through the State of Mississippi at a time when two years earlier in 1963 Byron de la Beckwith from Greenwood, Mississippi killed civil rights leader Medgar Evers. And shortly before Beckwith killed Evers, the Freedom Riders, civil rights activists who rode interstate buses into Alabama and Mississippi in 1961 and the following years to challenge the non-enforcement of the Supreme Court decision which ruled that segregated public buses were unconstitutional, put tensions on the boiling point.

## Byron de la Beckwith, Greenwood, Mississippi...

It wasn't until they got a ride from an old black man in a pick up truck 10-miles south of Greenwood, Mississippi, and, learned when he dropped them off on the outskirts of town with this advice, "boys what ever you do, don't let them know you are from the north" that Jay told me he began to not only practice his best "you all's" and come up with a story of why they were hitchhiking through Mississippi and Greenwood in particular. Jay said they knew it was no laughing matter and that both became very frightened, Plus, they had no money

127

in their pockets to call a cab. On top of that, they were stand out white guys from the North and young white guys to boot. Jay said they looked like they were from out-of-town and that is why the very next guy that picked them up, a friend of Byron de la Beckwith, "old de-lay" the guy who picked them up called Beckwith, immediately asked where they were from and what they were doing in Greenwood. Our boys told the guy they were from New Orleans visiting a friend. If it hadn't been for the fact that Jay knew a girl who actually worked in the library in downtown Greenwood, where they got dropped off by "de lay's" friend, no telling what would have happened to them. To this day, Hank still talks with disdain about Mississippi. But the good people of Mississippi finally saw the light years later and convicted Bryon de la Beckwith, old "de lay" for murdering Medgar Evers. Too little too late...I don't think so. Timing in this life is everything. Squatman later recalled riding in a bus in Mississippi with all the blacks in the back of the bus and hearing their thoughts on what it was really like in the back of the bus. You don't learn stuff like that in college. You don't learn stuff like that unless you go to the back of the bus and listen to what is being said. You had to take your hat off to Squat and Jay for their trip to New Orleans and through the South in 1965. An experience that lasted both a lifetime, and 50-years later, when the subject came up, Squatman always said one thing, "it was a great trip". For them it was the trip of a lifetime in a lifetime of trips. And, while my Father always asked me in high school why I wanted to hang "with those two bums", it was adventures like their trip to New Orleans and The Big Easy that separated them from the average guys our age growing up in Western Springs. My neighbors were great guys and everything, but they weren't going to catch a southbound freight. Of the 700-or so students who graduated from Lyons Township High School in LaGrange, IL on June 15, 1960 you can bet your last dollar on the fact that not one of them ever jumped on a southbound freight train from Chicago heading to the Big Easy. They did things the average white guy from Western Springs would never think of doing. First, you have to know how to hop a freight and then, and this is the hard part, you have to get out there. For Squatman and Jay in the summer of 1965 the train pulled out of Kankakee. They rushed home to get back to Chicago by August 23, 1965 to see the James Brown show at McCormick Place's theatre. Arriving at the theatre, Jay said, "I hope there are a lot of Negroes at the show". In hopping a freight, our boys were advised that you select the car ahead of time as it is coming toward you and jump on the front of the car (the side closest to the front of the train) to greatly lessen the chance, if you happened to miss your grip and fall, of getting hit by the railroad car behind you.

Returning from the New Orleans trip in 1965, because the draft loomed and he couldn't find a "career-type" job, Squat got a job as a janitor in a huge apartment complex in LaGrange Park, Illinois. The thought of working in an office sent shivers up and down his spine. The janitor job was outdoors which he liked, and no one was breathing over his shoulder barking orders. Admiral Dan, also liking the advantages of working outdoors got a job as a tree specialist. He spent his days up in trees cutting down tree limbs. On Sundays, they loved to go to Comiskey Park to watch the White Sox. On the way home they would drive back into the City and have dinner at Ronnie's Steakhouse. For $1.19 Ronnie's offered a greasy steak, greasy fries and "oven buttered rolls" as Squatman called them. And, as a special treat, Ronnie's often brought forth a nice upset stomach on the drive out to Western Springs. But, they kept going to Ronnie's and years later Squat wrote about Ronnie's for a writing class he was taking at Northwestern University in Evanston, Illinois. We all could understand his love of Ronnie's but none of us saw him taking a writing class at Northwestern University.

# Chapter 17

*"The trouble is, you think you have time"*
*— Buddha*

## The Peace Corp...

THE NEXT SCENE for our boys---Squat and Jay---saw them in Albuquerque, New Mexico going through Peace Corp training. Ah yes, the Peace Corp experience. Jay emerged as a mid-year grad from the Great U of Illinois Journalism School, and secured a minimum wage job with R.H. Donnelly, loading trucks while weighing his options, which basically boiled down to Viet Nam or acceptance of his application for Peace Corp service. Meanwhile, he was deep in the throes of mindless infatuation with his first serious girlfriend, erstwhile Tri-State (Illinois, Wisconsin & Indiana) Toll way Oasis waitress Susan Wonderful, "swimming in glory" just like Fast Eddie Felson just before Minnesota Fats took him down in the movie "The Hustler". It was an unlikely pairing at best, since Susan was a serious Catholic with past aspirations to the nunnery, then sharing a Hyde Park flat with several white women of the same religious persuasion whose social lives seemingly centered on revolving guest assemblage consisting exclusively of Black males, other than myself that is. Be that as it may, Jay's lady love and he were talking marriage prior to notification from the Corps that he had been accepted for training in Albuquerque, NM for a Physical Education assignment in Columbia.

Intoxicated with romantic delusions, Jay spent most of his last weekend prior to his departure in the company of Sister Susan, throwing his parents into a tizzy by staying out to 6am the first two nights, and not coming home at all the third, which conceivably could have had something to do with his subsequent contraction of mono midway through his 3-month training period, prompting an administrative decision to send him home in good standing until his recovery was completed. He kept an uncharacteristically low profile well performing well in all Peace Corp tasks; he was almost a shoo-in for acceptance, which most probably would have changed his whole life course. Who knows, Jay could have become a Republican or married a wealthy Columbian beauty. For those of you not familiar with the beautiful women of Columbia, spend a little time in the "D" (cup) concourse of Miami International and see for yourself. The Columbian women all had olive skin and dark hair and all of them stunning.

The relationship he had with Ms Wonderful quickly and quietly disappeared during his convalescence, and he quickly sought diversion by recruiting his old time friend Squatman, to join the Peace Corp, even going so far to complete his application when Squatman asked him to do so. To their mutual surprise, Squatman received an invite to join Jay in his return to Albuquerque Unlike Jay, Squatman was not burdened with any idealistic illusions at the time and was ready to go home after the first month of training, but Jay managed to dissuade him from doing so, with eventual fatal consequences to Jay's own future in the Corps, since the two of them came to be perhaps the most easily identifiable members of a funky subset looked upon with considerable disfavor by the more respectable element, in particular several married couples whose acceptance was seemingly guaranteed. Jay talked about this one couple attending Corps training, Nick & Susan, or something like, that had reportedly already been designated for assignment as swimming instructors at a Columbia country club to teach "teamwork" American style, even though a knee injury prevented an physical exertion by champion swimmer Nick during the training period. Jay always talked about what a real crock it was.

"Go along to get along"
— Peace Corp credo

The general expectation on was for the Peace Corp training group to supposedly enhance their skills by socializing with the training staff after hours in nearby bars, i.e., slinging bullshit around, Senor Squatman and Jay, and several comrades, preferred other activities, e.g., weekend road trips to Juarez and formation of friendships with the ladies Jay said they found at the Navy Rose bar in the unique community of Juarez, Mexico. The general training credo was "go along to get along" which Jay told us he tried to do, despite appearances, but the shrink still wanted to know why he wore flip-flops to his Saturday morning interview. Squatman said the Saturday morning interview "was queer" after he went to the interview. Jay's slim chances for Peace Corp acceptance were probably doomed on an evening late in the training period when the visiting Columbian Peace Corp envoy, a guy Jay remembered as "Ellis" spied he and Squatman hitching to a James Brown concert when both of them were optionally committed to an evening class in Columbia folk songs. Like several others who were subsequently accepted, Squatman's Spanish never progressed beyond kindergarten level, while Jay, on the other hand, was ranked no worse than # 2 in the class in Anglo aptitude for the language.

The Peace Corp "de-selection" process was preceded by an evaluation tool known as "peer norms" in which trainees were asked to name, in so many words, whom they admired most and whom the despised. Some of the trainees, Jay said, including himself, declined to throw stones at the dipsticks, but the favor was not returned and final tabulated "peer norm" results placed Squatman and Jay, and almost all of their friends, at the bottom of the Peace Corp "peer norm" standings. All but Squatman and maybe 10-individuals, Jay remembered, were subsequently de-selected. They sparred Squatman because of his "superior hoop skills". Squatman went to Columbia, participated in an exhibition game, and the scurried back to the States within a month "looking for other ways to serve his country" as he mentioned, but we all knew Squatman was just waiting around to get drafted.

The Peace Corps Field Officer In Charge of de-briefing those who had been de-selected and castoff, an older guy Jay said, found that the Peace Corps found Jay to be unacceptably "hostile and defiant to authority". Maybe they had it right after all. Jay remembered tabbing one of the trainees who was accepted to be a future CIA guy that turned out to be the case. Every time Jay told the story of his Peace Corps training experience I knew how much it hurt him not to get accepted and how different his life could have been had he gotten selected. But in a lot of ways he set himself up for failure. Chasing the lovely Wonderful around all hours of the night prior to going to the Corps the first time did him in.

Jay's being de-selection by the Peace Corps cost him a trip to the country of Columbia noted later for its drug and beautiful women. Ask any business-man who travels out of the Miami International Airport what concourse in the airport has the best looking women walking through, and the answer would be unanimous...the D-Concourse. Affectionately dubbed by the business-men who knew, the "D-cup" concourse because the women from Columbia, Argentina and Brazil flew in and out of "D". If you have a delayed flight at Miami International, with some time on your hands, make your way over to the D-concourse for sightseeing MIA style.

When Jay got deselected and asked to leave before becoming a Peace Corp member, we all thought, in looking back on it, that it was his fork in the road. He returned to Chicago to look for a job and then, after a time, went down to Grand Cayman where his parents had a house on the beach and started "dating" all of the Cayman native girls. My brother, DK, around the same time Squat and Jay were going through Peace Corp training, attended a different training class and was selected and placed in a bank in Ponce, Puerto Rico. He didn't speak too favorably about his job as a banker and was transferred immediately to Central America.

I don't exactly recall the chain of events here but I do know that Jay spoke many times about the 1968 Democratic National Convention held in August 1968 at the International Amphitheatre.

"How many times can a man turn his head, and pretend that he just doesn't see"
— Peter, Paul & Mary, "Blowin' In the Wind"

## "Hell no, we won't go"…

1968 was the year of violence and civil unrest in the US, with riots in more than 100-cities. "Hell no, we won't go", in reference to the war in Vietnam, was echoed across the US. On a very personal, extremely sad note, a guy I played intramural basketball with throughout high school, George Jones, piloting a plane over Vietnam was shot down and never returned home. We all gained the utmost respect for Mohammed Ali, The Great One, for refusing to go to fight in Vietnam. It cost him 3-years during his fighting career, but he stood by his principles. Pro-Vietnam War President Lyndon B. Johnson was more worried about his new pants he was having made being big enough in the crotch for his "nut sack", as old Lyndon described it, than he was about the guys our age getting killed.

By bringing the Democratic National Convention to Chicago in 1968, Mayor Richard J. Daley intended to showcase Chicago and "The Windy City", but the Democratic Convention became notorious for the huge number of demonstrators and use of force by the Chicago Police Department. Riots took place between the Chicago Police Department, the Illinois National Guard members and peaceful demonstrators. Jay, who was there, said that residents living in the area getting off the El and heading for their homes ran into the middle of the police with sticks. Many got the shit kicked out of them. Jay said he never saw anything like the police swinging from the heels with their nightsticks. Journalists and reporters were caught up in the violence. Even veteran national TV reporter Dan Rather was roughed up a bit by Chicago Men In Blue. Jay was there along with 10,000 other demonstrators and told us that Grant Park had become a war zone. The Chicago Police used tear gas and sprayed the crowd with mace. "Hell no, we won't go" chants from the crowd turned to "pigs are whores". Jay said that Police used Billy clubs to knock the heads of residents who were just passing through or just happened to live in the neighborhood. On August 28, 1968 the last place on earth you wanted to be was in Grant Park in the City of Chicago. I think the great boxing champ. Muhammad Ali, said it best for all guys our age when he refused to be drafted said, "I ain't got no quarrel with them Viet Cong". We didn't either.

It wasn't long after that Jay returned to Grand Cayman, It wasn't long before that one of the natives he was seeing saw him coming and got pregnant. And it wasn't long before Jay, with wife and child in tow, headed north to the States to get a job. Jay's brother, Dick, a veterinarian lived in West Allis, WI, a suburb of Milwaukee. By the way, if you want to know if a guy is from Chicago or not, just ask him to pronounce Milwaukee for you. It isn't pronounced Mil-waukee it is pronounced Mau-waukee. The first job Jay got was as a Sports writer for the Milwaukee Star a black newspaper that showed promise but fell on hard times and folded shortly after Jay started. Before the paper folded, Jay did interview Oscar Robertson, the great Cincinnati basketball and National Basketball Association guard. Oscar granted very few interviews. The Milwaukee Star was the only newspaper Jay ever worked for. He would have made a great newspaper writer, especially a sports writer.

From Milwaukee Jay & Family, the Mrs. and sonny boy, headed to Chicago where Jay got a job with the Chicago Department of Children and Family Services (DCFS) as a case worker in adoptions and then child abuse. His territory was the Cabrini-Green high rises and the Robert Taylor projects, south and west. He always thought the west side of Chicago was the toughest. Jay had a thousand stories about the people he met in the ghetto on his DCFS job…one crazier than the next. One Saturday late morning, prior to our heading to the off track horse racing betting parlor in Indiana, Jay had to make a stop around 4700 south Cottage Grove area, known in the day as 47th & Cottage. When I pulled the car into the neighborhood all we could see was boarded up houses, and I said to Jay there wasn't anyone inside "Oh yes they are" he said. He told me to drive the car around the block while he went into this house. He said to be back in front of the house in 15-minutes. Most important, he said; do not stop for anything or anybody even if it meant running a stop sign or a red light. Sure enough 15-min later out pops Jay from the boarded up house and off we go to Indiana. I couldn't even begin to imagine doing his job, let alone doing his job in Cabrini & Taylor. No one could. So off to Indiana and the off-track betting parlor we went.  As luck would have it, it just so happened on this day that the great horse Cigar lost his first race, and we didn't have money on him to lose. "Oh so close" as we always described Jay's horse race handicapping and betting. But Jay always had an excuse for losing. His excuse was flimsy at best with Cigar because we always tried to beat the favorite. The reason for this is that most track experts will tell you the favorite wins approximately 33% of the time.

# Chapter 18

*"One more thing"*
— *Lt. Columbo*

### Back to Normal... a semester on the brink

I HEADED BACK to Illinois State Normal University in Normal, IL on a very cold day in January of 1966 carrying all of our family belongings in a panel truck and saying good-bye to my LaGrange, IL Post Office buddies thinking for sure I would see them again, but never did. It never ceases to amaze me, looking back, how much stuff you accumulate in a lifetime. By then, I had lost track of Squat who went from the Peace Corp to Sam's Army and stationed in Germany. I also lost track of BS, Mike, Dutchy and Baldy wondering if I would ever see them again. I had no idea on that cold day in 1965 that the Braidwood Bunch would get back together.

To find out what my Grade Point Average (GPA) was prior to school starting in January 1966, I ventured up to the Illinois State Normal Univ Administration office in the middle of the quadrangle just steps away from the segment of the quad we used for touch football to see the sins of my past grades. I was quickly informed that I was on probation and should I get a GPA of less than 2.0 the first semester, I couldn't come back. One and done as Jay later called it. There is no pressure on earth like getting grades and I knew that I had to pick my classes carefully. I also had to pick up my past studying habits even more. But, I had to take two dreaded accounting classes to get a minor in business administration a degree I started at Northern Illinois Univ in DeKalb in Sept of 1963. I had already failed Accounting 101 once at Northern and here I was taking it again only this time for all the marbles. A semester on the brink is what I called it. To make it a little more difficult and suspenseful, I knew I had to get a job in the evening and weekends to support my family. Further more, all of my buddies who started with me at ISNU in the fall of 1960 had graduated and were long gone. My playing days had truly come to an end. It was the football on Saturday morning in the Quad with Jay, Seaman with an "E", Duck, Harry Grass, Jim V, the Duke of Kankakee, Kenny K, Baggefy, et al that I missed the most. The ground we played on in the ISNU quadrangle, with the Milner library looking right at us, was just about as perfect as you could find for a touch football field. Our field had a manicured lawn, no trees or bushes in the way and room to run. On a return trip back to ISNU in 2011 it was painful to see that our beloved football field was dotted with big trees and shrubs. But the memories of those games on cool, crisp Saturday mornings will live with me forever. I can still see the speedy Hector "Bud" Harry Grass streaking down the sidelines and going deep for a pass.

As luck would have it, I got a job as a mail sorter/clerk in the Bloomington, Illinois Post Office 5-nights a week which paid decent money for part time work. After all, I was an experienced mailman. I also got a job waiting tables on Friday and Saturday night at the Bloomington Country Club wearing my little red jacket with the gold buttons they furnished with the job. At the Country Club, I had the privilege of serving dinner to McLean Stevenson, later Colonel Blake of "M-A-S-H" fame and his father, a prominent doctor in Bloomington. You could not have met a nicer guy than McLean Stevenson who always gave me a $5 tip that was a lot of money in those days. I was very saddened when I heard McLean had died. The Bloomington Post Office didn't have half of the characters the LaGrange Post Office had, but they were friendly and I only worked 3-4 hours per night. Probably the most memorable thing that happened while I was there was the 36" snow storm we got in 1967 which caused the highway post office, which ran from St Louis to Chicago and back every night, to shut down for the first time ever when it got to Bloomington. Drifts on US 66 were reportedly 30-feet high. And it began to get cold. Having been out there on US 66 when the temp dropped below freezing it felt 10-degrees colder than it actually was because of the wind and nothing to block it. The snow was so deep the wind pushed it up and over the snow fences put up along US 66 and when that happened it was all over for any kind of travel north or south.

My two stints working in the US Post Office system paid my way through college, and for that I was always eternally grateful. It also provided me with an opportunity to meet some guys I ended up respecting a lot. Unlike most guys in corporate America, who are climbing the ladder, the guys I met in the Post Office didn't try to be someone they were not. Each was a character and all I knew the meaning of hard work and teamwork. Hauling mail on your back with 10-12" of snow on the ground is tough even for a 20-year old guy.

I received a grade of "A" this time in Accounting 101, my first semester back. If you were happy with your grade going into the final exam, you didn't have to take the final. I can't begin to tell you how happy I was to hear the Professor say that. I did very good in the rest of my classes I thought and when I walked back to Administration to get my grades before they mailed them to me, I learned from the clerk that I made the Dean's List. The clerk offered congrats and said not many went from probation to Dean's List like I had done. Three more semesters to go and I would reach the Promised Land, but looming ahead was Accounting 102 and I needed a grade of "D" to be able to get my diploma. I got a "D" thanks to the help of a guy from Chicago who I had met in Accounting 101 who absolutely loved accounting and I think ended up in the accounting department of A.O. Smith in Milwaukee upon graduation ahead of me. I knew then there wasn't much I couldn't do if I put my mind to it. But I wasn't going to spend anymore time looking at and studying accounting principles. Trying to balance a checkbook was always tough for me. I had to pat myself on the back for handling the pressure of making grades while working two jobs in January 1966.

One of the last courses I took at Illinois State Normal University (go you Birdies) was an upper level sociology class because I heard the professor was good and everyone can be a little more social I thought, including me. In lieu of a term paper, the professor allowed me to do a program on prostitution whereby I would interview a Catholic priest, the Bloomington, IL Chief Of Police and a prostitute and tape all three conversations. The Catholic priest was easy to find and easy to interview. I knew what he was going to say about prostitution before I even scheduled the appointment, but I thought it would add something to the program, The Bloomington Chief of Police was nervous about being recorded, but we managed to get through the interview in about an hour and a half. Finding a prostitute in Bloomington-Normal was going to be difficult, particularly one who wanted to be interviewed even if we didn't record names. To interview a prostitute, it became very clear that I would have to go to Chicago or Peoria, IL (the same "Does It Play In Peoria" you probably heard about) to do it. But, not knowing anyone in Peoria, on a warm for mid-March day in 1967, for what would be the last time, I hitchhiked north to Chicago on my beloved US 66 to find a prostitute to interview in Chicago. "Each time I roam, Chicago is calling me home". They were beginning the build the new interstate (I-55) next to US 66. The new interstate did not go through the towns of Pontiac and Dwight like the old US 66 did. For me, it was a nostalgic trip up to Chicago and back knowing that this would be my last hitchhiking trip on the big one, US 66. You can only imagine all of those many memories from over 100-trips hitchhiking in Illinois and so much learned from the drivers who picked me up. It seemed that everyone who stopped to give me a ride, once they knew I was a college student, wanted to give me advice on life. I learned a lot and became a better listener. There was a sense of freedom hitchhiking on US 66, and while the scenery wasn't like driving from Denver, CO to Glenwood Springs, CO, Illinois had a beauty all of its own. Row after row of corn and soybeans in the summer and snow pressed up against the brown picket snow fences in the winter with corn stalks sticking up above the snow. The black dirt in Illinois, particularly at planting time in the spring, had a beauty all of its own. We are loyal to you Illinois.

Fortunately, when I got to Chicago, Jay knew the bars to go to see if we could find a prostitute to sit down and interview. In our effort to do so we went into this one bar on the near Southside where we ran into a little headwind from one of the patrons not taking too kindly to two white guys inquiring about prostitutes. Jay did the negotiating and I sat at a table near the front door. All I heard after about two minutes of "negotiating" was the sound of a chair hitting the ground and a black guy saying "you bleed red blood like I do, MF". With great negotiating skills somehow Jay got us out of the bar and on our way. Finally, we found a prostitute by the name of Candy who agreed to be interviewed for $10. The taped interview, when I played it in front of the central Illinois born co-eds at Illinois State Normal University, was an instant hit. Not only was it an eye-opener, but for most was a taste of the real world, i.e., what it took for this young, very attractive black woman, high school drop out to survive in the big city of Chicago...the City that works, Mayor Daley used to say. The Sociology professor, with my permission, kept the tape of my interview with Candy and played it for every class when he discussed prostitution. Candy taught us all a lot in the interview...an education for the co-eds on what guys liked and why they visited her instead of having sex with their wives. As only Candy could put it, she worked hard for the money and worked very hard to please the guy. The different things her clients wanted her to do shocked the class (tastefully described by Candy) and I watched the mouths of the co-eds dropping in the class while I watched from the front of the classroom as they listened to the tape. Candy was a street-smart Chicago girl who knew how to get around and how to please a man.

# Chapter 19

So in June of 1967, with no cheering from the crowd, sporting a 2.9 GPA I was proud of, I walked across the stage at newly built Illinois State Normal University Horton Field house and got my diploma, 3-years later than the guys I started with and, so far, never ever to see again. I said good-bye to the Menkins as I walked up to get my diploma. A long train running I thought, but I wasn't thinking too much anyway because I had this wicked hangover from downing one too may at the Polar Lounge on Main Street Bloomington the night before the graduation ceremony. I always thought it was interesting that I only saw one of those guys that I started college with ever again after leaving ISNU in June, 1964. The only guy I ever saw again was a guy from Kankakee who I saw at Gulfstream racetrack in Hallendale, Florida (just north of Miami) in the summer of 2005. Harry Grass went back to his high school (Maine High School in Park Ridge, IL) and was their cross-country coach for many years before dying in about 2005. I have communicated via email with my former roommate, "Seaman With An E" many times and we hope to plan a Menkin reunion before every Menkin, like gherkins, have dropped from the tree…long time passing.

Just before graduating to get a teacher's certificate, I had to do 8-hours of Student Teaching. I was assigned to doing my student teaching at Springfield High School in Springfield, IL to see if I was cut out to be a teacher. I passed and Springfield High offered me a job starting at $5,200 a year beginning in September of 1967. The pay was so low that Sears wasn't going to loan me the money for a clothes washing machine and a gas range. Is it any wonder almost 50-years later that the once mighty Sears, who wouldn't loan me (a new teacher) money, was struggling for customers. I paid off the appliances and never shopped at a Sears store again. We set up a system of envelopes where we kept the monthly money for rent, utilities, clothes etc. We went to the grocery as soon as I was paid to get enough food to last the entire month. Rarely did we have money for a show and never did we have money to go out to dinner.

## The Ray Biggs story...

To make ends meet I took a job nights pumping gasoline at Ray Biggs' Marathon gas station right adjacent to the Illinois State capitol building. For the career I went on to pursue after quitting teaching in 1970, without a doubt, I learned how to communicate with a customer the most from Ray Biggs. Ray ran a very successful Marathon gas station and garage with 4- gas islands, two lifts and two mechanics who were busy from 7am to 7pm everyday during the week, His location next to the state capitol and statehouse buildings meant a customer could drop off their car in the morning and pick it up after work on the way home. The location of Biggs' Marathon was perfect for most people. Ray's two mechanics were top notch and Ray only used quality parts to repair. But, the customer paid for Ray's excellent service and guarantee if something went wrong, and, many were floored when they saw the bill Ray handed to them when the work on their car was completed. About 50% tried not to show their surprise. Ray was at his best when he handed the customer the bill. Not only did he tell them what parts they used in the repair and amount of labor it took to put in the new parts, but what that was going to do for the car moving for-ward. In other words, the benefits of having the work done by Ray's mechanics far outweighed the cost of the bill. Ray didn't just hand the customer a bill... he used the bill as a sales tool to bring the customer back to get his or her car repaired by Ray's mechanics again.

Ray was a good looking guy with a full head of white hair and glasses that he wore when he handed a bill to a customer, When presenting the bill to the customer, he always stood it seemed about 4-6" inches or so closer than the normal conversational distance and looked the customer right in the eye. I always thought that the position gave him a step up on the customer. I never asked him about it and I might be wrong, but it is something I observed him do time and time again. I also learned from Ray to let the customer do as much talking as they wanted to do without saying anything, and pausing a little longer when the customer finished talking which I described as a "pregnant pause" but had the customer on the edge of his chair, so to speak, waiting for Ray to respond. His office was dimly lit with wall-to-wall papers and files. How he found anything in that office was amazing. He remembered every customer's name and the history of problems their car might have had. He always had a smile on his face to greet the customer and a certain twinkle in his eye. He treated me very well the two years I worked for him. We closed the pumps and the station down at 9:30pm each night. There wasn't too much to clean up after work so I got home and got to bed around 10:30p or 11:00pm just in time to get up at 6:00am and make the first bell at school at 7:30am. I would wake up as the Rascals were singing their big hit, "It is a beautiful morning". The worst part of the job at the Marathon gas station was doing a service call to jump start a car on a cold, cold Springfield evening in January with the wind howling, the temperature outside below zero and having to walk into those unlit garages. I did become very good at jumping cars and Ray made a nice $25 profit on each service call. Sometimes I worked all day Sunday and remember to this day missing the first Super Bowl in which Bart Starr and the hated Packers beat the Kansas City Chiefs. The Packers were clearly the better team and with Lombardi coaching them you knew it wouldn't be much of a game. And, it wasn't. I heard many years later, and don't know if it was true or not, that when Ray passed away, his daughter turned the station over to her husband who quickly ran the business into the ground. Ray Biggs Marathon…a business in which Ray worked many, many years building. As Warren Buffett said years later, "it takes 30-years to build a reputation, and 5-minutes to destroy it". I'll always remember Ray Biggs and to this day I'm thankful for his teaching me how to meet and communicate with people; and, while Ray had a style all his own, the basic principles of communication and dealing with people meant everything. Every time I came into work, no matter how busy he was, he always took a minute to say hello and ask how I was doing... and he was sincere about it. But the thing I remember most bout Ray was his smile. It could light up all of Springfield.

To supplement my teacher salary and Ray Biggs Marathon salary, neither amounting to much, I was employed as a certified Illinois High School Association high school basketball ref during the season from November to March and ran the umpires for the City of Springfield Little League during the summer. Why I ever accepted the job of running the Little League umpires remains another mystery to this day. I used mostly high school juniors and seniors to umpire games all over town. These were clean cut, college bound high school kids trying to make a little pocket change who, many, many times during the long baseball season, did their best to endure the wrath of some parent in the stands yelling obscenities at them, or worse yet, coming down on the field to get belly to belly. And, as much as I told them to call the game immediately when something like that happened, they endured the verbal abuse and kept right on going. I think hey were scared shitless of forfeiting the game and dealing with the parent as they tried to leave the diamond. Somehow we made it through and I called the balls and strikes behind the plate in a hotly contested championship game. I got verbal abuse beginning in the 2nd inning, but no one walked on the field to confront me. I had to smile on one pitch thrown by the pitcher when the little catcher said, "you missed that one". To which I replied, "yes I did". It was a special moment that stays with me to this day. What made it special is that the young catcher knew it was a bad call, and I also knew, and we kept on playing. After that Little League season, I never ragged an umpire, or ref even, when they made a bad call. Things happen so fast in sports that it is almost impossible to be perfect on every call. As the late, great American Baseball League umpire Bill Klemm once said, "it ain't nothin' till I call it". How true...50% of the people like the call and 50% of the people don't. I learned in situations where people are upset that it is best to let them talk it out...don't interrupt or ask questions, let them get it out.

Tommy The Ref from Springfield High took me under his wing to teach me how to referee high school basketball games and the two of us worked a couple of games together before I ventured off to ref by myself. The most memorable basketball game, played by football players, I ref'd pitted Greenville against New Berlin in the winter of 1970. With 4-minutes left in the game, one of the Greenville players took a swing at one of the New Berlin players and all hell broke out on the court as both teams came together to duke it out. To this day I don't know how I ducked this one punch as I was standing between two players trying to beak up the scuffle before one guy threw a devastating right. New Berlin just didn't like Greenville and I suspect lost to them in football that year too. For $10 pay a game, I decided that there was a better way to make money, not that I didn't love basketball. The experienced refs got the good games to work and I could see it was going to take a long time to get to that experience level, I don't know when Tommy The Referee died, but he was well remembered in central Illinois for being a top high school basketball referee. As was a friend of mine from high school, and LaGrange Park, IL Little League team mate, who went on to ref some of the championship games in the Illinois High School basketball finals in Champaign, IL at the Univ of Illinois. In 2010, Jay, Squat and I watched as he ref'd the game at the Univ of Illinois/Chicago basketball court between Jabari Parker's Simeon High School in Chicago team and big Frank Kaminsky from Benet Academy in Lisle, IL (suburb of Chicago) who went on to star at the Univ of Wisconsin and then for the Charlotte, NC Hornets in the NBA. Jabari Parker went to Duke and then on to the Milwaukee Bucks in the NBA.

Some financial help for me came when the Springfield High Athletic Director giving me the golf coaching job which paid $300 for the golf season. My job was to drive them to various meets around central Illinois. As I remember, we fielded a pretty good team, no coaching from me of course, and we went on to compete in the State Golf Meet in Champaign, Illinois. I realized with the golf team that encouragement can go a long way. We were a team.

I played 12" softball for Lorenz For Attorney General with some fellow Springfield High teachers in 1968 and our third basemen played the same position for the old Washington Senators. Dick Schofield was from Springfield. Present Washington Nationals outfielder Wertz was related to the Schofield family. Famous National League umpire, Jocko Conlon, was from Springfield. Dave Robish, who held the Illinois High School Association basketball final 4 scoring record, went to Springfield High, Class of 1967 before heading to the Univ of Kansas and the Cleveland NBA team. He could not be stopped in his high school playing days. In the championship game for the state of Illinois basketball title they lost to the Pekin, IL Chinks, and the Chinks put their two 6'5" starts both in front and back of Robish to deny him the ball. They were so tight on him that he couldn't even breathe. Verdie Altizer, Springfield's coach, complained to the refs who did nothing. In 1960 Rage Page's Springfield Senators won the Illinois High School championship. Ray went on to stardom in politics, but it was John Sowinski's scouting the opposition that was a big part of the reason why Springfield won.

It was the start of the 1969 school year when I began looking at houses to buy in Springfield, IL and quickly realized I couldn't afford one. The housing investigation lead me to begin thinking about finding another job outside of teaching, But what was the $64,000 question. Not that I didn't like teaching in the Quonset hut known as building 34 "A" and 34 "B" at Springfield High, it was because I didn't see any opportunity to make enough money to buy a house for 5-10 more years at these wages.

# Chapter 20

*"Originality is unexplored territory, you get there by canoe, you can't take a taxi"*
*— Alan Alda*

Did I want to sell pharmaceuticals to doctors or dog food to grocery store managers?

WITHOUT ANY FANFARE, in September 1969 I began writing companies to see what jobs were out there that paid a little more or had the potential to pay a lot more. I had offers from Moore Business Forms in Peoria, Ralston-Purina in St Louis, Union Oil of California and a British pharmaceutical company called Burroughs Wellcome (B.W. Co). It must have been fate that I ended up accepting the job with Burroughs Wellcome Co because if the phone hadn't rung just as I was leaving the placement office at Illinois State Normal University in Normal, Illinois, I would have never looked at the brochure about Burroughs Wellcome Co sitting on the placement officers' desk resting under my elbow. Following the final interview with Burroughs Wellcome Co., at the old Parkmore Hotel in the 400 North block of Euclid in St Louis, MO, I was offered a starting job. I thought I'd go with the Ralston job calling on grocery stores, until the interviewer for Burroughs Wellcome Company, as I was getting up to leave, asked if 5-years from now I wanted to be calling on doctors to sell a new break through drug or calling on a grocery store manager trying to get more shelf space for dog food. Plus, B.W.Co offered a company car. The territory they wanted me for was in St Louis, MO…The Clayton, MO actually. How many towns do you know that actually put "The" in front of their name?" The citizens on Naples, Florida thinks they should be called "The Naples". Even if they don't always say "The", I always do. On the long way home from the interview, the 1962 Chevy II I was driving, called Grape, started coughing just north of Litchfield, IL, and broke down as I returned to Springfield. As Fogelberg said in "Run For The Roses"…fate was delivered, my moment was at hand. I started out in pharmaceutical sales at $5,200 per year with no bonus. Today reps make $5,000 in a quarterly bonus. The chickens, I thought, came home to roost one evening after a dinner-speaker program I co-sponsored with Clifford Samuel the Gilead Sciences Rep for Ft Lauderdale, Florida. After the program, Clifford and I walked over to Starbucks to review the evening festivities over a cup of coffee. Somewhere in the conversation the subject of how Gilead Reps, who started when the company was in its infancy, would make over a million on the stock options they received. I complained to Clifford that it was my generation of drug representatives that made in possible for the Gilead Reps to make so much money. Gilead Rep Clifford Samuel laughed and his reply stayed with me to this day, "it ain't your daddy's Oldsmobile anymore, Ron". Clifford Samuel was very good at what he did.

It is easy to look back 45-years later and ask myself why I made the decision to quit teaching, and the answer always comes back the same…I needed to make more money, or at least I thought I did. . But money does not buy happiness, and we had enough money to "get by" as they say. The students kept you young and the sports were great. I was most happy teaching and working as a teacher at Springfield High School. If I had to do it all over again, I would have stayed a teacher and, at the same time, invested my money wisely. I bought my first stock mutual fund in 1968 and it was perhaps the smartest thing I did. I missed driving all over central Illinois from November to March scouting basketball games in towns like Mattoon, Champaign, Decatur, et al with Don Yutzy a PE teacher at Springfield. I missed coaching the sophomore baseball team and watching their successes. I learned a lot coaching. First, is the importance of communication and not turning "trust" into a four-letter word. If players did not respect and want to play for you they weren't going to give 100%. And, you needed to be a 110% clear on everything you said or asked a player to do. Play favorites and everyone loses. Teaching high school, too, keeps you thinking young. And, back then you didn't have a buzzer to push in the room to bring an armed guard to your classroom. Kids then showed respect and manners. 30-years after beginning teaching I went back for a day to substitute teach in the Denver Public Schools...how kids had changed. When I gave them time to study they studied all right, but it wasn't homework, but gun magazines. How important discipline had become. Why did most of the kids even bother to come to school...they really weren't interested in learning anything. And, the first thing the principal showed me was the buzzer to get help into the room in case of an attack.

If I could turn back the hands of time, as Tyrone Davis from Chicago said in his big hit, to 1970, I would have and should have stayed a teacher. What lay ahead was not a reward for good work while working for Burroughs Wellcome Co., a British Pharmaceutical Co., but jealousy, control maniacs, back stabbing and watching guys get promoted not on what they did, but how well they were liked by upper management. The problem was upper management had absolutely no idea how to recognize ability. And the guys that were liked rose to the top in management jobs. When Joe Hecker retired in 1986, I got a new boss who was not the same as the old boss and who climbed the ladder playing the game. "Meet the new boss, not the same as the old boss" as The Who put it in their song. If you wanted to learn how to "kiss ass" as they called it, this was the guy to learn how to do it from. To this guy, it did not matter what he did for the reps working under him as long as he could get time to interact with the right people at meetings. He also knew fully well exactly whom he was competing against for the next upper management position. If you were positive, cheerful and full of enthusiasm, you moved up the Director of Sales' bean stock. One thing he was good at was promising everyone that he managed that they would be the next who would be promoted. Who gets promoted, and why they get promoted, in corporate America is the subject for another book. But I can't begin to tell you how difficult it is to work for and work with a manager who you had no respect for and actually did turn "trust" into a 4-letter word.

In 1995, in an effort to compete with the other major pharmaceutical companies, Burroughs Wellcome Co decided to start a much needed Medical Science Liaison Department of Pharm D's calling on physician thought leaders in infectious diseases, oncology, respiratory and virology and the Director of the Medical Dept had recommended me for the job. Just as I was about to get my resume together, here came the best job of all that took me miles away from the Sales Department loaded with guys who stole ideas and excelled in babysitting and selling themselves. The chickens had come home to roost for me, but let me start at the beginning because if you are reading this, and want to make a career out of working for a company in corporate America, you are going to get some of the best advice you ever got. As Charley Watts said in the back of the US Post Office parcel post truck over lunch…"one day you will know".

What mattered to me the most, as a District Manager, was to fight like hell to get the Reps working for me promoted. And, I did… two of my Reps promoted to the Marketing Dept and one went on to be in charge of launching and marketing AZT. The other went on to become Vice President of Marketing for many years. 3-guys went on to be outstanding District Sales Managers and deserved to be promoted. The Denver District gave me a plaque when I transferred to San Francisco. The heading read "You Know You Work For Ron Sheeley When" and each of them wrote a paragraph on what the liked and remembered about me. To this day, the cup Joe Hecker gave to me when he retired (inscribed "It Is Party Time" coming from a question I always asked as one of our meetings was closing down---"tell me General is it party time?" I still have that cup. The plaque the Denver hospital District gave to me I also kept. It was difficult watching this lack of talent get promoted, but like my Dad always said, "the hardest thing to learn in corporate America is the ability to recognize ability". All one needed to do is look at how poor Jack Welch of General Electric did at recognizing ability with the 3-guys he hand-picked and selected to take over his CEO position. All of Jack's choices to succeed him were poor choices, particularly the guy who almost single-handedly ran Home Depot into the ground.

We moved to St Louis following school finishing in June 1970. They sent me to Boston for basic training. Because I didn't have money for an expensive cab ride, I had to hitchhike out to Bedford, Mass where the training was to take place. The further I went, the more things stayed the same. Basic Training class in Bedford, MA, just outside of Boston, lasted 2-weeks and I flew back to St Louis, MO to start my new job in my new sales territory. And, so here I was in the Gateway To The West, starring at the St Louie Arch wondering what happened from here...I had no medical background and the only sales experience I had was selling magazines from door-to-door during an 8$^{th}$ grade contest. I finished second in the class in that contest. The winner sold all of his magazines to a couple of dentists' offices. This was an excellent lesson to learn as early as I did...go after the big potential customers and concentrate your selling efforts on them. As I quickly learned in pharmaceutical sales, 20% of the doctors prescribed 80% of the drugs. I also learned that if you didn't know the answer to a product related question a provider asked, it was suicide to try to bluff you way through. "I don't know, but will find out" was the only way to go. I also learned that follow-up was of utmost importance. If you told a provider you were going to do something, you better do that thing.

"He doesn't have to"
— as said by Jockey Chris Antley to heckling rail bird fans screaming
that Charismatic, who just won the Kentucky Derby at 21/1 odds, that
he would never again win another race The Kentucky Derby, Churchill
Downs Louisville, Kentucky, the 1$^{st}$ Saturday in May 1999

No sooner had I started calling on doctors to sell Burroughs Wellcome Co drugs---Actifed, Sudafed, Neosporin, Cortisporin Otic, allopurinol, Cardilate, Septra, Lanoxin, to name a few, then I learned that Bristol-Myers just laid off 600-representatives. Would I be headed to Ralston on my hands and knees to beg for the job I just turned down? Burroughs Wellcome, founded by two American pharmacists, was headquartered in London, England and Research Triangle Park, NC. There were 200-reps selling Burroughs Wellcome Co products in 1970. My first territory had me calling on the ivory-tower doctors in The

Clayton, University City and West County St Louis, up and down Ballas Road. The "Palaces on Ballas" as they were rightfully called. University City was the home of the great Cub pitcher Kenny Holtzman. The providers I called on that batted against Holtzman in high school said he was unhittable. I agree. He had a curveball like Clem Labine and control like Warren Spahn. One fourth of my territory had me running out to the boondocks where it was a lot easier to see doctors. Eureka, Pacific, Sullivan, Cuba, Hermann, New Haven, Owensville were a few of the towns I called on outside of St Louis. While the drug reps today would never believe it, doctors in the "country" part of my territory in those small towns used to call my house if I missed a 4-week rotation and missed calling on them in their offices. "Everything ok, Ron. "Family ok?" There were only 12-companies competing then and rarely did you ever run into another drug rep in the country. I always admired the general practitioner with an office in the country in those days. They got calls from patients at 6:00am and 12-midnight and still maintained sanity. When I called on the providers in rural areas, I was always sent back to their office where we talked for 20-minutes across their desk. It was a break in the day for them and a chance to catch up on what was going on in surrounding towns and St Louis. Business was always first, and, in those days, we reviewed new articles and studies from medical journals, reprints as they were called. They always appreciated the information I provided on new studies and information pertaining to my drugs versus the competition's drugs.

> "If everyone believes it, it probably is not true"
> — a sign posted on the wall in PhD Ernie C. Hermann's office at the
> University of Illinois School of Medicine, Peoria, Illinois, circa 1982

The amount of studying and new information on the job never ended...it was like college all over again. The providers in The Clayton, MO, primarily Jewish, taught me a lot of defending my position if I knew I was correct and had the right information. Easily intimidated by them at the start of my career, I quickly learned that knowing one's product information was very important. The doctors in The Clayton were no bullshit providers...tell me what you've got, tell me why it is better and tell me how it compares to what I'm using in cost and effectiveness. It took a long time to get a provider to use your drug for the first time. But, when they did start using it, the competition would pay the piper to get them off of your drug.

In 1972, I got a promotion from territory representative to hospital representative and began calling on the big teaching hospitals in St Louis (Barnes, Jewish, and St Louis Univ) and the Univ of Missouri in Columbia, MO. While I was prepared to call on the providers by calling on the ivory-tower providers in The Clayton, MO, I hated giving up my "country" doctor call run. Life was so much more laid back in the country, doctors loved to see you and all the drug reps got a share of the business. If you made your calls on the country doctors, you were rewarded with having your drug prescribed. It was as simple as that. We were a family. If you called on Washington University doctors and St Louie University doctors you competed against the best competitive reps each company had in St Louis, MO.---Merck, Pfizer, Eli Lilly, Upjohn, Sandoz, McNeil, Roche to name a few companies.

In the big cities there were more drug reps calling on the same providers and as time went on during the decade of the 1970's, the competition got more and more fierce. Because I sold 12-drugs, I called on a number of different specialties and competed against several of the major top companies. To this day I still remember the names of the reps I competed against...Ray with Bristol, J Cubes with Upjohn, The Deeker and Virg with Eli Lilly, Donnie with Pfizer, the Big Bopper with Schering, Gary with McNeil. My boss split up Barnes Hospital because of its size and importance---I had ENT, Urology and Pediatrics. My Burroughs Wellcome teammate had medicine and surgery. We were much smaller than most of the companies we competed against and didn't really have any "big" drugs until Septra (trimethoprim and sulfamethoxazole) was approved and released in 1972, first for urinary tract infections and prostatitis and in 1978 for acute exacerbations of chronic bronchitis and acute otitis media.

In the spring of 1972 in Sullivan, MO two department stores were being built right along Interstate 44. You could see both of them being constructed from the I-40 highway that ran right next to the town. Store "A" beat Store "B" to completion by about 3-months. As I called on Sullivan, the doctors and drug store there, every 4-weeks, it was interesting to first see the building progress made each month and then, after both stores were finished, who got the majority of business. The clear-cut winner for having the most customers was Store "B" which garnered so much of the business that Store "A" closed six months after Store "B" was built. Store "B's" parking lot was so full one night that I stopped to see what was going on. They had to be giving something away.

The only thing store "B" was giving away as far as I could see walking the aisles was rock-bottom prices. And the little store "B" was named WalMart in Sullivan, Missouri in 1972 went on to join about 3,000 other WalMart's to become the biggest of the big. Had I purchased a few shares of WalMart in 1972 when I first saw it go up in Sullivan, I could have retired by 1992 a very, very wealthy millionaire. Sam Walton knew how to merchandise and treat customers. He was the first store to have a guy greet you as you walked in the front door welcoming you to WalMart. The greeting made you feel like you were part of the WalMart family. Can you imagine a store actually showing interest in their customers and thanking them for coming into the store…how novel. It didn't take the pharmacy in Wal-Mart to crush the Sullivan drug store, which had been charging high prices for prescriptions for years and getting away with it.

As the 1970's opened, Jay was starting his job at the Department of Children & Family Services in Chicago in the adoptions department. Mike was heading to AIG to become a successful insurance guy. Squat returning from Germany and the Army, got married, and started with All State Insurance where later he became an investigative auto accident adjuster and drove all over the city of Chicago investigating accident claims. He could spot fraud a mile away. I lost track of Dutchy and Baldy, and, thought BS was out in California working as a computer programmer for Visa. It wouldn't be until the 25th high school reunion in 1984 that I would see those guys again.

1972 was also the year I started playing tennis with a wood Wilson Jack Kramer racket. Little did I know at the time how much it would help me in pharma sales. By 1975 I got good enough to play in city tournaments once losing 7-5 in a match after leading 5-0. You don't forget those matches.

I liked the competitive nature of pharmaceutical sales. Because the provider [physician] you were calling on to sell he/she on prescribing your product didn't buy the product directly from you, but had to remember to prescribe the product for someone else [the patient]. It was different because you didn't know leaving the sales call if the provider would "buy" the product or not by prescribing it when he saw the condition. It is much easier to over come a buyer's objections if you know at the end of your sales presentation whether or not the buyer was buying the product. If the buyer said "no", you had the advantage of asking why not. With pharmaceutical sales, 90% of the providers, at the close of the presentation, would tell you that they would prescribe or "buy" your product the next time they saw the condition. I only recall a handful of times that a doctor actually told me "no" I won't prescribe your drug. They all wanted to make you feel good. It wasn't until 1975 when DDD came out that we learned how successful we were in selling our products because for the first time ever we got a comparative report showing how much market percentage-wise we had vs. the competitor's in each zip code in our territory. A lot of guys who looked good and sounded good at sales meetings didn't look so good when DDD came out. The bullshit and the glorified stories featuring glorified successes were over and done. You could run, run, run but you sure can't hide from those DDD numbers. District Managers, who had their favorite Reps because they sounded good at meetings, gave them the highest raises, didn't look so good. As Buffett said, "when the tide goes out you can see who is swimming naked".

So it was with DDD…the many false success stories crumbled and for the first time ever, you knew where you were positioned in sales in your territory. And all the bullshit sales success stories at District Sales Meetings came to an end. If you didn't have the DDD numbers, no one was going to listen to your ideas anyway. I often think had DDD come out earlier I would have quit and moved into selling something on a commission basis. By 1975, the DDD numbers proved I could sell, and, sell very well. The District sales in Septra were 2$^{nd}$ in the USA and I called on the largest number and most important Urologists in St Louis, the specialty that used the most Septra. How I went from selling magazines door-to-door in 8$^{th}$ grade at Forest Road school to one of the top pharmaceutical sales reps in the country proves that it can be done by anyone who works hard and learns as they go. And, I might add, anyone who listened to Joe Hecker.

"Abbott: Who's on first. What's on second. I don't know is on third
Costello: You know the fellow's name?
Abbott: Yes
Costello: Well then, who's playing first?
Abbott: Yes
Costello: I mean the fellow's name on first base
Abbott: Who
Costello: The fellow playing first base
Abbott: Who
Costello: The guy on first base
Abbott: Who is on first?
Costello: Well, what are you asking me for?"

# Chapter 21

*"Once upon a time there was enough time"*
*— Anonymous*

IN 1972, BURROUGHS Wellcome Co launched a new antibiotic called Septra for urinary tract infections. For some reason, which remains puzzling even to this day, they cross-licensed the product with Roche [of Valium and Librium fame] and Roche launched Bactrim, the same product as Septra, at the same time we launched Septra. They were identical products under two different trade names, sold by a big pharmaceutical giant (Roche) and a little British pharmaceutical company (Burroughs Wellcome Co). There was only 1-problem for little Burroughs Wellcome Co, and me. The problem was that Roche had twice as many Representatives as Burroughs Wellcome Co did and I competed against 6-Roche Reps (calling on 2-times as many reps was a big deal; I had 6-times). I was killing Roche so badly with Septra vs. their Bactrim on Ballas Road and West County St Louis; they called in their top female Rep to try to get a little business. Even though she dressed for success and brought all kinds of little gifts in, the Urologists and top-prescribing doctors stayed with me. When I was promoted into the home office in 1979, I had 90% of the business in my territory.

What it meant to me competing against 6-Roche Reps, calling on all the attending Urologists and Residents at Washington U Barnes Hospital and all the urologists in West County St Louis, MO, was I had to figure out a way on the day the two drugs (Septra & Bactrim) were released to see as many urologists and big prescribers as possible. In west St Louis County the biggest hospital was

St John's Mercy Med Center ("Have Mercy" we called it). St John's allowed drug representatives to hold a display at the doctor's entrance of the hospital. From 6:30am till noon you could see a lot of doctors. The night we received word Septra was approved, I called up the McNeil guy who had the St John's display the next morning and asked him if I could trade tomorrow's display for a display I had scheduled approximately two weeks out. No problem. So at 6:00am in a hot and steamy August morning in 1972, I dressed up in overalls over my shirt, tie and suit pants that made me look like a plumber. On the display case I had Septra product information, comparative studies and a small toolbox painted pink the same color as a Septra pill. On my pocket I had affixed a small sign that said "Septra...the plumber's friend". Septra was approved for urinary tract infections and the targeted physician specialty were urologists.

Years later, when I was promoted to the home office to see if I was management timber, in saying farewell to doctors I had called on for 10-years, the one thing they remembered most was my plumber's uniform. Lesson learned, and a good one, a gimmick never hurts, The only time I actually called on doctors' offices on a Saturday was the week that Septra was approved by the FDA and we began selling it. In one day I went from Eureka, MO all the way down I-44 to Cuba, MO and then up Missouri 19 to Hermann, MO and on to Union and Washington, MO before heading home at 6:00pm. My very first call that Saturday morning was on a dispensing doctor in Eureka, MO who acted as his own pharmacy buying drugs from a St Louis wholesaler and then dispensing to his patients...just like Walgreens did. When I finished my Septra presentation that morning I asked him if he would stock a bottle of 100 to give it a try. He purchased a bottle of 500, unheard of in selling a new drug. I knew 2-things after walking out of that provider's office in Eureka, MO that Saturday morning...I could sell and I was going to sell a lot of Septra. 99% of the doctors I called on did not dispense meds so this was a bell weather case---was he going to buy or not. Most of the time you never knew even if a doctor said he would prescribe. I never knew when I started selling drugs to doctors if they were really going to prescribe the drug or not as it was so easy to say "yes", but it was "yes" or "no" with a dispensing doctor. The reason why I always thought the best salesmen in the world were drug reps because you sell information. The doctor does not buy the drug from you, but prescribes it for someone else. How to get a doctor to start using a new product, usually for a long time and usually higher priced than what he was using, is for a chapter later on in this book.

## The Joe Hecker story…

And it just so happened the concept I learned how to get a doctor to try a product for the first time and use a new drug from of all companies, McNeil, a company belonging to the big holding company---Johnson & Johnson. And a company, 35-years later, I went to work for. Why other companies and pharmaceutical reps never picked up on this sales concept remained a mystery my entire career in pharmaceutical sales…but it didn't remain a mystery to my first boss, Urban J "Joe" Hecker, District Sales Manager, Burroughs Wellcome Co. (BWCo.) Joe Hecker started selling drugs for BWCo in 1946 in Louisiana and Alabama. He was the 108th guy to be hired by the Company. A medic in the Pacific in World War II he returned home to pharmaceutical sales because of his degree from Tulane in pharmacy. He often stated his college degree I think to let providers know that he was a brighter bulb than your average rep. Anyway, he often led his sales presentation out with "Doctor, I'm a pharmacist".

The first thing you observed when he was sitting across a provider's desk ready to begin his presentation after the provider sat down was that he moved "up" in his chair to the front of the chair to where he was almost off the edge of the chair. And, with great enthusiasm, he began talking about the drug he was selling. He was a master at providing information on what types of patients other providers he had recently seen that week were using the drug he was selling. "We just talked to Dr Hugabone, and Dr Hugabone told us that he loved Sudafed because it didn't cause any drowsiness and didn't dry them out…let their noses run, get rid of the mucous". "And, it had to be safe doctor because NASA selected this decongestant to take into space in the form of Actifed which consisted of Sudafed plus an antihistamine/".

He always drew a picture and used an example provided by another doctor of a specific type of patient who would benefit from taking the product. He absolutely hated reps who asked the provider, "doctor, will you use a little of my stuff". Joe would use as many stories as possible during his sales presentations… people remember stories he always said. How true. He stressed a lot of things and taught more. Go where the business is he used to say "20% of the doctors prescribed 80% of the drugs". One of his favorite sayings was "If you do your homework every night you never have to worry about a test". In other words, know what you are talking about when you are in front of the doctor by studying what is written in the medical journals about your drug and your competitor's drugs and product information prior to seeing the doctor. Don't practice on your customers is something he always preached.

As soon as he said "Doctor, I'm a pharmacist", it was like a switch was thrown and he was on stage…enthusiastically sitting on the edge of his seat, leaning in and bringing up stories about specific patient examples and discussing benefits, not facts. He loved the job and the thrill of the sale because as he used to tell us nothing in the sales arena is tougher than convincing a doctor, who had used a drug successfully for a long, long time to switch to using your drug. If you can do that, you can sell anything. How true.

And, the longer I sold pharmaceuticals, and competed against the best of the best, the more I realized how right Joe Hecker was. It is hard to explain but when Joe started talking to a provider it was like the providers instantly trusted him and they hung on every story he told. They loved his enthusiastic approach that meant to the provider he believed in his product, how it worked, how effective it was and how safe it was. To the home office personnel, he was "poor old Joe Hecker". Ten years after I was hired, I was promoted to District Sales Manager in St Louis, supervising 12-Reps and I reported directly to Urban "Joe" Hecker who was now the Regional Sales Mgr with an office in Rolling Meadows, IL a suburb of Chicago. The first thing he taught me as a new District Sales Manager was to eliminate the word "but" and substitute in its place the word "and". Joe felt that as soon as reps heard the word "but" everything you

Ron Sheeley

said before "but" was thrown out the window and all people remembered was what you said after you said "but". He taught me to work hard on teaching reps how to sell, use the sales literature, understand reprints, improve their product knowledge and to realize that the reps you supervise may not do things the way you did them. Trust was very important to Joe Hecker. The District Managers who reported to Joe always trusted him.

"You miss 100% of the shots you never take"
— Wayne Gretsky, Edmonton Oilers

One of Hecker's favorite management stories that he shared with new managers was the one about the old male bull and the young male bull in the pasture. Two pastures over were several female bulls. Noticing the female bulls 2-patures over, the young bull says to the old bull, *"let's run over and meet some of those female bulls."* To which the old bull replies, *"let's walk over and meet them all".* That story summed up Joe Hecker. As they say in New Orleans his advice, stories and teaching skills were "lagniappe".

**"Yes, this is the doctor speaking"**
— Your Truly, Renaissance Marriott Hotel, New Orleans, March 2013

New Orleans, outside of Chicago, was one of Jay's favorite towns. He liked the bar scene, some of which were on the seedy side, and the smell of Creole cooking. I think the bars reminded him of Lyons, IL. He often commented that if he ever struck it big at the Fair Grounds racetrack the first home he would buy would be in the French Quarter of New Orleans. In 2013 we went to the NCAA basketball tourney in New Orleans. As the games were played on a Friday and Sunday it gave us time to go to the Fair Grounds Race Track to play the horses. We decided to stay at the big Renaissance Marriott downtown. Buck made the reservations for us under his name, "Doctor Buck". Jay and I roomed together. Before we headed to the Fair Grounds, Jay stored his "stash" in the Bible placed in the drawer in the nightstand. When we returned from the racetrack to the hotel later in the afternoon, we discovered that the "stash" was gone and someone removed

162

the shower curtains from our room. When I called the front desk to ask for a manager I received a telephone call about 10-minutes later from the hotel manager asking if, when I first said "hello", she was speaking to the Doctor. When I replied, "this is the Doctor speaking," Buck, who dropped up to our room to investigate the missing "stash", when he heard me say to the hotel manager that "this is the Doctor speaking" almost fell off his chair he wasn't even sitting on. Because of the missing shower curtains, and no telling what else was connected with the room, the Renaissance hotel manager elected to "comp" the 3-night stay for us. To this day, I'm still puzzled as to why they searched the room and took the shower curtains and stash. We didn't win or lose that day at Fairground racetrack, and, true to expected New Orleans form, the food they had to eat there was the best ever. The town wasn't the same after Katrina, but it was still The Big Easy. I remember while we were there for the NCAA basketball tourney on Saturday night we ventured to this little hole in the wall restaurant and had some authentic New Orleans cuisine. To put a little "pep in the gumbo" as Jay liked to say.

## "If the job is worth doing"...

When Joe Hecker retired, the manager who took his place didn't trust anyone and absolutely could not be trusted. He climbed the ladder on the Director of Sales coat tails and, learned from him not to trust reps. I think that happens a lot in corporate America, get to a position when you honestly know you are over their head, and don't trust anyone and control the information and decisions yourself. It was extremely difficult for him to make decisions and often times delayed so that the whole issue passed. For example, a Rep who reported to me set it up so that we could have the keynote speaker on herpes simplex at a big St Louis convention to be attended by 5,000 providers. It was a slam-dunk opportunity and I explained it that way when I sent it up (and followed up with a call) to my new "Not Trusty" boss. "Not Trusty" waited two weeks to make a decision which should have taken 5-minutes. It was all about control, "Not Trusty" wanted me to wait for his answer. By the time he called me back to approve the speaker, the convention had found another keynote speaker. Here is what I learned...if you have a boss you do not respect and do not trust, who works hard to promote himself and people who kiss his ass, you can play the game, hoping your ass kissing is better than the next guy, or you can look for a transfer to another division or look for a job with another company. In my experience, a manager who you do not respect is extremely difficult to work with. A manager who is a control freak is also difficult to work with. You can try to change the way he makes decisions, but you aren't going to. The best way to tell if you should be in the position you are in is to ask yourself this question…is your boss teaching you anything? But, if you are babysitting, as most managers in pharmaceutical sales are doing, than who cares if the boss wants to make all the decisions and can't be trusted. You don't plan to challenge him anyway even if you know he is wrong. "Yes men" are easy to find in corporate America or corporate Europe for that matter.

My Dad, a long-time manager at General Electric, in the range component division, and Elfun President for one year in 1968 (GE's elite management society) told me that "if the job was worth doing, it was worth doing right" If you want to get promoted you must, at every corporate meeting opportunity in which the big bosses are present, walk up and talk to the big bosses. Those are the guys over your immediate boss. Tell them how much you are learning and tell them how much you look forward to beating the competition this year. In other words, make sure they know who you are. You can be the best lower level manager in the entire company, but if you don't spend time selling your self to the top guys, or at least letting them know you are alive, there is no way in hell you are going to move up.

Joe Hecker always stressed the importance of listening and telling people what they were doing right. "Look for things they are doing right", he used to tell his managers. More so than any manager I ever had. He said not to get involved in your reps personal business unless the rep brought it up. Sell benefits of your drug in specific patient types he preached. If you sell by personality some guy with a better personality will come along and take your business. But, if you sell by product knowledge and benefits of your drug in specific patients you will be hard to beat. Watch how the rep planned a day and what happened around

4:00pm, he said. The rep that rationalized the 5:30pm possibility to call on a certain provider would sooner or later start rationalizing the 5:00pm call and the sales numbers would begin to reflect the rationalizing. Who was the rep trying to see during your working trip with the rep…hard-to-see-internal medicine providers or easy to see pediatricians. I learned a lot about managing people working under Joe. I learned how to be fair, but firm. I learned if a rep was not working, it was time to let them go. A fair number of my manager colleagues found it easier to let the failing rep ride along, but not Joe. Joe was undoubtedly the best team-building manager I ever worked for…as a rep under District Sales Manager Joe Hecker, we were known throughout the Company as "Hecker's Hero's".

As a District Manager reporting to Regional Manager Hecker, I was a member of Joe's "Board of Directors". Everything was about team. He motivated by telling stories of what successful reps and successful managers did…he had a lot of stories.

He was fair and he was experienced. As excited as he got at something you had success with, you knew in the back of your mind that he had already done it. I quickly realized when Joe retired and his replacement came on board, it took about two meetings with him to realize that I had zero respect for what he said. Plus, he could not be trusted which is usually the case of guys who got promoted above their level of capability. We went from telling the Rep what he was dong right to trying to catch him doing something wrong.

## Joe Hecker on how to make a decision…

In training his managers on how to make decisions, he developed a large square of an 8 ½ x 11" piece of paper. Inside the square there was a horizontal line and a vertical line which formed 4-boxes within the large square. In the upper left square he wrote "too soon", in the upper right-hand square he wrote "too little" in the lower right-hand square he wrote "too late" and in the lower left-hand corner he wrote "too much". In the center of the 4-squares a circle he printed two words---"JUST RIGHT". I put this diagram on the bulletin board in front of my desk and every time I needed to make a decision, I looked at the diagram to see was it "too much, too soon" or "too little too late" or was the decision I was making "just right".

He constantly preached taking care of the small details…*"if you don't take care of the rust on the bow of a boat, you could be in trouble in high seas when real trouble comes"* he always said. Take care of the little things, he taught us. When he worked with you as a Manager he would stay out making calls with you until your day was finished. We once called on a GP in Sullivan, MO at 9:00pm. Joe had to be in Kansas City the next morning. You always knew that he was working as hard, or harder, than you were. His enthusiasm over a rep presenting a good idea was priceless and motivational. His replacement would sit in the back of the sales meeting catching up on his memo reading and paying little attention to the reps. Who do you think they admired and trusted more? To this day I can hear him say, *"every time you knock the competitor's product, it is a plug for the competitor"*.

Forty years selling pharmaceutical products had taught Joe Hecker a lot. He worked in the days when 99% of the doctors would see drug reps and 90% of the doctors talked to you sitting down at the doctors desk in the doctors office. Not so today. This job, he once told me over lunch at a Jewish deli on Central Ave in The Clayton, Missouri, is like delivering a baby…99-times out of 100 you and I could deliver the baby, but that one time when complication set in that is when they need a trained OB/GYN doctor to deliver the baby. And, so it was with pharmaceutical sales, 99-times out of 100-times when you present a product to a provider, the provider doesn't ask a question or asks a question that is easy to answer. But it is that 1-time a provider does ask a tough question, and the rep knows the answer, that makes all the difference. As one rep put it, "product knowledge, there is no substitute". One of the greatest compliments I received was from a well-known and extremely busy urologist at Faith Hospital West office complex on Olive Street Road in Creve Coeur, MO two weeks into the launch of Septra the company's new antibiotic for urinary tract infections. And my boss was with me when I called on the urologist, but the doctor didn't know that because I always introduced my boss as a co-worker. When we got to the providers office I knew his waiting room would be packed with patients waiting to see him, but I proceeded to the front desk and I gave my card to the provider's receptionist. We waited for less than 5-minutes and the receptionist said the doctor would see us now. We walked back to the doctor's office where his desk was and in about 5-minutes the doctor came in. As soon as the doctor got to his desk he picked up the intercom to the receptionist and nurse and said, "hold all calls, I'm with Mr. Sheeley". I bet over my 41-years career calling on doctors I called on 50,000-60,000 doctors, and never did I feel more important than that day…"hold all calls, I'm with Mr. Sheeley".

## "Obvious Adams" & "The Elements of Style" …must read for corporate America

I learned from the VP of Marketing of Burroughs Wellcome Co., Peter Howsam, that one of the best books on management ever written, that few people know about, was a small book called "Obvious Adams". If you have aspirations for a future management position, or even if you do not, this book should be high on your list of future books to read. Joe Hecker, like Howsam, also worked hard on stressing the importance of communication. He suggested that his managers read the "Elements Of Style" which is a short book on how to write. A Trip Report written by the District Manager following 2-days of working trip with a Rep in the field were extremely important at yearly evaluations of a Rep's progress or lack of. If the Trip reports weren't clear and concise they could quickly come back to haunt the manager should performance slip and termination proceedings begin. The proper use of the 2nd person on trip reports was paramount. We wrote a trip report every time we spent 1-or 2-days working in the field making physician, nurse, pharmacy and hospital calls with a representative.

"If you don't throw it, they can't hit it"
— Lefty Gomez

## "Just checking the radiator"...

The first guy I had to fire for not making calls was in Columbia, MO. I "staked" the Rep out for two days parking my car (not the company car) at a spot down the street but in view of his house and driveway to clock when he left the house and when he returned to the house. This rep lived on a short, dead end street making in difficult to just go "park" for fear that the neighbors, seeing a suspicious car parked in front of their house with an unknown guy in it, would call the local police. To avoid this scene, I parked along on the 4-lane highway running from Columbia, MO to Jefferson City, MO. This provided me with a view of the reps' house but was a little further away than the dead end street in front of the reps' house. I arrived at 7:30am just in case the rep left early I did not want to miss the time for documentation on the report. By 9:30am the coffee I had at 6:30am was calling and I had to wiz in the worst way. So I decided to lift the hood up on the car and get on my hands and knees in front of the car and go. No sooner did I start and the warm pea hit the very cold highway forming steam, then a Missouri State cop pulled up behind me and got out of his car walking to toward the front of mine. I just got my fly zipped as he was standing there next to me. *"Need any help?"* he said. *"No, just checking the radiator"*, I said.

With that vantage point eliminated, I took the chance of parking down from the reps house on the dead end street about 4-5 houses from the rep's house. When I got there I went up to the door of the house I parked in front and explained to the woman answering the door what I was doing. "No problem" she said. At 10:30am the rep departed his house. He had a house with the garage underneath the house accessible by driving around in back into the garage. This meant that I had to watch the house like a hawk for fear I would miss seeing him pull out. I was parked on the wrong side of his house and could not see his full movement out to the street. I had to stay to determine what time the rep came home. The rep returned home at 2:00pm, but I had to wait to see if the rep went out to work in his territory again. When the clock struck 5:00pm, the rep was tucked safely and comfortably in his warm house while Your Truly was both cold and hungry.

I had to stop the car on Interstate 70 on the way to Columbia, MO to terminate the Rep so I could toss my cookies on the side of the road. After terminating him in person, I had to pick up his samples and literature. But I knew I was doing the right thing. When I got to Columbia to pick up the company samples and literature he would not let me step on his property, and his wife kept throwing the literature, almost piece by piece on the street. I left at 6:30pm. We started at 10:00 am. The job should have taken 3-hours max, but this was his way of getting even. I always thought that if he had worked as hard making calls as he did throwing literature at me in the street in front of his house there is no telling what he could have done. What made it difficult was the manager before me had placed this rep on a pedestal for future promotions into management. That was until the company had DDD...a way to measure your sales compared to your competitor's sales in a territory by zip code. The Columbia territory was the worst in the District in sales yet it was very, very easy to see providers in this territory stretching from Kirksville on the north to the Lake of the Ozarks on the South with the two big cities being Columbia and Jefferson City. A lot of Casey's Gas stations in between. Years later I bought Casey's stock. Good hotdogs.

# Chapter 22

*"To everything there is a season"*
— *"Turn, Turn, Turn", The Byrds, 1967*

## The change it had to come...

JOE HECKER WAS promoted to Regional Mgr in 1972 and moved from St Louis to Chicago. Gone were Hecker's Hero's and the manager who hired me. My new boss, from Georgia, was a lot different than the old boss as the musical group The Who put in their big hit "Won't Get Fooled Again". While you would want him next to you if you ever got into a fight, he was not long on communicating, motivating or product knowledge. He fired some guys I would have never fired, hassled some guys who did not deserve to be hassled, and hired some guys I would have never hired. One guy he hired for the north St Louis territory was a hiring mistake from day one. "Doc, would you use a little of my stuff" is about all he had to say on a sales call. But, as long as the new boss liked him, all was well. Because a District Mgr might have worked with a Rep on average 5-6 times per year in the field, it was very easy to start procrastinating a 5:00pm call because no one was these supervising you. Once you procrastinated on a 5:00 pm call, it was easy to do the same with a 4:00pm call and begin quitting at 3:30 pm. It wouldn't take long for the sales figures to begin dropping.

The new boss promoted me to the position of Medical Center Rep which had me calling on the urology, ENT and pediatric residents at Washington U and St Louis U hospitals which included Cochran VA Hospital on North Grand and; my favorite, St Louis City Hospital called the "Citz" by the ENT residents. I was also responsible for all of the private practice doctors on Ballas Road and West St Louis, MO County and the University of Missouri Med Center in Columbia, Mo and the Veterans Hospital across the street from the University of Missouri Med Ctr. At these two institutions I called on all of the specialties. It was a big territory, but I liked it that way. There was never a dull moment and a lot of providers to see. Plus, there was a nice mix of providers in private practice and physicians in teaching hospitals.

The attendings and residents in the Urology Dept at Barnes Hospital (Washington U School of Medicine) taught me a lot about urinary tract infections and selling. Dr Bill Fair had put together a great staff and as busy as they were, they always took the time to see me if I had something new. I learned how to sell Septra from them and I used the knowledge I learned to sell to urologists in private practice on Ballas Road in west county St Louis. The "Palaces on Ballas" Rd the drug reps called the many doctor office buildings. Hoping to do 70-30 against Roche, who sold the same drug as Septra under a different trade name, I did 95-5 to completely beat them. I look back on it now and realize I should have gone into commission selling because I learned I could sell and it wasn't until 1975 that I got my first bonus check. Believe it or not, my first bonus check amounted to $500. 25-years later pharmaceutical sales reps were hauling in bonus checks of $70,000. Some they do; some they don't. It didn't hurt to play tennis with many urologists in my territory and the Chief RPh at Barnes Hospital in the early morning before work that decided only to stock one drug. That good decision was close to 100,000 Septra tablets per year in business.

## 1978...a trip back to Wrigley Field

Jay came down to St Louis to visit in the fall of 1972 bringing the "Missus" along with him. The Missus didn't say much the entire time she visited, but she made up for the absence of words many times after her 1972 visit to St Louis, MO. I could tell immediately that their marriage was a true mismatch. Once she opened her mouth and started firing those nasty bullets, and she was nasty, it all changed. We got along at the start fairly well as long as I didn't see her very often and when I did stop in to visit, I usually took them out to dinner. As they say at the racetrack, the Missus was a "do-er" (translated…she loved to eat). But toward the end it became almost unbearable to watch her rage and mood swings.

I didn't see either of them again until 1978 and a trip to Wrigley Field on a Saturday to watch the Cubbies play Atlanta and Joe Niekro on a postcard day. In 1978 Wrigley was much more crowded then it was in 1962. The ivy on the outfield walls was still there, but gone were the little old men sitting in the grandstand with their brown paper lunch bags and stories watching batting practice before the game. A whole new group of fans now occupied the bleachers in left and right field. Wearing sleeveless tee shirts they tormented the left and right fielder yelling nasty stuff throughout the game. It seemed like most of the younger crowd attending the game did so to drink beer, get drunk, chase women and care less about the ballgame. It just wasn't the Wrigley we knew and loved, and this positively convinced us that if you missed Wrigley Field in 1962, you missed Wrigley Field. And we thought the Cub players of 1962 would have agreed. As I write about what Wrigley Field was like in the early 1960s, the noise level about the Cubs not being in the World Series for over 100-plus years became deafening. But it was summed up best by a Dr. Leo Weinstein from the Chicago Institute For Psychoanalysis, commenting on the 108-years said, "every year, we are just waiting for justice to occur".

## Mama Crow…one of a kind

Jay's Mother, Ann "Mama Crow" Crawford, was one-of-a-kind. An avid reader she could hold her own with anyone on politics and world affairs and passed the love of books and reading along to her son who later became a true wordsmith and gave all of us a vocabulary lesson, it seemed, every day. "Bolixed" was one of his favorite words in later years. Mama Crow had a piercing voice that you could hear for blocks and, as much as Jay tried to get away with stuff, Mama Crow appeared to always be one step ahead of him. She walked to the A&P for groceries pulling a cart like many elderly women had who rode the route 80 bus east and west bound in Chicago did many years later. She was always there to listen and pass along advice on life in general and the dating game in particular. She was the one to find this little unheard of (in 1963) little island in the Caribbean called Grand Cayman where she and husband Fred retired. There was nothing like beachfront property on an island that hadn't been discovered yet by the vacationing horde of northerners looking for a little beach in the winter. Jay told me his folks paid $25,000 for beach property on Grand Cayman in 1965. It is worth $10-million today.

## Loblolly Bay & The Big Bamboo Bar...

If you are going to find your beach, find one like Grand Cayman was in the 1960s and 1970s. Most of the beaches I saw in the 70's and 80's have all been discovered and prices for a house on those beaches have gone from $90K to many, many millions of dollars.. There is one beach left that very few people have found, and probably never will because it takes an experienced sailor to get past the coral reefs and sail into the island. The name of the island is Anegada. It is the northern most island in the British Virgin Islands. Anegada is 15-miles north of Virgin Gorda and the world-renowned Bitter End resort. And when you park your sailboat, head quickly by bike or taxi to Loblolly Bay and tell me that isn't the most beautiful beach you have ever seen. If you are looking for a peaceful, beautiful, white sand beach, with turquoise water and not a lot of idiots running around, get to Loblolly Bay. There aren't many beaches like this left. From that beach you look directly at Africa. The Big Bamboo Bar at Loblolly Bay serves the best rum punch you will have in your lifetime. A long ways to go for a rum punch, topped with Meyers rum, but very much worth the trip. A rum punch at The Big Bamboo will set you free.

"Some times I will,
Then again I think I won't,
Some times I do,
And then again I think I don't
Looked at my watch and it was quarter to nine,
She said Chuck baby this sure feels fine,
We were reelin' and a rollin',
Rockin' to the break of dawn"
— "Reelin' and Rockin'", Chuck Berry, 1958

On one trip to Anegada, my brother who is a world-class sailor, and I, after dropping anchor, decided to get in the dingy and drive to the island and head to Loblolly Bay. In doing so, we got in the dingy and pushed off before getting the engine started. We quickly drifted past two other boats moored in the harbor. Realizing that if we did not reach out to the next boat moored we would be a drift into the Atlantic Ocean, we yelled to the young lady as we drifted by to throw us a line. She did quickly and we learned that our gas tank was empty. Her husband went with my brother to get gas and I had a chance to ask the young lady on board, their boat was called "Moose", where they were from and where they were going. She told me that she and her boyfriend were from Curacao, a small Dutch island in the Caribbean, known for being a diving-spot because of the beautiful coral and underwater caves. She said they were leaving Anegada tomorrow and heading across the Atlantic to Spain. We bought them dinner on the beach that night and thanked them again for bailing us out. Dinner on the beach consists of freshly caught lobster, corn on the cob and salad…a real treat. About 6-months later, I was in the Dallas Ft Worth Airport (DFW) and had time to stop in a news stand to look at the newspapers and magazines for flight out of DFW that evening. And whom do I see on the cover of Sail magazine? Yes, it is true, a picture of The Moose and our friends from Curacao who saved us from drifting in our dingy out into the Atlantic The article in Sail magazine told of their experiences about crossing the mighty Atlantic Ocean over to Spain. By the way, I asked her which Caribbean island she thought was the most beautiful and worth seeing…The Grenadines hands down.

2$^{nd}$ choice for the best beach I've ever seen would be the beach on Peter Island just across the Sir Francis Drake channel from Tortola. A guy by the name of Bomba made the island of Tortola in the British Virgin Islands very famous. Bomba's claim to fame was his Full Moon Party. Bomba holds his monthly party when the moon is full at the Bomba Shack on the west end of the island on Apple Bay. It is a party not to be missed. Put it on your Bucket List and be prepared to drink a lot and watch the sun rise.

Squatman, Baldy, BS, Buck, Munch and Dutchy Van were gone now, not to be seen again till the 25$^{th}$ high school reunion in Lagrange, IL in October 1984. And then we were like lost relatives. You know they are there but don't make an effort to go to see them or call them for that matter.

## The University of Missouri, Columbia, MO...

I had the University of Missouri and the Columbia VA Hospital added to my territory in the Fall of 1972 when Burroughs Wellcome elected to change Columbia being called on by a Hospital Rep coming out of Kansas City to one coming out of St Louis. In 1972, Columbia, MO was a small little college town with a big football stadium and a school most renown for journalism. Every drug rep calling on Columbia and the University Hospital, whether from Kansas City or St Louis stayed at the Best Western on the east side of town right on Interstate 70. As I recall, the room rate was $19 per night, and while far from glamorous, the rooms were clean and so were the bathrooms. And if you spend any time on the road, a good bed and a clean bathroom are worth their weight in gold. I quickly learned on the road to tip the maid rather than the guy with his hand out wanting to take your luggage to your room. For the maid can make things awfully comfortable.

There were a lot of characters masquerading as pharmaceutical reps calling in the Univ of Missouri Hospital in those days. The God Father, or so he thought he was, was a blustery bull shit artist by the name of Bernie the Big Bopper out of St Louis who ran with two reps out of Kansas City. I don't think the two KC

Reps ever made a call on a provider while they worked Columbia for at least 3-years. But, Bernie's Kansas City friends woke up at 5:00pm and they knew how to party at night in the local bars. And party they did. Disco was just coming in then and every woman wanted to dance. The KC boys were good looking and well dressed and that put them miles ahead of the local boys in Columbia most of whom frequently the disco bar scene were blue collar guys. You got an education watching them in action. They had an 80% success rate in making a connection. How they got away with not working remains a mystery to this day, but they loved Columbia because it was their hammock green. Everyone who stayed at the Best Western on Interstate 70 went to the hotel restaurant around 8:00am for breakfast before starting the day. The Pfizer Rep, Donnie Weiss, an experienced rep who looked like he could deal blackjack in Vegas, when leaving breakfast always said the same thing. "It is time to go save some lives". To which I always replied back to him with "yes, your own". The camaraderie within the drug rep set was what made the 120-mile trip from St Louis worthwhile. There was, and I say this from the bottom of my heart, never ever a dull moment in the 8-years I worked Columbia. Very few bosses worked Columbia, MO. I know mine never came out because it meant a late arrival home and an overnight. For many, it was a license to party until companies started getting competitive sales data by zip code. In other words, my Actifed sales by zip code were compared with Ornade and Dimetapp. Things began to change in 1975-76 when the comparative sales data were placed on the table. Guys who never made calls on the Univ of Missouri started to. One problem...they had no clue of where to go and most of their reckless calling cost us access into several key departments. All it took was one McNeil Rep to put up Tylenol posters in the wrong places and we were barred from seeing attendings and residents in that department. Most of these reps hadn't the slightest idea of where to go and what to do when they got there. But the Univ of Missouri Hospital tolerated a lot that they didn't need to tolerate thanks to a levelheaded Chief Pharmacist, Garth Thomas, who knew what he was doing. If only all hospital chief RPh's knew what they were doing, oh what a wonderful world it would have been for the drug representatives.

# Chapter 23

I BID FAREWELL to Columbia, MO and the University of Missouri Hospital in March of 1979 leaving many, many good memories and times behind. 9-years of selling to hospital-based physicians, city office-based physicians and rural country physicians had taught me a lot. There is a big difference in selling to residents vs. selling to rural physicians. As Mark Twain said, "the difference between lightning and the lightning bug". The thrill of beating my competition was what kept me going those 9-years.

## The T.O.P.S. Program...Turkeys On Parade

In the 1970's and early 1980's Burroughs Wellcome Co upper management came up with this idea to bring reps aspiring, and recommended by their District Mgr's, to be promoted to a District Manager Position by bringing them into Research Triangle Park, NC for a 2-year assignment to see if they were management timber. They called the new position TOPS (Temporary Office Personnel). The candidate had to give up his/her territory and move his/her family, wherever they were located in the USA, and relocate to Research Triangle Park, NC. This meant selling your existing house, relocating your family and buying a new house in Raleigh-Durham, In other words, shine your shoes, floss your teeth and smile. Some guys overplayed the smile, i.e., over did the bullshit, couldn't write and were deselected and given the choice of where they wanted to go. If you had a territory in northern Alabama and called on country doctors, but no territory existed at the time calling on doctors in rural Alabama, you might have to accept a job in Chicago. It costs a lot more money in Chicago (all Reps were paid the same regardless of where they lived) and it is a lot different calling on a big city doctor than one out in the sticks of rural 'Bama. The thought of getting deselected had some candidates breaking out in hives because it meant you would never go any further than a sales representative. Not that it wasn't a good job, but for those TOPS candidates who were interested in becoming a manager and were deselected for becoming one, it meant you were going no further. For the guys who were qualified to come in to TOPS in the first place, the biggest issue was transferring into Raleigh-Durham-Chapel Hill, NC and pulling your children out of the school system they were in.

To this day I remember a Chicago guy named Kenny, who had practically graduated from the TOPS program, when Upper Management called a meeting at the end of his TOPS 2-year evaluation period, With other TOPS members present at the meeting, Kenny commented calmly and clearly, when asked by Upper Management for his comments, on the TOPS program He matter of factly told Upper Management how much the TOPS program had hurt his 5-children in different grades in school. It had been very stressful for three of his children to move from Ohio to North Carolina. While his statements were factual, and his children emotionally devastated, he was immediately deselected from TOPS and never promoted to District Manager, although he would have been an excellent Manager. He went back to a territory as a sales rep and waited by the phone for 10-years thinking he would get a chance to manage but never got a call. Once you crossed Upper Management; there was no going back. You were no longer on the "team". To destroy a guy's career because he spoke from the heart when they asked for his honest opinion about the TOPS program, and if his Family was OK, is what corporate America and especially military style "my way or else" Upper Managers were all about. It is called survival of the game players. The other TOPS candidates, who attended that meeting, knew the program was tough on their families, but didn't say a word and let Kenny hang out to dry. "Players only love you when you are playing". I had zero respect for the TOPS guys who attended the meeting and even less for the Upper Managers.

Again, out of the blue, and with less than 10-months into my TOPS program sentence, Upper Management called and asked if I wanted to go back out into the field as a District Sales Manager. I hated leaving Dr Dave Barry, Dr Bob Desjardins, Kathy Pattishall, et al, in the Medical Department but I always wanted to try my hand at management and accepted the job. It would be 15-years before I went back into the home office to head up the "newly created" position of Head, Medical Science Liaison Division, Once I accepted the job as District Sales Manager, I learned the job was to be District Mgr in St Louis, the same District I worked in as a rep for 9-years. Nothing could have been worse because I knew who was working and who wasn't, but I told the St Louis Reps at the start that what happened in the past, was in the past. Like what happens in Vegas, stays in Vegas. They were being judged on their future sales efforts...but one thing for sure, the Rep who closed his sales presentations with "Doc, would you use a little of my stuff" knew he had changes to make because I was his new manager. Changes he needed to make in a very big hurry.

It was in January of 1995 that Burroughs Wellcome Co. developed a Medical Science Liaison Division, and pulled me out of my job as District Sales Manager to run the new Division. Fifteen long years had gone by since the Company began talking about developing a Medical Science Liaison Division. Some think it was years and years later because upper management had no clue about the value of such a division. Most of them never called on thought leaders in teaching hospitals or knew how to develop relationships. Bye-bye Miss American Pie. It is easy to see why companies fail. From 1995 to present, Glaxo-Wellcome and then Glaxo Smith Kline still do not get it, even with new management.

## Back to good old St Lou...

So in March 1980, back to St Louis I went to manage the same Reps I worked with for 9 ½-years. Fortunately, Joe Hecker was my boss again, and, without saying, I learned how to manage from him. How to do appraisal sessions, write trip reports, conduct sales meetings, build a team and the more I learned, the more I tried to put into practice. I remembered the words of Joe Hecker..."if you do your lessons every night you never had to worry about a test". I emphasized to the St Louis District the importance of product knowledge, specific patient type selling and how to analyze, interpret, read and use a medical journal study comparing our products to the competition. Selling by a specific patient type meant selecting a patient in which our product had an advantage for that patient over the competition. I taught that to get a patient to use a drug for the first time required this type of selling. We had to move beyond the tell-tell-tell-close selling technique our Sales Training Dept taught. I used McNeil's example of selling Tylenol brand acetaminophen to doctors for a specific type of patient, i.e., a gout patient taking Benemid could not take aspirin, but they could take Tylenol's acetaminophen. There weren't too many patients taking Benemid for gout, but what was important to McNeil was that the doctor would remember that their drug, Tylenol, had an advantage over aspirin in that specific patient type. Why not do the same things for our products...find advantages of our products in specific patient types? And instead of trying to get the physician to use our product for all his patients, let's point out advantages of our products in select patients. This way the physician gets used to using our product, and, we learned it is much easier to get a physician to expand his usage of a product than trying to get the physician to use the drug for the very first time. Most reps went in, told some facts about their product, asked the doctor if they would use the drug on their next 5-patients and leave. This approach is totally meaningless to the doctor. Today, the selling environment is completely different. With little to use other than some company approved literature, reprint use taboo, it is easy to see why representatives are asking questions and pressuring doctors to use their drug rather than providing good reasons for the doctor to use their product. And, what is most telling in the pharma sales arena is that the managers of these field sales reps are putting more and more pressure on the rep to make their quota. It can get very ugly very quickly in a provider's office when the Rep's manager makes a call on a provider and starts pressuring the provider. It was interesting that certain medical specialties were called on by fewer sales reps. Representatives calling on those select specialties got in the door because of their product knowledge. If you were a sales Rep calling on an infectious disease provider selling an AIDS drug, you had better know what you are talking about because your competition did. "Doc, would you use a little of my stuff" wasn't going to work in an infectious disease doctor's office selling an antiretroviral.

## Off to Denver, Colorado and the great Rocky Mountains...

I worked with some great people in St Louis, but when Hecker left to the retirement pastures, my position as District Mgr in St Louis was looking very bad with Hecker's replacement coming on. I knew Hecker's replacement when he was a Rep in Kansas City and knew back then what a bull shit artist the guy had become. If and when it was coming out of his mouth you couldn't trust it, and I had too many years left to put up with his bullshit brand of management.

It was with great fortune that a hospital mgr position was open in Denver so off I went leaving the new Regional Mgr (Hecker's replacement), Mr. Non Trusty, behind and forming a "bond" with a new mgr who worked for two hours in the morning and then immediately headed for the golf course. How could I respect that? He taught me nothing, but then I wasn't looking for anything from him either. The Denver Hospital District was man-for-man the best hospital district Burroughs Wellcome Co ever had at calling on attendings and residents in teaching hospitals. They turned sales meetings into journal clubs and there wasn't a competitive company or product they couldn't compete against. Three became District Mgrs and one, who I fought like hell to get into the home office, moved all the way to the position of VP Marketing, the top marketing job in Burroughs Wellcome, later Glaxo Wellcome and today Glaxo SmithKline. They liked each and helped each other. Everyone seemed to have a nickname, "Our Man In The Heartland, "In The Fold", "Carts" were a few of the nicknames.

# Chapter 24

*"We skipped the light fandango, turned cartwheels cross the floor"*
*— Procol Harem, "Lighter Shade Of Pale"*

### "The only car like it in Chicago"...

THE NEXT TIME our "First Call For The Burley Express" Boys (aka "The Braidwood Boys") got together was at the Lyons Township High School 35th reunion held in a hotel across the Chicago River from the Marina Towers on Wacker Drive. I always loved the names of Chicago streets, Halsted, Touhy, Wabash, Wells, Sheffield, Addison were a few of my favorites. The best was Wacker Drive. We played cards the first evening (Friday night) in a suite rented by BS who never saw a reasonably priced suite he didn't like. Saturday night saw us at a sit down dinner, followed by dancing, as I recall, and could easily be corrected on this, about 200-classmates attended. In high school, the women who made up the homecoming court and the popular cheerleaders and clique girls who never even looked or talked to us in high school, at the 35th were now not only sitting at our table and eating with us, but dancing with us too. Jay, of course, was cheek-to-cheek on the dance floor with Diane B. We were a long ways from LTHS. Who would have guessed it? But the Braidwood Boys, none a high school football hero, had grown to be as big and in much, much better shape than the high school football heroes who attended. I think the other thing was that several of the Braidwood Bunch guys had very successful jobs in corporate America. And, our graduating class women, most entering their 53rd year on God's Green Earth, wanted no part I was told supporting some over weight ex-high school football player. A lesson learned. You don't have to be a football hero to eventually have the best looking women in high school knocking on your door at age 35 to 50. At the 35th high school reunion, we thought, and justifiably so, that we were the Duke of Earl. The 35th reunion provided Jay with the best chance he ever had to corral Diane B. But, you can't pull up to the hotel on Wacker Drive in a car loaded with Daily Racing Forms and exit through the passenger side rear window to make an impression on any woman. Squatman spotted Jay's car pulling up as we were standing at the front of the hotel by the smoke coming out of the exhaust, the grime on the body yelled out that the car had never been washed, and Squatty said "the only car like it in Chicago". The car served him well in the ghetto for few people were going to spend the time trying to break in. But for Diane B, used to the upper middle class, and riding in The Lexus luxury automobiles her adult life, she as any woman would, had a hard time stepping down to Jay's car even though it was fully equipped. As long as the car ran is all Jay cared about and as long as it could get him to the Mudbug, or on occasion, Arlington Park, is all Jay really cared about. Jay was complex, but not when it came to his choice of automobiles.

Around midnight, the women we danced with wanted to go to Uno's for a pizza and we walked over to the pizza joint from the hotel. Diane told Jay on the way over that she would pay him to begin writing. That's right, she would pay for him to write. He was flattered immensely, but never did, instead wasting his time writing in the LTHS website his political views which were extremely foreign to 95^ of the classmates to say the least. It was a complete waste of his time, nobody after a short while read what he said anyway. The best opportunity he had later to write something that easily could have made a great story was his trip out to Vegas the annual Striptease Queen convention and interview with Tura Satana, the same Miss Japanese-American we saw stripping on South State Street in 1959. Jay interviewed Tura around 2007. He took great notes from his sit-down interview with Tura. Instead of writing about her times, he chose instead to go after his high school classmates for which he could run circles around, and look good, on foreign affairs. The Tura Satana book never got written.

The Diane runway for take-off was wide open that night for Jay as we returned back from Uno's pizzeria, and he should have driven home for the bunny, but once again dropped the ball. I guess it just wasn't meant to be. You will find that timing in this world is everything.

I was also amazed that evening at how the quality of their once proud pizza restaurant had faltered. While Jay never seemed to agree with my choice of the best pizza parlor, when in Chicago go to Pat's Pizza on Lincoln Ave if you like thin crust pizza. We never seemed to go in for that deep-dish pizza, but it sure was popular in The Big Onion of Chicago.

## "Ketchup maybe harmful to your taste buds"...

To digress just a moment to talk about Chicago food, you owe it to yourself to have a Chicago style Italian beef sandwich when you are in Chicago. Jay Leno, when visiting, always made it a point to have his limo driver drive him down to Mister Beef on Orleans in downtown Chicago for an Italian beef sandwich. Mister Beef is located at 666 N. Orleans to be exact and worth the trip. Our favorite Italian beef Chicago sandwich was Al's Italian beef that competed with Mister Beef. We always liked Al's broth better. We ordered the sandwich "dipped". Highly recommended. I've had 3-excellent steaks in my life---the Stockyards Inn in Chicago, a restaurant in downtown Kansas City that I can't remember the name of and Gibson's on the near north side of Chicago on Rush Street. Of the three, Gibson's was the best of the best. If you like a great steak Gibson's is the place. A close second would be Gene & Georgetti's restaurant on north Franklin in Chicago. They have been there since 1941. Frank Sinatra, when he was in town, would buy up the entire restaurant for the evening to entertain his friends over a steak,

Famous for it neighborhoods and family owned restaurants, if you liked Polish sausage you knew that the best was in the Polish neighborhood on Milwaukee Ave. If you liked Italian, there were hundreds of restaurants to eat in. If you liked German food, you headed to The Berghoff on West Adams, which first opened in 1898. Watch the parking meters when going, as parking on the street, thanks to Morgan Stanley runs $6.50 for 30-minutes. And, so it seemed, on every corner there was a neighborhood tavern where everyone knew your name, particularly lively during football season.

I can't leave the dining out in Chicago section of this book without paying tribute to the Chicago Vienna beef hotdog. They sell more hotdogs in Chicago than any other major city in the USA and one of the reasons is that the Vienna beef is extremely tasty and the condiments put on top---pickle, onion, mustard, tomato, peppers and relish---made it seem like you were eating a salad with your dog. In later years, Barry's place on North Clark became my favorite because they had char-dogs. It is definitely worth the trip to Barry's for a char-dog. But, if you live in Detroit, Michigan you will argue that Kowalski's hotdogs with natural casing were the best. Although hard to find outside of Michigan, Kowalski's are worth hunting up to buy. Whether it is a Vienna Beef or a Kowalski's hotdog, if you like to put chili sauce, mustard and onions on your dog, the chili sauce of choice, no competitor's come even close, belongs to world famous National Coney Island Chili. National's chili sauce can be ordered on line directly from National and makes the best chili sauce topping for a hotdog, but also can be enjoyed in a mouth-watering and savory bowl all by itself. A bowl of chili in the winter is heaven sent.

At the time of his death, Jay still had the sport coat he bought at Dad-And-Lad's men's clothing store on LaGrange Road he wore on his very first date with Diane after high school. She remained the love of his life throughout his entire life. He had his chances as they say at the racetrack. "Missed it" as the old man at the Mudbug said talking about a long shot that won and Jay didn't have it because Jay overlooked the fact the horse was wearing blinkers for the first time. Once in a while he missed blinkers or a past work, but not very often. Win or lose, he always went back and dissected the race. Sometimes there was just no reason for a particular horse to win or lose and I think this was the case with Jay and Diane.

The Braidwood Bunch, before leaving the 35th, vowed to meet the following October in Las Vegas, and hold the meeting the weekend of The Breeders Cup horse races. The Breeder's Cup is a two day affair with the best horses in the world running at different distances. And, we did. Three reunions in Vegas quickly went by, and three years later in Vegas, Shorty aka Diego Jim, who we hadn't seen since graduating in 1960, graced our presence. It was a good time... lot of stories, but the favorite was the reminiscing about the trip down US 66 to Braidwood that overcast, dark night in March 1961. A couple of years later they moved the Braidwood Boys reunion to Palm Springs and Diane B herself showed. I wasn't able to attend and neither was Jay, but the boys said they spent a lot of time cheering Diane up.

In July of 1995, Glaxo, a little dermatology company in Ft Lauderdale, who rode the coattails of the terrific sales of one drug they purchased, seized Burroughs Wellcome Co for $15-billion in a hostile takeover. I had two choices...stay and work for Glaxo, who knew nothing about a medical science liaison division, or take the retirement package they offered. I took the retirement package. I had no respect for Glaxo. As a matter of fact, Glaxo had recently hired a Rep that I had recently fired for not working. That said volumes about what Glaxo had going for themselves.

# Chapter 25

*"The lion and the calf will lie down together, but the calf won't get much sleep"*
*— Woody Allen*

## They'll be no cheering from the crowd...

ONCE AGAIN, WITH no cheering from the crowd, I walked out of Burroughs Wellcome Co's main office in Research Triangle Park, retirement check in hand, for the last time on July 1, 1995. It was 6-months after moving to Research Triangle Park to accept the job as Head, Med Science Liaison Division. It was like the guy in Ocean's 11 who, driving out of Vegas with a big score and a large sum of money, had a heart attack and uttered "never the luck". Finally got to level and a job that would be challenging in the medical department working with Ed and some very good people, and out of the blue Burroughs Wellcome Co was bought out by Glaxo. The same Glaxo pharmaceutical company who had a bunch of used car salesmen masquerading as Sales Reps. "Doc, would you use a little of my stuff" was their sales pitch. They didn't know if they were selling technical pharmaceutical drugs or used cars, and from what I could tell bumping into their Rep staff on the road in different doctor's office buildings, it didn't bother them. Glaxo disbanded the Medical Science Liaison Division we put together immediately after I left Burroughs Wellcome Co pharmaceuticals in July 1995 I knew they would. Money doesn't mean you are smart and most of Glaxo was made up of reps calling on community-based doctors who never set foot in a major teaching hospital like the University of Missouri in Columbia,

MO or Barnes Hospital (Washington University School of Medicine in St Louis, MO). In other words, how would these guys know what to do with a Medical Science Liaison Division?

About 1-year later I received a telephone call from one of the VP's at Glaxo asking me to come into Research Triangle Park, NC to discuss with them how to set up a Medical Science Liaison Division consisting of Pharm D's, PhD's and an occasional MD who would be calling on physician thought leaders in different specialties. I decided to go. Upon arrival, and walking down a hall to the meeting room, I passed the Sales Department. The Director of Sales, a young guy who attended the meeting, had a sign prominently posted above his door for all to see that said, "What Have You Done For The Rep In The Field Today". After the meeting, and listening to him talk about establishing a new Medical Science Liaison Div, I came to a quick conclusion that he wasn't doing anything today or the next day to help the Rep in the field.

Hearing from former pharmaceutical representatives that more and more doctor are closing their offices to representatives prompted me to ask my own internist one day in his office if he saw pharmaceutical sales representatives. He said, "I used to, but stopped doing so". Why I asked? He went on to say that even the reps from the big companies (Pfizer, Merck, Glaxo SmithKline, Allergan, Roche) did little but press him with questions on what drug he was using for, say a urinary tract infection for example, and why he was using the competitor's drug and not the drug they made. Pressure-question-pressure. The reps offered him little information he could use to select one product over another. He stopped seeing reps all together. This information then prompted me to call my old friend Paul Snyder. Paul and I started out as Reps together in the St Louis District beginning back in 1970. We decided to write a book on how to sell pharmaceuticals based on our experience in calling on over 80,000 doctors as reps, teaching hospital reps and District Sales Mgrs. The book will be called "The Dynamic Big Book Of How To Sell Pharmaceutical Products" and anyone who reads and re-reads and studies the knowledge and wisdom that is written will learn how to sell presenting specific patient types to the provider where your drug has an advantage over the drug the provider is presently using. It is the section of the book discussing how doctors are trained to think and make drug selection decisions that is worth its weight in gold. For if a rep truly understands how a physician he calls on thinks and makes decision, he or she is in the best position to present their drug in a manner the physician will relate to and understand. To get a doctor to use a drug product for the first time is the most difficult thing to do in all of sales. This book teaches the reader how. And…it teaches the reader how to understand, analyze and interpret the medical literature by starting with the Material & Method Section of a study and breaking the article down from there. Even if the rep today can't use a journal article in a selling situation, the knowledge gained from knowing how to interpret and analyze the study is invaluable. Paul and I have 80-years combined experience in writing this book and it teaches so much. We have been to hundreds and 100's of Journal Club meetings, M&M conferences, grand rounds conference and specialty meetings and what we learned by listening to cases presented, and how they were presented and discussed, is this book. If you are reading this book and are a frustrated pharma reps or a frustrated pharma District Manager, look for this book on Amazon e-books.

What I learned in corporate America is to advance you need to get on someone's coattails and rise up. Be enthusiastic and positive at ALL times, and above all keep your mouth shut about your opinions. Upper management doesn't want to hear negatives nor do they want to really hear your opinion even if you are asked. I watched some of the best in the business at selling up and they always, and I mean always, talked to upper management guys at every meeting. Outspoken guys go out with the dirty laundry. Unlike Lee Iacocca at Chrysler in the 1970's, who wanted a management team with guys who would disagree with him, 99% of the time in corporate America, upper management always thinks they are right. My Father spent 40-years at General Electric. He closely watched Jack Welch move to the top of GE by being what my Dad described as a "stem-winder". A stem-winder is French for a guy who sold himself and was enthusiastic when he did it. A bull shit artist if you would, with an outgoing personality…"hey gang, how are we doing" type of guy. The ability of most upper manager's, the guys who decide who is getting the promotion, to recognize ability is sorely lacking. Just look at Welch's selection of Jeff Immelt to replace him. For 15-years Immelt has done little. But he looked good in meetings, and that is what Jack Welch was looking at. Books have been written on the subject of advancing in corporate America, and while I've never read one, from personal experience, look good in meetings, talk to upper managers (don't lay back) and keep your mouth shut. Lastly, it is dog eat dog so don't confide your deep thoughts with any co-workers. Your "friends" can turn on a dime. Upper management wants to hear positives so feed them with how well things are going in the field or in your section, how you are enjoying the job and look forward to the challenges ahead. That's all you have to say. You might have to fight your way through the ass kissers to get to talk to an upper manager but stay the course. And start with "just wanted to say hello and let you know how well things are going in _____department and I'm really learning a lot working with _____. Keep it brief and positive and say "pleasure talking to you". You are on your way, and when your name pops up for a promotion or they are looking for someone to start a new division, upper managers know your name. This advice will save you from reading all those books on advancing in corporate America. Of Byron Wein's "Life Lessons", which I read in Barron's weekly magazine, the one that jumped out to me is his lesson on not trying to be better than your competition, but try instead to be more imaginative. The same thing Joe Hecker stressed to me years ago. Bring new, fresh ideas on how to do your job more effectively. Too many guys try to compete and that leads to back stabbing and lies. Stay away from negative comments about you and the negative comments about the Company you work for. As Charlie Watts told me in the back of the US Post Office parcel post truck, "nobody wants to hear them anyway"

# Chapter 26

*"On the strength"*
— *a saying in the Chicago ghetto*

"The Pelican Principles"...

IN AND AROUND 2001 we decided to buy a small investment condo in Ft Myers in a newly built condo and subdivision called Pelican Something. At the time I was working for Virco selling HIV drug resistance tests---genotype and phenotype---and covered the Southeast USA and the Caribbean working out of my house. The condo was painted Florida off-white on the inside, with a sand colored tile floor throughout. I spent a little money on furniture in several different local furniture stores. I hate looking around furniture stores, but the Tommy Bahama look was in and that made shopping a lot easier. And the Naples-Ft Myers Robb and Stuckey's (dubbed Rob & Stick You by me) had a large selection of Bahama. You could relate Ralph Lauren to Tommy of the Bahama or Tommie of The Anaegada for that matter. The place looked great with white furniture, some color and a lot of style. Jay came calling about 3-months after the "Pelican Place" was completed. The Pelican Principles took life with Jay using too much toilet paper after taking a huge dump. Trying to flush with too much toilet paper cause the toilet to run over and 2-3" of overflowed water and shit was now all over the bathroom door. You can appreciate shit all over the new light sandy colored bathroom tile with light tan grout. Good friend Jay passed on the bathroom clean up leaving his shit up to me to clean up and process. By the third day, he had spread his horse track papers over every table he could find. One the 5<sup>th</sup> day, about 4:00pm, in the afternoon waiting for us to go out to dinner, dressed in a 3-piece brown suit (vested and all) he decided that it would be a good time to smoke his pipe. To do so, he walked outside under the carports 50-feet from my front door. This smoking location put him in plain view of all the residents in the 24-condos within my 3-story building unit. He always thought that no one would know what he was doing but he was absolutely clueless. By the 7<sup>th</sup> day, he didn't want to hear any comments from me about tidiness, got pissed off, and decided to leave the Pelican really to my surprise. Because the weekend was coming up and I would have more time to spend with him. I repeatedly asked him not to go, but Jay was always a headstrong guy and after years of being bossed by his Mother, Mama Crow, just didn't want to be told what he could and could not do. After returning to Chicago, Jay wrote the "Pelican Principles" for all of our friends to chuckle over. I would like to remind the reader that this was the same guy who was called "the house guest from hell" by Buck's wife. He was never taught manners growing up and he had no dinner table manners the rest of his life. He threw his food down and talked with his mouth full of food throughout every meal. And Gentlemen's Quarterly was never going to call him for tips on what looked good in men's clothing. If you could have seen that 3-piece brown suit you would know what I'm talking about. It dated around 1940. That is a little background for the reader before the start of Jay's "The Pelican Principles".

## "The Pelican Principles"

1. Dress Sharp. No brown suits. The neighbors will notice.
2. Stay out of sight, No neighborhood strolls, Community vigilance is constant...be it for deadly dogshit or other foreign substances
3. No slobbering in sleep to screw up very expensive bedspread. If you MUST use the bed, make t promptly upon arising. Just because, okay?
4. No bulk deposits in the guest toilet. Medium Dump+Expensive sheets (translated toilet paper)=Apocalypse. Consider leaves in the woods but remember to stay out of sight.
5. No splashing in the bathroom sink. Floor gets wet.

6. No reclining on the furniture. Coaches not for snoozing, except by host. Best to stay clear of the furniture altogether.

6. Smoking permitted on the porch but remove all cigar wrappers immediately, Fire hazard.

7. Keep you feet off the rugs---not for wiping.

8. Don't go near the golf course unless you shirt has a collar.

9. No loitering on premises, Plans of host do not revolve around guests. And, stand up when a lady enters the room (Betty's Rules)

## Virco Lab & HIV drug resistance testing...

I received a call from a guy who I worked with in the St Louis District (#59) of Burroughs Wellcome Co pharmaceuticals back in 1970, who had been contacted by Virco, a European Lab company headquartered in Mechelen, Belgium to hire 4-guys to promote their HIV drug resistance tests and get them officially Medicaid approved and coded in each State in the USA. In other words, getting State Medicaid to pay for the resistance test called a virtual phenotype. We had one competitor who only had a phenotype that was much more expensive than Virco's virtual phenotype. So everywhere the competition went they tried to make sure that the Medicaid bigwigs did not approve the virtual phenotype test. And they told some wild stories to prevent the virtual phenotype test from getting approved. This was for me the first time I had sold laboratory tests. As a pharmaceutical rep, I had little to no respect for lab reps because I thought that they were mainly order takers much on the order of a drug wholesaler rep. Our job was to visit Medicaid departments to convince them what these tests, even though they cost $500 to $1,500, would do as far as saving money in the long run. When a patient began failing one of the 23-AIDS drugs on the market at the time, the provider would order a genotype; a virtual phenotype or phenotype test on the patient to determine which of the 23-drug choices would work best. A virtual phenotype provided the results of a phenotype with the cost of a much less expensive genotype. My area of responsibility, because there were only 4-of us, was the Southeast USA and the Caribbean. The job took me to Birmingham, AL, Jackson, MS, Atlanta, GA, Tallahassee, FL, San Juan,

PR, Raleigh, NC, Little Rock, AR, Nashville, TN, Columbia, SC, Austin, TX and New Orleans and Baton Rouge, Louisiana. Growing up in Chicago, we didn't see or even know what grits were, but the local café's in the South had them featured on every breakfast menu. Calling on the Medicaid Directors and the Medical Directors of Medicaid to get them to approve resistance testing and assign a price and code for phenotype, genotype and virtual phenotype. A typical sales call saw me reviewing slides outlining the benefits of the virtual phenotype HIV drug resistance test in front of 5 to 25 from the Medicaid department personnel. Louisiana was the first State in the South in my territory to actually approve resistance testing and they approved all 3-tests thanks to my insistence that they do so. They liked my presentation so much that they were going to code the test "RS" in my memory. They were quick to realize that these HIV drug resistance tests (like virtual phenotype) could save a lot of money on AIDS drugs which were very expensive and getting more expensive with each approved drug. Texas, which was no surprise to me, was the last State to approve testing. Finally, with help from a special woman within the Medicaid office, we had a chance to present the advantages of resistance testing to the top Medicaid officials and the Medicaid Medical Director and his Staff in Austin, TX. Of all the presentations I made over all the years and miles, the presentation I made that afternoon in Austin, TX to the top brass was, without a doubt, the best ever. I had no idea whether or not they would approve when I departed the meeting, but one thing I did know, "I felt a groove coming on". Texas approved. So did Florida, which was another long, long epic struggle. At the meeting when they announced approval, two guys came up and hugged me for the work I had done to gain approval. Once they saw how these tests would save money, the light bulb came on and so did the approval. For me, this job made me realize how much I missed selling. It had been 20-years since I was a rep. and I enjoyed every minute of making the sale. However, in 2001, Virco decided to hang up their shingle and the company put on the market. Hanging it up, just after I got Texas, Louisiana, Florida, No Carolina/South Carolina to approve testing by Medicaid. Once the State paid for testing, providers could order it for patients in the Medicaid system. The 4-reps who started were all let go. One of the four, Gary (G-dot I called him), had just left a well-paying job at Bristol

Meyers Squibb and said going with Virco cost him $500,000. It mattered little to Virco and the pompous Belgians. It was amazing how little respect I had for the Johnson & Johnson the management people working in Belgium. They couldn't make a decision without having 10-conference calls. After 10-conference calls they still did not know what to do. They thought they knew it all and knew nothing about selling lab tests in the USA. Selling in the USA pharmaceutical market, and the laboratory market, was totally different than selling in Europe. But they weren't into listening to the guys who were selling the product in the USA…let's have another conference call. They thought they knew everything.

In 2003, mighty Johnson & Johnson, realizing they were going to be purchasing a couple of AIDS drugs, decided to buy Virco Lab. They also decided to hire some sales reps, and get back to selling virtual phenotype an HIV drug resistance test. We stopped selling virtual phenotype in 2001. They also decided to hire me. With some reservation, I accepted. Their McNeil Reps (part of J&J), who I competed against in the 1970's, were used car salesmen. Their hospital rep in 1978 got the medicine department at John Cochran VA hospital on North Grand Ave (just down the street from the old Sportsmen's Park where the St Louis Browns played baseball) closed to drug reps for plastering McNeil literature on walls where it should not have been plastered. My reservations were well grounded…not only did they make the mistake of hiring two J&J pharma reps, with no knowledge in HIV/AIDS and who ended up selling nothing, but the first manager we reported to had the biggest inflated ego of any manager I'd ever worked with. In a matter of 6-months as our Manager, ego boy couldn't stand it, and retreated back to what he had been doing. VP Manager # 2, my new manager, who had no experience managing people was promoted by J&J to manage the 4-Sales Reps. Unfortunately, he was influenced by co-workers who he thought looked out for his best interests, but he should have done a better job questioning some of which was told to him. It seemed like everything became a control issue. The good part of the job is that I called on some of the top physician thought leaders in infectious diseases and HIV. Joe Eron at the Univ of North Carolina, Dan Kuritzkes at Harvard, Corky Steinhart in Miami, Molly Eaton at Emory, Jeff Nadler and Don Kutyka at the Univ of So Florida in Tampa, Dr Jay,

Rafael Campo, Gordon Dickinson at the University of Miami, Julio Mendez at Shands Univ of Florida in Jacksonville, Harold Kessler at Rush in Chicago, IL, Ana Puga and Joey Wynn in Ft Lauderdale, Bob Catalla in Jacksonville, Edwin DeJesus in Orlando, Jorge Santana in San Juan were all top notch people and a real pleasure to call on. I would be amiss not to give a "shout out" to all of the hard-working AIDS treaters in Bayamon, San Juan and Ponce, Puerto Rico who treated me so graciously every time I visited the island. They brought back memories of how this job was when I started in 1970.

"But February made me shiver, with every paper I'd deliver, Bad news on the door step, I couldn't take one more step"
— Bill McLean, "American Pie"

## From selling HIV drug resistance tests to selling a HIV medical record system...

By 2010, I was closing in on calling on 60,000 doctors in my career, which began in St. Louis, Missouri in 1970. Johnson & Johnson decided in that year (2010) to stop selling virtual phenotype because they were getting beat and to begin selling a HIV Medical Records System they bought from LabTracker, a medical records systems designed for AIDS treaters. Shortly after making the bad decision of purchasing and over paying for LabTracker, they changed the name of the electronic medical records system to AVIGA.

I don't know the first thing about computers or electronic medical record systems and now I had to begin selling a system that would be ready in 6-months, and to continue to sell virtual phenotype 20% of the time (which turned out not to be true). The reason it would be finished in 6-mos was because LabTracker was not complete and features needed to be added to get the system up-to-speed to compete better in the marketplace. To this day, I'm not sure why they decided to buy Lab Tracker and begin selling it when the system was not finished. It did come as no surprise that they did not ask for my opinion in making the decision to buy Lab Tracker in the first place. A few hospitals in the Southeast USA were using Lab Tracker, but it needed serious updating and the home office computer geeks in Belgium with J&J were going to enhance the features. As our manager said, "once updated, LabTracker would sell". The only problem was that the manager who made this forecast had no clue of what the competition looked like. And based on working with them, we knew that J&J Belgium rarely got anything accomplished on time. The story we had to tell was that we, as a company, knew HIV and what should be in a medical records system. As I had been calling on infectious disease physicians for a long, long time. I knew the key infectious disease physicians and had developed a strong rapport with almost all of them. The hard part for me, with very elementary skills in using the computer, was being able to explain the "ins and outs" of this electronic system that had screen after screen for the provider to store data on a patient that Belgium kept updating on the fly.

Guess who sold the most AVIGA systems? That's right...Yours Truly. A provider in Ponce, Puerto Rico, who I called on for a long time, liked what I presented and bought the system. A small HIV clinic in the Caribbean bought AVIGA from me. And a small rural HIV clinic just north of Atlanta, after overcoming a number of their objections at the start, also bought the AVIGA System from me. As I was retiring from J&J the other 3-Aviga Sales Reps calling on providers, clinics and hospitals had not sold one system anywhere in the country.

# Chapter 27

*"Be fearful when everyone is greedy, be greedy when everyone is fearful"*
— *Warren Buffett*

I RETIRED FROM J&J in 2011 after 8 ½-years of working for them covering a sales territory from Raleigh to Galveston, San Juan to Little Rock. On my last day of employment, I remembered all of the places I had been and the great people I had been able to work with over 41-years. And, I remembered what Charlie Watts said to me in the back of that US Post Office truck in LaGrange, IL while we had lunch together back many, many years ago. Why did you quit corporate America, to drive a post office truck Charlie?" I asked. "One day you will know", Charlie said. On June 1, 2011 I knew.

He came to play…

Back to the Boys In The Band, aka The Braidwood Bunch. For the last 10-years of reunions in Las Vegas we met at a hotel on the Strip or a hotel out in the Summerlin area. In later years, Summerlin had fewer crazies and we usually ended up at the JW Marriott or the Sun Coast. Some of the strip hotels, like New York New York for example, in our opinion, were really going down hill to the "dump" category. We always met during Breeder's Cup so those who wanted to play the horses had the super bowl weekend (Friday/Saturday) of horse racing. By the millennium, Jay stopped using a green garbage bag to carry his clothes and had moved up to a dark blue, cloth weave Yves St Laurent bag with a handle that he proudly displayed to all who were interested in seeing it. BS was in his element in Vegas and, after retirement, worked at Home Depot in Hawaii to make enough money to play Blackjack and the slots 3-4 times per year. He was "comp'd" at the 3$^{rd}$ tier hotels on the strip and downtown Vegas. Hotels like the Aladdin were BS' style. We would all meet for breakfast each morning before the golfers went golfing, the slot players went gambling and the guys playing the horses went to the Sports Book. John BS or "Maximum Leader" as Buck called him moved to the slots and Blackjack without wasting a minute of time. Blackjack... interesting name for a card game I always thought. BS loved his slots that we always thought were the worst bet in Vegas, but it made no difference to BS. It was the action he liked. I don't ever recall seeing him win any real money, but he said he did. Go to Vegas and lose your money. Go back home to Maui and work at Home Depot to make money to go back to Vegas. Seems simple enough. I often heard Jay call BS "The Great One" because of his relentless resilience. In the words of the late Cub manager Leo "The Lip" Durocher, BS is a "gamer", because he comes to play. Jay said he would follow BS straight to hell when the time comes. As Jay put it way back in 2011 when speaking of BS, "until then, Hail To The Chief, after him there can be no other".

"I have always believed in the therapeutic value of understanding horse races. It fills the lungs and empties the mind"
— A.J. Liebling

For Jay, the Sport Book was his office. He loved to handicap horse races and after 50-years of doing so got to be an outstanding handicapper. We often thought the handicapping was much more important to him then winning money. He was raised by Fred & Mama Crow to save every penny and instead of betting $25 on a horse to win, he would bet $5. Had he put place money on every horse he bet to win, he would have made a fortune at the track. Instead of place bets he loved to play the exotics as they were called. He spent his money playing exactas (the top two horses) and trifectas (top three finishing horses) and superfectas (top four finishing horses). Because any horse in the race could finish 3$^{rd}$ or 4$^{th}$, and because Jay didn't want to spend money on throwing a number of horses in the race to finish 3<sup>rd</sup> or 4<sup>th</sup>, he often lost because he didn't spend the money,

A perfect example of this, that still makes me mad, was a $6-million dollar Pick Six at Santa Anita following the Breeder's cup weekend at Santa Anita in 2015 that we decided to play. We had 5/6 horses, but Jay didn't want to spend an extra $128 dollars throwing in more horses in the 5<sup>th</sup> race. We looked at the horse that won the 5<sup>th</sup> race, he was on our radar, but decided not to spend the money. Instead of $6-mil we won $1,500. Another time, at a northern California summer Fair race at the Fresno Race track we lost $190,000 on a superfecta simply because we didn't want to throw two more horses in to the bet. It would have cost $76 to throw the 2-horses into the bet.

By 2010, Jay spent most of his time at the Chicago off track parlor called The Mudbug, located just south of North and Sheffield, betting the day away and exchanging comments with two guys who also loved their racing, Barry and Freddie. If you wanted to meet two Chicago guys, Barry and Freddie were your guys. They spoke Chicagoese and brought that Chicago air with them wherever they went. Like Chicago itself, they were no bullshit guys. The Mudbug, in 2012 or thereabouts decided to move across the street to new digs and was never the same again for Jay. Freddie, a charismatic degenerate gambler friend of Jay's, moved from the old "Bug" to the new "Bug" and set up shop once again to unofficially administer his new table and the room. Freddie was another character in a city full of characters. In an article he wrote for a small Chicago newspaper "The Heartland Journal", Jay described Freddie as a "gambler in the Groucho Marx tradition heading a clique that habitually bets several different tracks at once. In the summer of 2004, Jay wrote an article in this same newspaper, describing in full detail how he left off a horse in a trifecta bet to save $10. Jay hated NASCAR and auto racing of any kind and noted in his article that the "demented American public preferred racing by autos rather than horses". He told me that he jumped for joy when the Chicago Bidwell family tried to convert Sportsmen's Park (one time home to Al Capone) to a car racetrack only to go belly up and lose all of their money. Al Capone would have rolled over in his grave had Sportmen's been turned into a NASCAR track. Jay talked about Tommy a lot in his Heartland Journal article about the racetrack and how much he valued his opinion on horses, odds, track conditions etc. Tommy was one of Jay's best friends and they spent a lot of time at the track and on the phone discussing big races. Like Jay, Tommy always thought that the big win was right around the corner and every year was going to be his year.

## "Let's see if we can beat the favorite"...

If you were a pupil wanting to learn how to handicap a horse race, and Jay was the teacher, he would first talk about "race shape". The pace of the race, what horse would take the lead, could the speed horse hold the lead, how many speed horses were in the race vs. the number of horses called "closers" (won a race by coming from behind) is what he looked at first and foremost. He used BRIS (Bloodstock Research) for his pace numbers and final numbers. He couldn't afford The Sheets, as they are called, which provide you with a final number for every race a horse has run...the lower the number, the better. But, he loved the Ultimate Past Performer on BRIS, especially the pace numbers. When he first started handicapping races there were no pace numbers available and one had to look at times and a horse's running style. One of the big questions for Jay was who was going to take the lead. Jay never thought the jockey to be that important, but he thought the trainer was very important to look at. There are good trainers and bad and they can make all the difference. Jay's betting style, in addition to playing the exotics, consisted of always trying to beat the favorite and he scoured each race to look for a horse with a price (translated means finding a horse who could beat the favorite with odds of 4/1 or greater). "Let's see if we can beat the favorite," he would always say. In addition to trainer stats, Jay looked at who rode the horse last time, were they switching from a bad jock to a good jockey? Was the horse wearing blinkers for the first time? What was the horses record at the distance? Was the horse dropping in class from say a $12,500 claimer to a $4,000 claimer, a big drop and it meant the horse would now be running with slower horses. How had the horses' workouts been? What was the trainers record on drops? Jay put a lot of weight on the horses' trainer. The trainers' record at different distances and on dirt and grass was important. On and on he went by the hour looking at the stats for each horse in a field of 8-12 horses in the average race. But he was a genius at remembering a horse, and if the horse lost, did it get a bad trip the last time out? He kept mounds and mounds of records for every race every day. He liked to play Gulfstream in Hallendale, FL (between Fort Lauderdale and Miami) and Churchill in Louisville, KY. "Churchy" as he called it. He hated the nags at Golden Gate and Bay Meadows (which has been closed) but knew who the good trainers were and the good trainers with the good jockeys. My guess is he spent $40-50,000 per year at the track. I don't think he lost that much but he lost plenty over the years. Without something like the track and betting pro football, where he could keep statistics to his heart's desire, I think he would have gone nuts. BS declared around 2005 that "he (Jay) has a problem" meaning he was spending every day gambling at the racetrack. That was like the kettle calling the pot black. Jay was betting the horses till the day he died. To listen to him break down a race by looking at all of the information in front of him should be made a board game or a game for corporate America to play to see how potential manager candidates could analyze data and make a decision. Sort of like case studies. Set the game up with 5-horses and put down each horses' workout times, records at the distance, was the horse wearing blinkers, was the horse dropping in class and different parameters like that. Then set up the race as to distance, run on dirt or grass and have the potential manager decide which horse was going to win the race.

## I didn't want to forget this...

How does corporate America determine who is getting promoted and who isn't? After watching for 45-years, the answer is simple...it is who they like and feel most comfortable working with. The promoted manager could lack imagination, could have trouble putting two sentences together in a memo, could lack the potential to teach, could be a 9-5 guy and not lead by example, could be a cold fish and not show empathy or look for what his people were doing right. But if they liked you, you were in. If you are ever called to provide reasons why you should get promoted over other guys, make absolutely sure that some where in your list of reasons why they should promote you (or in a job interview, hire you), you have the ability to work with all kinds of different personalities, communicate with them and motivate them. Cheer them on and provide advice when asked. TEAM and a positive attitude is your DNA.

## The 50<sup>th</sup> Annual high school reunion...nametags required

Approximately 350-classmates and their spouses attended the 50<sup>th</sup> high school reunion. I had to spend hours convincing Jay to go. It was only after I paid his way for the weekend festivities did he agree. Once again the Braidwood Boys were followed to their dinner table and joined for dinner by the best looking girls in the class. The worm had turned. We became the football heroes and looking down at some of the old players who attended, all dining together, I could easily see why. Ed Bear who played football for 4-years was always taller and bigger than I was in high school, not so 50-years later. I was at least 4" taller than the Bear who just couldn't get over it. The Bear hadn't changed much, and that was to his credit, because most of our classmates were difficult to recognize. As Walt Whitman said, "the years teach much which the days never know". 50-years is over 18,000 days so we all knew more, but we didn't look the same. Ricky Nelson's song "Garden Party" rang in my head a couple of times the night of the 50<sup>th</sup>. The Braidwood Boys looked good, and, all except Baldy made it. Dutchy Van and Willie The Wop both looked the same and both had aged well. They would have preferred being on the golf course rather than making small talk with a lot of people they just didn't remember and said the hell to catching up with. Lennie B of cross-country days walked by and I didn't even recognize him. John Poly, who was the ringleader and event planner for every reunion, asked everyone to stand, say their name and where they live. This took a lot of time. When it was time to roll back the carpet and start dancing to the likes of the Platters, the Drifters, Lloyd Price, The Crests and many, many more, the No-Tell Hotel, where we held all the reunions at except one, rolled up the carpet at 11:00 pm and began tearing down the existing tables to get ready for a planned event on Sunday. No dancing at the 50<sup>th</sup>. Poly had an early morning root canal to take care of. But, it was hard to get too mad at Poly; he kept the entire Class of 1960 together. Jay headed home Sunday morning after breakfast instead of going with Squatman and me to McClure Jr High School where Squat had arranged a McClure reunion and tour of the school. I went so I could see the gym one last time in which we played many a heated game in the Western Springs League in 1958-1959. Bert Kraus of Lyons Township High School Corral burger fame was the ref. Bert let the players play. You would have to have a broken leg before Bert would call a foul. He had things to do at home.

When I called Jay from McClure Jr to tell him that SB was attending the junior high reunion Squat had set up, he was already at home smoking his pipe. As soon as I told him SB was taking Squatty's McClure tour, he practically went nuts because next to Diane, SB was like Elizabeth Taylor to Jay. "Missed it" is what he said later. In an effort to see SB, he wrote her a letter entitled "The Wind In The B Tree" and sent it to her. She was so touched by the letter that she called him and invited him to a Univ of Illinois basketball game. As Bill Murray said in Caddy Shack, "at least I've got that going for me". He bought some new duds and rented a car just for the trip to Champaign and meeting with SB. And that is as far as it went. SB was too busy for a follow up date, and even an invite to attend the Univ of Illinois versus Northwestern game in Wrigley Field did not bring her out. One and done.

# Chapter 28

*"A billion here and a billion there, and pretty soon you are talking
money"*
*— Senator Everett Dirksen, Republican/Illinois*
*Where is Everett Dirksen when we really need him?*

The train pulls out of Union Station in Chicago...

IN 2014, JAY and I decided to take the Amtrak from Chicago to Austin, Texas,
There is something hard to explain about getting on a train leaving Chicago's
Union Station. We were going to meet Buck and drive from Austin to San
Antonio, TX to watch the NCAA men's national basketball championship. We
had tickets for the round of 16-teams remaining in the tournament. Before we
left, with Squatman pointing the way, we drove out to the Sky Box on the south
side to watch the stripper action. Because it was there and because we had some
of our best conversations in peeler bars it was an easy decision to make. In
between games in San Antonio, they played on Friday and again on Sunday, Jay
went to visit this peeler bar in Austin with a little more action and immediately
fell in love with this stripper who played him like a fiddle. Jay thought she had
fallen in love with him, and as soon as he left the establishment, it was like he
just had to get back to see her. Jay also told us that he had fallen in love with her.
I don't remember the timing of the return to the peeler bar, but this time I went
and it was clear to me, in watching the new "love of his life" flirt with other patrons, that she wasn't in it for love. On his return, Jay spent $150 for a lap dance,

but when it came time for "more", she brought out a chubby little thing to pinch hit for her in doing the deed. Jay passed. Out $150. By then he was, in his words, "blowing his nose on twenty dollar bills". "We learn by doing" is what Jay said to summarize the event.

I usually talked to Jay every other day on the cell phone…. he was up or he was down. Down when he had a knock down drag out with Rodriguez who he really liked. She was a very attractive Puerto Rican who worked in the Department of Children and Family Services in a different division from Jay. On many, many occasions he tried to get something permanent going with her, but she always seemed to find some "stem" to go out with instead of Jay. By early 2015, they had some very rocky calls and one morning announced to me that he would never be talking to her again. I didn't at the time think it was true, but it ended up being so. Too bad. When they got along together they really enjoyed each other's company, but underneath it all, Jay felt like she was taking advantage of him and just throwing him little bones from time to time.

When he didn't answer his phoney for hours I knew he was on the phone with a woman he called "Phony Sex" who loved to hear sexual explicit stuff said to her on the telephone. The dirtier the thoughts were, the better for Phony. I think it got old Jay worked up talking to her as well. But she ran extremely hot and extremely cold, e.g., when she was "on" she could go all morning. Jay kept thinking that she could be the woman he had been looking for, he liked sluts, but it never panned out". Toward the end of the "relationship" she got more and more guarded and less mysterious. But while it lasted he said the talk was as good as it gets. Phony Sex didn't attend the funeral I don't think.

"Knishes make the able more able"
— on a sign next to the knishes in a Jewish deli on Olive Street Road
in Creve Coeur, Missouri, circa 1975

The 55th High School Reunion…bring your reading glasses to read the name tags

At the last minute Jay and I decided to go to the 55th high school reunion. Neither of us knew at the time it would be the last for Jay. While taking a lot of heart meds, and told he had a small hole in his heart, he was in good spirits and had loss some weight. His sleep apnea condition had seemed to worsen and he promised to go in for testing. "When" was going to be the big question. One day before he died, Jay went into the hospital for sleep apnea testing. Mahoney picked him up at the hospital after the tests were run, dropped him off to his apartment on Irving Park Blvd. Mahoney was the last guy to see him alive.

There weren't any women attending the 55th that Jay was interested in, but knowing he liked to tell stories of the past, he attended. About half who attended the 50th attended the 55th, which was held on 55th Street at LaGrange Road in the Poly Palace Hotel aka The William Tell Best Western. We sat together and had a good chance to recall old tackle football in the snow at South Campus days with good friend Bob Ferguson. Bob could run in 1958 and it looked like he was just about as fast at the 55th as he was then. Jack, who beat Jay up n 3rd grade, attended and didn't say anything to Jay. Jay hadn't talked to him since 3rd grade. A good stamp collector, Jay remembered many things about people who snubbed him in high school, didn't pay off their poker bets or played dirty on the basketball court or football field. At the 55th, we talked about driving from Chicago to Bloomington on as much of US 66 that we could, have breakfast and Brandtville Restaurant where US 66 met Illinois 150 and then drive east on Hwy 150 to Champaign, IL before heading north on US 45, stopping in Kankakee to see old friend from Normal days The Duke of Kankakee, before continuing the journey north to The Big Onion. Jay even mentioned the name of the hamburger stand he liked and stopped at in Leroy, IL about 20-minutes from Bloomington. If time permitted while in Bloomington, IL, a trip out to Lake Bloomington was justified to see just how stupid we really were 50-years ago in swimming across that Lake.

It was a good night at the 55th reunion. Barb V, hands down the best looking woman there, sat with us for dinner. She had opened a very successful business at the Merchandise Mart in downtown Chicago. Squatman, attended, danced several times with Barbie V, and was still muttering 2-days later how she got away in our high school days. Nobody lived back in the high school days like the Squatman and couldn't talk enough about people and events. Easy I thought. Old friend Marshmellow, who was class President, attended and it was good to catch up with him after many years. All of the trying to impress one another was gone as were several classmates. My close Forest Road grade school buddy Carl Rydin died. My grade school friend and neighbor Bob "Repel" Brockob of "private party on the northside" never showed. He was allegedly looking for a bigger meaning to life. It was the last reunion for Jay also. Some classmate by the name of Paul wrote in the high school website when the news of Jay's death first was known, that he was glad to see Jay go because of all the stuff he wrote on the high school website belittling everyone, or so he thought, The women in our class, who frequented the high school website, quickly told him not to speak badly of the dead. I agree...never speak badly of the dead.

## The Braidwood Boys reunion in Vegas...

The 2014 Braidwood Boys annual reunion in Las Vegas on Breeder's Cup weekend was one of the most anticipated reunions of the past 20-years. The thought that these same guys who knew each other from High School beginning in 1956 absolutely amazed our high school classmates and people we knew and didn't know. To this day I think one of the reasons for the long lasting friendship, besides retelling some very good stories, was the fact that absolutely no one was putting on any airs. The best storyteller of all time was Jay. He never forgot the name of a restaurant, a town, a date or the like. No one was there to try to sell you on his or her own agenda. Everyone made it, I played in a USTA tennis match while Squatman watched the match talking on the phone to his former junior high school coach, Stevie Stelmack. Jay, couldn't sit still, and wandered around the grounds. Overweight and somewhat tired I went down 6-2, 6-0 to the eventual champ but vowed in my own mind to play better, meaning moving my feet more, in 2015. Don't play tennis to get it shape; get in shape to play tennis. Words I planned to live by. So he didn't need to spend money on a hotel room, or split the hotel bill with someone, BS opted for staying at some fleabag hotel on the strip where he was "comp'd". And he was proud of it.

On Saturday night of each reunion we had our annual dinner. We always decided on the restaurant in advance based on ideas brought forth by group members. Nothing too fancy, just a good meal at a reasonable price. Early in our reunion days BS picked out the restaurant and his choices left most of us gagging. We selected Outback Steak House for the 2014 reunion formal dinner. It became a dinner to remember when Squatman forgot his manners and started hitting on the restaurant manager. There is a fine line between flirting and being overly aggressive, and Squatty stepped over the line only to embarrass himself in front of us and other restaurant patrons. BS also pulled a neat little trick at dinner, and we wondered after Buck caught him, how long he had been doing the neat trick. While we each ordered our dinner selection usually consisting of a wedge salad with Roquefort dressing and a decent steak for around $15, BS sitting at the end of the table, out of earshot of the group, ordered a lobster and Outback's most expensive steak. BS was no dummy because he knew we always split the bill at the end of the dinner. This time, however, Buck caught him doing it. BS just laughed it off.

At the end of the dinner, to keep BS in his usual and customary "free digs" we (Buck) drove him back to the Strip. A trip that took ~ 1-plus hours if the traffic cooperated. In America, the traffic only cooperates from 11:00 pm to 5:00 am. I was surprised by the traffic heading west from downtown Vegas during rush hour. Jay was flush with BRIS info to handicap the Breeder's Cup and Tommy sent him The Sheets. For one race day and one track, the Sheets run, I think, around $35. Lagniappe we called it. However, the fabled Sheets do not have pace figures, i.e., what horses would go to the front at the start of a race, which horses would stalk and which horses were closers. I had a feeling Jay had the races, the toughest in the world to handicap because the best horses in the world, at different distances, on dirt and grass, run, pretty much mapped out in a way only Jay could. Over dinner the night before, the Boys said to put some money on a horse named "Texas Red". Jay's $3 bet still haunts me, but before the race went off I asked Jay how much win money he put on good old Texas Red. When I heard the amount Jay bet on Texas Red, I walked to the ticket window and put $100 on Red to win. Red won all right but my $100 bet lost because the clerk at the ticket window punched in the wrong race number. What bullshit we thought. Of course the Sport Book would not give me my money back for their error. "You had time to look at your tickets," said the angry male supervisor who delighted in screwing the public. I think he had his job for that very purpose. Reminded me of some TSA guys in airports being jealous of well-dressed young businessmen and giving them a hassle particularly if Mr. Business Man was running late. If you are a businessman never let them catch you looking like you are in a hurry. *"Games people play"* by Joe South. I stepped in front of a young businessman who was going to charge a TSA guy and brought him to his senses before anything happened. Besides losing his job, there is no telling what else could have happened.

My favorite hotel story occurred in Tulsa, OK. I arrived into Tulsa from Denver about 7pm. For January, the weather was mild but still cold. I immediately called Marriott to have them send their shuttle bus come out to the airport to pick me up. So did a lot of people. As it got later and later, the crowd headed for the Marriott started building, and by the time the shuttle bus arrived there must have been 25-people waiting. We got to the Tulsa Marriott and there was one clerk at the front desk to check us into our rooms. By the time I exited the bus I was in the back of the line. When I got within two people of the front desk to check in I heard the guy in front of me ask the clerk for the phone while he got out his credit card information. All I hear him say on the phone was "you told me to call if I had a problem". He then handed the phone over to the desk clerk. Her eyes told the story that whoever was on the phone had some clout with Marriott. So much so that whatever the guy on the phone said immediately prompted the clerk to go through the door to the office behind her and pull the assistant manager on duty out to talk on the phone. Where had he been when 25-people were waiting to check in? I asked about the assistant manager on my return trip to Tulsa and I was told the assistant manager had found employment elsewhere. It had to have been Bill Marriott on the phone. Where did the assistant manager go, Motel 6?

## "What are you going to do about it"? — Chris Chambers, Springfield, IL

In August of 1984 I drove from St Louis to Springfield, IL to work with Chris Chambers. I had a room reserved, or so I thought, at the Holiday Inn hotel on the south side of Springfield by the old US 66 Drive-In theatre. When I got to the front desk the clerk told me that I did not have a reservation and the hotel was sold out because of the annual Illinois State Fair which ran for 10-days every August. "How can that be"? I asked. "I'm sorry" was all the clerk would say. What 6-foot 6-inch Chris Chambers said next to the front desk clerk stuck with me for my next 27-years on the road in corporate America, and to this day. What Big Chris Chambers did next was very cool. He walked up to the front desk and asked the clerk "what are you going to do about it"? Chris' question to the front desk clerk was etched in my memory. I quickly picked up on it and repeated to the front desk clerk, "what are you going to do about it?" He then said he would pay for my room at a hotel down the street. Thinking it was the Ramada Inn, I went along with the idea. But it wasn't the Ramada Inn. It was an old, flea-bag hotel that should have been torn down years ahead of my stay. The shower floor was so dirty and grimy I had to take a shower with my running shoes on. By the way, about 10-years after Chris was hired, he was promoted to Burroughs Wellcome Co's home office. While in the office he was encouraged to get his master's degree in business. He took the GMAT national test and finished first out of 40,000 students taking the test. Kellogg School of Business at Northwestern wanted him. So did the famous Wharton School of Business and Duke. He decided on the University of North Carolina.

From that point further in my corporate America career, if I was going to be treated like that on the road or if I had a problem caused by a hotel, airline or rental car I always uttered that famous quote---"what are you going to do about it?"--- to hotel clerks, rental car agents, airline agents and other people I came in contact with as Chris had done at the Holiday Inn in Springfield, Illinois. I figured over 41-years I stayed 1,500 nights in hotels, took 3,500 flights, rented 5,000 cars (80% AVIS) and took 500 cab rides. The road is absolutely no picnic.

## "Running down the road trying to loosen my load" — The Eagles

While taking a shower at 5:00am before heading to the Ft Lauderdale Airport in 2005, the ceiling at the Ft Lauderdale Renaissance Hotel collapsed on my head and plaster fell down on me because of a faulty roof. The front desk manager raced up to the room to find out how I was, but true to form, said nothing about what he would do for me until I asked "what are you going to do about it'? Knowing he had a potential lawsuit on his hands, and I could have sued Marriott, he gallantly came to the forefront with 100,000 Marriott points worth about 2-3 free nights in any Marriott only after I bitched and bitched.

Traveling from San Francisco to Raleigh, NC on a Monday in 1993 to give a talk in corporate America on Tuesday at 9:00am, the 2nd leg of the trip from Chicago to Raleigh caused a significant delay when the left engine of the plan caught fire on take off at O'Hare. Arriving at the Marriott in Raleigh, NC (the hotel close to Research Triangle Park, NC) at 3:00 am I knew in an instant looking at the front desk clerk that they had sold my room. It is that Oh My God look. "We are all sold out" (which meant he sold my room thinking I was a "no-show"), said the desk clerk. "I have a reservation…what are you going to do about it"? I asked. "What do you want me to do about it?" said the young, inexperienced desk clerk. I quickly came to realize that the harder I worked to get them to say "what do you want me to do about it?" the better the bargaining position I was in, especially being a Platinum Elite guy (meaning you stayed at least 75-times a year in a Marriott hotel and were on the top of their pecking order) as I was with Marriott. For my inconvenience, and the fact that it was 3:00 am in the morning on a workday, I ended up with 3-free days at the Marriott of my choice. The years on the road taught me that if you don't ask for it, the hotel, rental car or airline would not just give it to you.

In early 2000, my evening flight into Cincinnati from Atlanta, Georgia was delayed and we did not arrive into Cincy until 4:00 am. A dreadful hour to land any where in any city. AVIS, who told me before I left Atlanta, that they would have an agent at the Cincy airport when the plane arrived, must have had their wires crossed because when I arrived at the Cincinnati/Northern Kentucky Airport located in Hebron, KY, there were no AVIS agents to be found. And there were no cabs either. The first cab pulled through the airport at 6:00 am. "What are you going to do about it?" I asked AVIS Customer Service. 16-$25 certificates was the answer.

# Chapter 29

*"Many a tear has to fall, but it's all in the game"*
— *Tommy Edwards*

My rules of the road:

- Always keep you bag, computer any anything else you are carrying in front of you at all times. Never lay anything down behind you so you can't see it. Particularly important when stopping to grab lunch and checking bags at the front ticket counter
- When going through security at any airport, put your wallet, watch and any other valuables you have in your briefcase or backpack. Don't put them in an open plastic bowel provided by TSA where anyone can grab them. I've seen laptops stolen at security check points particularly when it is congested with long, long lines to get through the screening people x-ray.
- Write down on the palm of you hand with an ink pen the number of bags you brought on the plane. You would not believe how much stuff I've left on airplanes, including fresh salmon from Seattle and steaks from Omaha, Nebraska.
- So you do not have to wander around the airport-parking garage looking for your vehicle, write down the aisle location when you pull into the spot and put the location info in your wallet or in your smart phone. And a good working habit is to always park in the same spot or as close to the same spot every time. Once you spend an hour looking for you

car in the Chicago airport parking lot at 10:00pm in January, you will better understand why I'm passing this little pearl of wisdom along to you.

- When riding the "El" in Chicago, or any subway system, I noticed that Jay always stood up. I asked him about it one day and he said just in case he had to make a quick exit. He also said never make eye contact with anyone.

- Always sit in an aisle seat near the middle of the plane where the wing is. The wing area is the strongest spot structurally on an airplane. And try to sit as close to the exit door as possible.

- Best hotel chain…no question, the Marriott chain. Best service, cleanest bathrooms, best beds and absolutely best pillows. You might pay a little more, but when it comes to hotels, and I know hotels, if you have a problem, Marriott is the best in the business. If you travel for business and routinely go to the same cities, try to stay at the same hotel. Introduce yourself to the front desk mgr and the general manager. When you need a room and things are tight, you will be glad that you took the time to do so.

- Best airline…Southwest. Up until 1998 I never flew anything but Delta, Continental and American. In 1998, the service on these airlines was so bad that, on some advice from an old, experienced traveler, I tried Southwest. While to this day there are some things I don't like about Southwest, especially when the changed their frequent flyer program, I knew one thing for sure about them that was so important in 1998 in corporate America, they worked their butts off to be on time. By 1999 more and more businessmen were traveling Southwest for the first time and then sticking with them.

- Always tip the maid $2-5 everyday. A clean bathroom is worth millions.

- Ask for low mileage rental cars and what upgrades they can give you. Don't under estimate the power of an agent in helping you get what you want. If you travel into the city regularly, introduce your self to the managers and the guys who work in the lot where the cars are parked.

- If you are getting cash at an ATM in the airport, cover the hand that is punching in the security numbers. Also, buy a wallet that can't be scanned by someone standing next or near to you. For double protection, wrap your credit cards in tin foil.
- Best airport for watching beautiful women…no contest; the "D" Concourse (affectionately called the "D" Cup by seasoned business travelers) at the Miami International Airport
- Worst city to drive in…hands down the rudest, boldest drivers in the world travel on I-95 from Ft Lauderdale to Miami and back. The driver's get ruder the closer one gets to Miami. Year after year Miami wins USA Today's survey of the worst cities to drive in. A word of advice…doesn't engage these guys.
- Don't engage a TSA agent even if you are mad and have a genuine complaint. You will not win and it could cost you plenty.

## Back in the fold…

My return trip to Tulsa was going to be a good one for Charlie McLeskey, MD, Professor of Anesthesiology, University of Colorado Health Science Center, was scheduled to speak early the following morning to the anesthesiologists at the biggest hospital in town. We sold a muscle relaxant called Tracrium and we were losing business to a competitor by the name of Organon. My Tulsa Rep, Davey, picked Charlie and I up at the airport and on the ride to the Tulsa Marriott Charlie asked Davey what he needed for him to cover in his talk the next morning. While driving, Davey went on and on about how he was losing business. Then he paused and said one of the classic lines of my 35-years in pharmaceutical management, "Charlie, we've just got to get these guys back in the fold". Charlie, never hearing a request like it, roared with laughter. Charlie departed immediately after his talk and I worked the rest of the day with Davey. An old school guy who was good at selling on personality and just showing up, but when it came to selling technical information like muscle relaxants, especially to teaching hospital anesthesiologists, he fell down a lot. Actually he wasn't comfortable with the job that required knowing how to use medical journal reprints to sell. The competition used reprints to sell and Davey was getting beat. What did Davey's former manager do in helping him learn how to interpret and analyze reprints and use them on sales calls? In this case, I was close enough to the situation to know who Davey's manager was before I was his manager. His former manager, a guy by the name of Mr. B, was only interested in one thing... promoting himself in front of Upper Management. He did a good job of selling himself, but nothing to teach poor Davey how to use a reprint in a sales presentation or even how to read a reprint for that matter. Yes, Mr. B moved up the ladder, but left Davey to fend for himself. I thought it was a reflection of Upper Management to promote Davey in the first place. But Mr. B. looked good in the shower and was very good at selling himself. He knew the right things to say at meetings and no one in Upper Management ever checked the credibility of what he was saying. He didn't help Davey, but he got promoted. This is what made me sick about corporate America and why I was sorry I got into all of this bullshit in the first place. Who cares about Davey or company sales as long as one keeps moving on up? More money and more prestige, hey Mr. Bob.

## "Reprint Ron"...

So I decided to see what was written in the literature on how to interpret and analyze a study appearing in a medical journal to have it read and reviewed at our sales meetings. Not much. So I sent the troops out to sponsor dinners at Journal Club meetings and watch and study how physicians broke down a study among their peers at a Journal Club Meeting. A journal club was a meeting, usually held in the evening, set up to review and present current medical journal studies. It became quickly apparent, that with every study discussed, the reviewer would start with what is called The Material & Method section of the study. The nuts and bolts if you will. Was it a double-blinded study? Was it a cross over study? What was the population of the study (How many people were involved in the study?). In what journal did the study appear? Where was the study done? Who did the study? We studied how to read, interpret and analyze the medical literature very hard.

The studying paid off and we learned and we became the best Sales District in the Company at interpreting, analyzing and using a medical journal study on a sales call. We even went so far as to become experts in whether or not there was bias in a study. Most important of all, the analyzing medical journal studies provided each of us with confidence in presenting the study to a physician. It gave us confidence on each and every sales call. In the technical world of pharmaceutical sales nothing is more important than confidence. When you know how to break down a study, you know how to present a study. So instead of reviewing the Marketing Departments Madison Ave, NY, style and written sales literature at our Sales Meeting, we reviewed studies from current journal articles. I became know as "Reprint Ron" (reprint was what we called a journal study) and sales soared. Instead of trying to get the doctor to switch all of his patients over to the drug we were presenting, we discussed specific patient types where we had a documented advantage. We asked for a small part of the provider's regimen for treating, for example otitis media, on a specific type of patient, not all patients, where we had an advantage. We followed the advice of General Creighton Abrams, "when eating an elephant, take one bite at a time".

One of the greatest success stories I've ever witnessed in providing value to the physician on a sales call, occurred in Cape Girardeau by our Rep who became know as "The Live Wire In The Cape". The "Live Wire" story is worth mentioning because to this day I still do not believe what happened. On the highway half way between Cape Girardeau and Popular Bluff, Missouri, our Rep did not see a wire on the road and ran over it, allowing the wire to wrap around his car's rear wheel. When he pulled off to the side of the road to inspect, he quickly realized that this was a very dangerous wire. How correct he was. Apparently, a farmer plowing in the field dug up, quite by accident, a live electrical wire that stretched from Cape Girardeau to Poplar Bluff. He was all right, but had a lot of questions to answer from the Missouri State police as to how the electrical wire got wrapped around his rear wheel. It is still hard to believe.

When "The Live Wire" started with Burroughs Wellcome Co., Roche, a large pharmaceutical company, which had the same antibiotic for urinary tract infections as Burroughs Wellcome Company's Septra, but went by a different trade name (Bactrim), had sales in the Cape of at least 10-1 better than Burroughs Wellcome Co had. Slowly and methodically our Man In The Cape made his calls, provided doctors up to date information on the drug from current medical journal studies. He knew how to analyze the medical literature and he taught the providers in The Cape and Poplar Bluff new uses of the antibiotic. And, little by little Septra sales went up. Two years into it, "The Live Wire In The Cape" had changed the picture and was leading 10 to 1. Naturally, the Roche Rep, who sold on personality, lost on product knowledge was looking for a job he could use his personality to sell. We heard he ended up selling used cars in Poplar Bluff, Missouri. As U. J. Hecker told me the day I started in pharmaceutical sales, "if you sell on personality, you can get beat on personality. If you provide the physician with reasons as to why your drug is better in specific patient types, that is pretty hard to beat".

"You move it to the left, yea, and, you go for yourself, You move it to the right, yea, if it takes all night"
— Bob & Earl, "The Harlem Shuffle"

## Put it on your bucket list...

Jay and I attended the Breeder's Cup at Churchill in Louisville, KY in 2007.

Most of the betters in the grand stand at Churchill Downs, at least those within earshot around us, as happened many times, overheard Jay's selections for each race and boxed 5-horse exactas. As Jay played non-favorites, these bystanders won some big money. Thousands of dollars as a matter of fact. They thanked us for the great tips. We played the exotics and dribbled our money away. The Breeder's Cup is a 2-day event. On the final day (Saturday) the last race run is The Classic. As they were loading the horses into the gate, the crowd of > 100,000-plus stood as one and began cheering for the horses in the race and all of the horses who participated in the two day event. By the time all of the horses were loaded into the gate to start The Classic the roar was so deafening it raised the hair on the back of my neck. It was a once in a lifetime scene and one I never forgot. At Muhammad Ali's eulogy, someone got up and said, "know the rules, you can't bet on a horse while it is in the winner's circle, you must bet on the horse when it is in the mud" (meaning before the start of the race). You would be crazy to miss seeing the Breeders Cup in person at least once in your lifetime. It is the Super Bowl of horse racing.

# Chapter 30

*"…when it is cold outside we have the month of May"*
*— The Temptations, "My Girl"*

By EARLY 2015, Jay was selling his home on Mozart. His son and wife packed it up for Grand Cayman. Buck and I helped pay for their airfare down to Cayman. Never the best of housekeepers, and now that The Mrs. was gone, the inside of his house looked and smelled horrible. Rafael, Jay's bird, had the run of the place and there was bird shit all over one wall. He finally got my hint and got some bleach and cleaned it. Poor Rafael, while packing Jay's stuff so he could move into an apartment in Chicago, the daughter of Jay's fantasy baseball partner Bennie somebody, first class ass that he was, left the front door of the house open enough for Rafael to run for daylight. I began feeling sorry for Jay as he sat in his little wicker chair in front of his TV just as he had done in the early 1960's. He loved Rafael, TV and particularly loved football, baseball, basketball and movies; "The World Of Suzie Wong" was one of his all time favorites. So was "The Pope of Greenwich Village". "The Cincinnati Kid" and "One Eyed Jacks" He often quoted lines out of movies…"I've seen the other side of your face". He truly was a one-of-a-kind guy. He pulled people toward him with his stories and intellect. Mahoney often came over to Jay's house just to talk. So did Tommy The Bookie. Jay was a great guy to talk to. Versed in many, many subjects, and opinionated in all, he was tough to beat in a debate. Many of his high school friends disliked him on the LTHS website because he was a stickler for facts. I spent a week with him in Chicago to try to help in move his stuff to a storage locker before the demolition team leveled the house. We had a good time going to breakfast at the Golden Nugget on Irving Park. The "Nuggie" he always called it. He would always order the same thing, waffle, bacon and chocolate malt. My visit to Chicago was a week of remembering all of the stories of our misspent youth. I don't even think we even bet on the horses during the week. Mahoney came by for a visit and sat there in Jay's living room while Rafael buzzed about from time to time. They too, Mahoney & Jay, had old memories. Thanks to Tommy's help, Jay finally finished the project of moving out. After that Jay headed to Grand Cayman and then met Buck and I in March in Omaha for the NCAA Basketball tournament. He returned to Chicago after basketball and a visit to my house in Florida before he rented an apartment on Irving Park Blvd where he died in June 2015.

I don't know officially where my brother got the following, or who wrote it, but it popped up on my computer in box in early 2013. I decided to include it in the book because it is looking for a sign:

"The folks who are getting free shit,
Don't like the folks who are paying for the free shit,
because the folks who are paying for the free shit
Can no longer afford to pay for both the free shit and
Their own shit
And, The Folks who are paying for the free shit,
Want the free shit to stop
And, The Folks who are getting the free shit,
Want even more free shit on top of the free shit
They are getting already!
Now...the people who are forcing people to pay for
The free shit,
Have told the people who are RECEIVING the free shit,
That the people who are PAYING for the free shit,
Are being mean, prejudiced and racist.
So...the people who are GETTING the free shit,
Have been convinced they need to HATE the people

Who are paying for the free shit because they are selfish.
And they are promised more free shit if they will vote
For people who force the people who pay for the free
Shit to give them even more free shit.
Me…I'm tired of all this shit!

It has now been over a 1 1/2-years now since Jay died and I started writing "First Call". When asked how I happened to write this book the answer was simple…I just started writing. But, more importantly, I stayed with it because I wanted to share our stories, what we learned in corporate America, what we all learned from each other and the advice Jay gave us all. Not many guys spent a career going in and out of the Chicago projects like Jay had. Writing the book also helped me grieve the loss of my friend. When we were young, we didn't know what we didn't have, but we knew that Chicago was in our backyard. In 1960 we knew that our playing days were over, but somehow they really never ended. We were still playing whiffle ball at 70-years of age, and Jay's slider was better at 70 than it was at 21. Or maybe I was getting slower. The luck of the draw for all of us was our taking advantage of what The Big Onion provided. At Jay's funeral, people attending were amazed how eight guys from high school days would still be hanging out together. Between speakers at the funeral it was easy to think back to all of those trips---from Amsterdam, Netherlands to Mahomet, IL to New Orleans---we didn't miss much. Jay never owned a new car; in fact, his 1992 Dodge Dynasty might have been the newest model he ever owned. Cars and speed were not important to him. While dating Anne "The Sheriff", as Jay called her in 2010, the 7-UP Company's poster child of the 1960's, Jay met the Sheriff's daughter and her husband. The Sheriff's daughter lived in the wealthy suburb of Oak Brook, Illinois. The daughter's husband drove a Hummer and the daughter drove a brand new BMW. The daughter asked the Sheriff what kind of car her new boyfriend Jay drove. "A 1992 Dodge Dynasty" is what she said. When the Sheriff said, "the car was an upgrade", the daughter and her hubby just roared. I think that said volumes about our man Jay, because driving fancy cars and wearing Nordstrom clothes were not important to him. He graduated from high school and his parents gave him at 1949 maroon colored Dodge he named Johnny Blood. Johnny Blood was the nickname given to John McNally, a NFL halfback who played halfback for the Green Bay Packers in the late 1920s. What was important to Jay was keeping up with current and foreign affairs in "The Nation" weekly magazine, The New Yorker and Harper's so he could pimp the high school yahoo's who frequent the high school's Yahoo website and sent out a lot of bullshit daily. .Jay would spend hours putting the Hall of Famers and the regular grads in their "proper place" as he called it. It is too bad we did not keep all of Jay's writings on the high school website because it would have made for excellent reading. What was important to Jay wasn't owning a BMW, but which horses were running where on that day. The Daily Racing Form and betting on pro football using the stats found in the Monday issue of "USA Today" took up most of his early week's time. The statistics he kept on horse racing and betting National Football League games would fill a room. Book after book of pace and past performance notes were piled up in his office. In his office, he had a picture of Muhammad Ali and stacks and stacks of former past notes. Had he learned how to use his computer better he could have save himself a ton of time. Sometimes I felt the record keeping and the handicapping itself was more important to him than the possible money he could have won on each race. He usually spent 3-hours handicapping a 9-race card horse race, and longer if it was the Breeders Cup. Even in the rain, on his 70th birthday, he played whiffle ball, always "stepping out" the virtual diamond. The last time we played, his slider was overwhelming, and I lost easily. He never learned how to invest his money, and he didn't trust Wall Street or the stock market. After what the banks did in 2008 in bringing the financial world to its knees it is understandable why he didn't. If you haven't seen the movie "The Big Short" take the time to do so. Outstanding movie about money and one that every American should watch. Subprime mortgage. In America today, a Mexican farm laborer in Southwest Florida picking tomatoes makes 80-cents for every bucket he picks. Eighty cents. Yet Wall Street cheated and got caught on the subprime mortgage scandal. Yet, the bankers were bailed out. How were they bailed out? By the American public using our tax dollars to cover the debt. How many bankers went to jail? Just ask Jaime Diamond of Chase because he can tell you. Everyone loved to hear Jay's stories, and, the only the good Lord knows how many stories he told. Nobody did it better. There are friends of Jay's to this day who miss talking to him. He was a very interesting guy to talk to.

## "No, no. no. no, I don't smoke it no more; I'm tired of waking up on the floor" — Ringo Starr

The Braidwood Boys, like the swallows returning to Capistrano, once again will gather in Vegas for the 21$^{st}$ time in November of 2016. BS will pull the "slots' and again proclaim "I'm right where I want to be" even if he is down $1,700. Buck will try to do his best to put a star on what the Republican Party is doing. You just can't make these stories up. The guy who threw his clothes in a Hefty Trash 30-gal green bag and used it as a suitcase will be missing, but his stories will be repeated. Jay did have a certain kinship with BS that came as no surprise to most of us. Buck called BS the "Maximum Leader", knowing full well he would have trouble leading a 2-man band. Volumes could be written about BS, but the morning he ordered an All-American breakfast at an all-you-can-eat restaurant on the Strip, and came to the table with two eggs and 12-pieces ("a slab" we called it) of bacon, will hopefully save me from writing additional volumes about him. How many guys do you know in this day and age who start breakfast with 12-slices of bacon? Admiral Dan, Dutchy Van and Willie will play golf...some things never change and that is good. Squatman will watch his Northwestern football on the big screen at the Sport Book and research which peeler bar we should go to that evening. Squatman knows what to look for when it comes to analyzing and comparing peeler bars. He has been there. The years have taught him much and he has seen enough. Dutchy Van will play golf and remember the words his Mother said to him in Champaign, IL as he started his college career in September 1960, "Dutchy, don't try to out eat the other boys, it isn't good for your health". We will gather together for dinner on Saturday night as we have for the past 21-years. It is always a joyful occasion. Jay's sayings, such as, "thanks much", "ok good", "hello-helloooooo", "it'll put a little pep in the gumbo" and "won't hold you" when he wanted to end the call, will all be missed. The old stories get better and longer, and some of them bring us to tears. It has been a long road for all of us.

"We are sick and tired of being sick and tired'"'
— Charlotte, NC Pastor speaking about police shooting of African-American males

Little did I know in 1956 what moving to Western Springs would bring to me in my life time. One thing for sure…these guys mean a lot to me. You couldn't have found a better bunch of guys to have all of these adventures with first in high school and then again for the past many, many years. Where do you find guys like that today? You don't. And while Wrigley is no longer the same and Comiskey Park has been demolished, Western Springs is still there and so are the Braidwood Boys. The train still pulls out of Kankakee. The Monsters of the Midway, the Chicago Bears, still play in Soldier Field. The great Chicago Bears players---Ditka, Butkus, Bill George, Joe Fortunato, Gayle Sayers, Johnny Lujack, Walter Payton---will always be remembered. Midway Airport, and the big one, O'Hare, still work and so does Union Station on South Canal in downtown Chicago. The Harold Washington Library continues to serve as the tombstone for the great Follies Theatre on South State Street. The El still loops around downtown. If you look carefully, and know exactly where you are look-ing, parts of the great Route US 66 from Wolf Road in Western Springs, Illinois to Bloomington, Illinois can still be seen and driven upon. Getting your "kicks on Route 66" would be another adventure I would recommend for your bucket list. My house in Western Springs was demolished and a palace built in its place by a guy who made his fortune hauling garbage. Wall Street and the bankers are still running free. And the times they are a changing…not long ago General Motors was building cars in Flint, Michigan and you couldn't drink the water in Mexico. Now General Motors builds cars in Mexico and you can't drink the water in Flint, Michigan. The Western Springs Tower remains and so does Kirschbaum Bakery selling the best sweet rolls in Illinois. Lyons Township high school, at Cossitt and 100 South Brainard, is still there, but because they received a grant from a wealthy grad, that had to have a building built with his name on it, the School Board made the mistake and removed the football field across the street from the bell tower. Vaughn Gym at LTHS still stands…a monument to the great 1953 team. Old US Highway 51, stretching from Cairo, IL on the South to Rockford, IL on the North, is still there, but only the locals travel on it. I would imagine they still like their beer in Minonk, IL. Like Route US 66, US 51 has seen its busier days, more speed and more accidents. More people are racing home to watch "Dancing With The Stars" on television. The Chicago Transit Authority 80 bus, which moves east and west on the historic Irving Park Blvd in Chicago still runs and more and more people are riding it. Kerry Wood and Kenny Holtzman don't pitch in Wrigley anymore, but Jake Arrieta and Jon Lester do. Al Heist and Frankie Baumholtz aren't roaming centerfield, but Dexter Fowler does. The Stockyards are gone, but Frank Sinatra would be pleased that the Wrigley Building is still there. Grant Park is still there, a memorial to the guys in 1968 protesting the Vietnam War at the Democratic Convention across the street from he Hilton. "Hell no we won't go". The Daley's are gone, having caused Chicago a lot of problems, but Sweet Home Chicago remains, and for a lot of us, that is all that matters.

# Chapter 31

*"Just as sure as God made little green apples, someday the Chicago*
*Cubs are going to win the World Series"*
*— Harry Caray*

IT HAS BEEN 60-years now since I moved to Western Springs. For what it is
worth, here is what we all learned from Jay and his daily work trips into the
Chicago ghetto, what corporate America taught us, what we learned from the
nameless little old men sitting in the left field grandstand of Wrigley Field in
the early 60s, what the Post Office guys taught me, what we learned at the
Follies Theater on South State Street in our youth, what we learned hitchhiking and hopping freight trains, what the old men selling their "wares" at
Maxwell Street taught us, and, most importantly, what we taught each other.
As they say in the Big Easy, here is a little lagniappe…a little something extra, A must word for your vocabulary.

**la . gniappe**

/ lan 'yap, ' lan . yap /

noun

Something given as a bonus or extra gift

## "Lessons Learned Along The Way"

- The best lesson to be learned in life is what Leroy "Satchel" Paige, American League Baseball Pitcher told us years ago, "don't look over your shoulder, someone might be gaining on you". Don't dwell on the past, work on the next thing and stay focused on the road ahead. No U-turns. No rear view mirrors.

- "It is what you learn after you know it all that really counts"— Coach John Wooden

- Listen more than talk…"talk about the other guy, not yourself" my Dad always said. People don't want to hear about your stuff, they want to talk about their stuff. This holds doubly true for corporate America.

- "If the job is worth doing, it is worth doing right". If I heard that from my Dad once, I heard it 1,000-times. Don't take short cuts; they can kill you in corporate America

- "If you can meet with Triumph and Disaster and treat those two impostors just the same"— inscribed above the entrance to the Wimbledon's Centre Court, Rudyard Kipling

- Best cities to live in…Chicago and Denver. Hands down; no contest

- Whatever job you go into or do in this life, you must read "The Elements of Style" by William Strunk (first edition 1918). You must learn how to write, whether it is a memo or letter, so people can understand what you are saying

- Just before the final game of the NCAA basketball tournament of 2015-2016 at NRG Stadium in Houston, TX pitting the University of North Carolina versus Villanova, coach Roy Williams of North Carolina, we called him "the pious one", uttered a sentence that made a lot of sense to all of us (even though we had all of our betting money on Villanova) when he said, "we didn't come this far, just to come this far".

- Read Warren Buffett's Berkshire Hathaway Annual Report every year… you will get a Master's degree worth of knowledge and information on investing your money. You can NOT get started early enough investing your money. Open up an account with Charles Schwab or Vanguard and begin slowly investing in companies you have researched. You can't be too rich or too thin.

- Meet as many new people as possible…treat them like a friend. Develop a network of friends, as you'll never know when you'll need them
- The Betty rules…(i) always stand up when a woman enters the room and (2) if you plan to take a girl out on a date, plan to take her out two times so as not to damage her ego if you decide not to ask her out for a third date
- "If you do your lessons every night, you never have to worry about a test" — Urban J. "Joe" Hecker, circa 1971
- You will encounter in your life a lot of guys smarter than you are. The key is not to be better but, as the Temptations put it in 1971, "Just My Imagination (Running Away With Me)" strive to use your imagination and be better that way.

  In January 2010, while departing Peter Island, BVI on a 41-foot sailboat, a 125-foot power yacht was pulling in and went right past us… the name of the boat, *"Harry's Game"*…. just my imagination.
- Finding your beach…there is no better beach to get away from it all on this planet than the white sands of Loblolly Bay, Anegada, British Virgin Islands. And The Big Bamboo Bar residing at Loblolly Bay serves the best rum punch in the Caribbean; make sure you take some time off to refresh
- "Be quick; but don't hurry — Coach John Wooden
- "If you have an opinion, back it" — Tommy The Bookie; whether the opinion be on a horse, a stock, a basketball bet, or a decision to be made in corporate America. Don't waffle, Back your opinions.
- The Book of Rules--- (i) drink a lot of water every day (ii) eat as many vegetables as you can (iii) stretch every morning (iv) exercise a minimum of 3-times per week (v) keep your bags in front of you at all airports (vi) travel extensively; try to get everywhere before you get too old to travel
- "It gets down to what it is all about, doesn't it Kid. Making the right move at the wrong time" — The Cincinnati Kid.

Be sure to read and understand Joe Hecker's diagram on decision- making. As the great horse handicapper, James Kuck, once said… "In all the important transactions in life, indeed those which have a relationship to the future, we must take a leap in the dark. We must act on sound information and make correct decisions. But how do we make sound decisions. By opening our minds and thinking".

- "The Man In The Arena" speech delivered in 1910 by Theodore Roosevelt…"who at the best knows in the end of triumph of high achievement, and who at the worst, if he fails, at least fails while daring greatly, so that his place should never be with those cold and timid souls who neither know victory nor defeat"

- Get enough sleep…at least 7-hours a day until you reach 60-years of age

- Read all the time. Have a point of view before you start a book or an article. I don't ever remember not seeing Jay with a paperback of magazine in his hand when there was time for it.

- When you are coming out of college or just making a job change always select the job that appears to you to be the most enjoyable even if it doesn't pay the most

- "If you don't have time to do it right, when will you find time to do it over" — a sign posted on the wall of Burroughs Welcome Co. Regional Manager Urban Joe Hacker's office in Rolling Meadows, IL, circa 1984, I don't think anything says more about taking the time to do it right the first time.

"If you don't know me by now"
— Harold Melvin & The Blue Notes

## The End…

I looked at Jay's urn sitting on top of the front table at the funeral ceremony in Skokie, IL that day in June 2015 and naturally remembered all of the good times, and especially all of the roads we traveled together. He rode the number 80 CTA bus to the Red Line El Station on Irving Park Blvd. till he died. Chicago was his kind of town. There wasn't much he hadn't seen in Chicago. He served a lifetime in the low security prison of Illinois bureaucracy and when most people couldn't tell you where Cabrini-Green was located, Jay worked there so long they thought he was a resident. He was very proud to be named as the all-star center fielder in a Chicago Public Aid workers co-ed 16-inch softball league. He loved his whiffle ball and always carried a ball in his bag so he could practice his deadly slider. Chuck Jackson's "Any Day Now", The Rolling Stones "Miss You" and The Dells' "Oh, What A Night" were three of his favorites songs. One of his last official act's before he passed was giving the ceremonial wedding party toast at my wedding held at the Verandah Restaurant in downtown Ft Myers, FL. Buck made the trip to the wedding and so did high school classmate Denny Boland, and can vouch for me on this one. It was a postcard evening in Ft Myers and we held the dinner and party outside on the Verandah's lovely tree-lined bricked patio. Sitting at the head table, which was round like the rest of the tables, Jay stood up next to me and began speaking. It was like he was giving a talk to me mumbling his words so that no one else in the audience could hear him. When I interrupted him to tell him to project out to all the people attending, it was the mistake of the evening because his "speech" consisted of things he and I had done together in our youth that no one could relate to. One of the stories he told was about the two of us playing basketball and picking players on each team from women in our high school class. So the speech became "Lenore from the corner" "Nan Nellie from the top of the key". I should have stopped him there, but figured no one could hear him anyway so what difference did it make. I was dead wrong. After Jay's wedding toast there were a number of questions about his sanity and "what the hell was he talking about". One guy even went so far as to ask who invited him to the ceremony anyway? It was good seeing Boland ("Denny Bo" as we called him) at the wedding. We agreed that Denny was the perfect example of a guy who took advantage of every opportunity that came his way in life. Just ask Alice.

As I was wrapping up this book, the 2016 version of the Braidwood Boys had just returned to Las Vegas for our annual reunion weekend. As we did on several occasions at reunion time, the horseplayers stayed at one hotel and the golfers stayed at another, and we would meet for dinner at night. Squatman, who brought his new golf clubs to Vegas, decided to stay with the horseplayers because there wasn't room at the Golden Nugget with the golfers. On Sunday morning following the Breeders' Cup final races on Saturday, the golfers decided to meet the horseplayers for breakfast at the JW Marriott in Summerlin where the horseplayers stayed for the weekend. On Sunday morning at breakfast, an event occurred that was proof positive the bricks were falling off the building for all of us. The golfers told Squatman "at least ten times" they would pick him up at the front door of the JW Marriott at 10am for golf. Somehow Squat thought he was being picked up at 8 am, and when the golfers arrived at the Marriott's restaurant breakfast buffet, they had to call Squat to tell him to now meet them at breakfast buffet instead of the front door. With golf clubs thrown over his shoulder and golf shoes on, Squat walked across a completely full restaurant up to the breakfast table where we were sitting. Because everyone in the restaurant stopped eating to look and laugh at this guy carrying golf clubs, looking both very lost and confused, I immediately asked him, "Senor, are you playing through?" Yes, the bricks were falling off the building for all of us, but we were, as Chuck Berry put it during our high school days and into our later years, "reelin' and a rollin', rockin' to the break of dawn". The bricks may be falling, but over the better-than-average buffet breakfast and the crowd noise the golf clubs causes dying down, we talked about our next adventure to meet in Kansas City, Missouri for the "Sweet 16" NCAA basketball regional tournament in March 2017. "Goin' to Kansas City, Kansas City Here I Come" as Wilber Harrison told us back in the day. One adventure away from the next adventure.

Jay was a brilliant writer and should have written this book. So my attempt to capture the story of Jay, one of the all-time characters in the history of Chicago, who worked with the poor and down trodden, who fought with Buck on politics, who loved his Cubbies, his Monsters of the Midway and who loved The Big Onion and the Braidwood Boys, has come to an end. After he sold his house on Mozart Ave, Jay could have moved anywhere he wanted to. I tried very hard to convince him that Florida would be a good place for him because of the weather and no state income tax. But he wasn't going to have any part of Florida or any place else for that matter. He was a Chicago guy. And each time he would leave, Chicago was tugging his sleeve.

One last thing…I remember back to college days in 1961 or 1962 that Jay recommended I read a book called "Too Much Sun" by Lee Olds. I read the book. It was a story of two close friends who went to Alaska to find work. At the end of the story one of the guys died, and the other guy, after the funeral, said "I left him there". But, in 2015 we weren't in Alaska, we were in Skokie, Illinois. I left him there.

"And when I see the sign that points our way
The lot we used to pass by everyday
Just walk away Renee
You won't see me follow you back home
The empty sidewalks on my block are not the same
You're not to blame"
    — The Left Banke, "Walk Away Renee," 1967

"My Kind Of Town"
     — Frank Sinatra's Lyrics

"Now this could only happen to a guy like me
And only happen in a town like this
So may I say to each of you most gratefully
As I throw each one of you a kiss

This is my kind of town, Chicago is
My kind of town, Chicago is
My kind of people too
People who smile at you

And each time I roam, Chicago is
Calling me home. Chicago is
Why I just grin like a clown
It's my kind of town

My kind of town, Chicago is,
My kind of town, Chicago is
My kind of razzmatazz
And it has all that jazz

And each time I leave, Chicago is
Tugging my sleeve, Chicago is
The Wrigley Building, Chicago is
The Union Stockyards, Chicago is
One town that won't let you down
It's my kind of town"

This book is dedicated to Jay and the Braidwood Boys for their friendship over the past 50-years. I would also like to dedicate this book to the nameless old men who sat in the Grandstand section of Wrigley Field from 1960-1964 and taught us not to take a win or loss too seriously as there will always be another day in Wrigley. I didn't realize until later how important this lesson really was. The completion of this book would not have been possible without the encouragement I received to keep going from my wife Diane, my brother DK, my daughter Stacy, Mike Monti, Dan Baldwin, Frank VanAelst and Hank Trenkle. My personal thanks to Dave Beckwith, an outstanding writer back in the day for Time magazine, for his guidance and editing along the way as I was writing this book. I would also like to thank and recognize the great people I worked with at Amazon's CreateSpace who assisted me with cover design, formatting and provided me with sound advice every step of the way. The book would not have been published without their help. Finally, to BJ who always said I would one day write a book and to Aldo Mungai, my senior English teacher at Lyons Township High School in LaGrange, IL, who gave me a passing grade of "6" when it just as easily could have been a failing grade of "7".

It is my sincere hope that the stories will bring back fond memories for anyone who grew up in Chicago in the mid 1950s and early 1960s. Looking back, everyone who lived through those days should agree they were the best of times. I also hope that whoever reads this book benefits from what we learned about life and what is important in it.

In the immortal words of Lt Colombo, "One More Thing"... of all the things in this life which don't come back, the thing we all learned that will come back to haunt you the most is a missed opportunity. The one thing I would like to leave with you is this...don't miss your opportunities because as baseball great Ted Williams taught us, "to be a good hitter, you have got to get a good pitch to hit". And when the good pitch comes, you do not want to miss it.

Made in the USA
Middletown, DE
03 April 2017